INDIAN TRAVELS OF APOLLONIUS OF TYANA, AND THE INDIAN EMBASSIES TO ROME FROM THE REIGN OF AUGUSTUS TO THE DEATH OF JUSTINIAN

Owing to the antiquity and rarity of this book, certain pages are regrettably absent, and readability is compromised due to the blurring of the original text. If you possess any insights regarding the availability of these missing sections, kindly inform us. Your assistance is crucial in ensuring the completion of this significant work for the benefit of future generations.

INDIAN TRAVELS OF APOLLONIUS OF TYANA, AND THE INDIAN EMBASSIES TO ROME FROM THE REIGN OF AUGUSTUS TO THE DEATH OF JUSTINIAN

OSMOND DE BEAUVOIR PRIAULX

GYAN

Published by

Gyan Publishing House
5, Ansari Road
Daryaganj, New Delhi-110002
Phone: 011-47034999, 9811692060
E-mail: books@gyanbooks.com

Distribution Network
gyanbooks.com
India, USA, Canada, UK, Australia

ISBN: 978-93-7014-283-1 (PB)

First Published, 1860

2nd Impression 2025

Printed at: Gyan Press, Delhi.

INDIAN TRAVELS OF APOLLONIUS OF TYANA, AND THE INDIAN EMBASSIES TO ROME FROM THE REIGN OF AUGUSTUS TO THE DEATH OF JUSTINIAN

Arthur OSMOND DE BEAUVOIR PRIAULX

THE INDIAN TRAVELS

OF

APOLLONIUS OF TYANA,

AND

THE INDIAN EMBASSIES TO ROME

FROM THE

REIGN OF AUGUSTUS TO THE DEATH OF JUSTINIAN.

BY

OSMOND DE BEAUVOIR PRIAULX.

LONDON:

QUARITCH, PICCADILLY.

MDCCCLXXIII.

PREFACE.

THE several pieces, all relating to India, which make up this volume, appeared some years back in the Journals of the Asiatic Society. I cannot say that they then or ever excited the least interest, and but that there were omissions and faults in them which I wished to supply and correct, I certainly should not have thought of republishing them. I now for my own satisfaction reprint a small number of copies.

With regard to the Indian Embassies I began the series in the hope that all of them would be as interesting and important as those to Augustus and Claudius; but when I found that they were only barely mentioned by historians, and the later ones so mentioned that it was scarcely possible to ascertain whether they were Ethiopian or Hindu, I was led on to enlarge my plan and to inquire into the Relations of the Roman Empire with India. My last paper had but just appeared, or was about to appear—it was read in 1862 and came out in 1863—when the late M. Reinaud, the distinguished President of the Société Asiatique published, first in the Journal Asiatique for 1863 and afterwards in a separate form, his "Relations Politiques et Commerciales de l'Empire Romain avec l'Asie Orientale."* If I had been aware of M. Reinaud's intentions, I assuredly would not have ventured on a subject which I regarded as especially his own. As it is, we travelled the same road and naturally enough read the same guide-books, but we read them with a difference. Our stand-points were not the same. He sees everywhere the Roman Empire; for him its wealth and civilization acted upon, and its majesty overawed, the most distant nations; from the heights of its Capitol he looked down upon a subject world. I on the other hand put myself in the Hindu's place—and this Empire spite its greatness then faded into a mere phantom, which still loomed large in the hazy distance, and which now

* The whole title of his work is "Relations Politiques et Commerciales de l'Empire Romain avec l'Asie Orientale (l'Hyrcanie, l'Inde, la Bactriane et la Chine) pendant les cinq premiers siècles de l'Ere Chrétienne, d'après les témoignages Latins, Grecs, Arabes, Persans, Indiens et Chinois." I do not know which were first published of the two journals, the English or the French.

and again, whenever some enterprising Roman merchant strayed to any far Eastern land, stirred up to wonder and speculation kings and princes, but never influenced their policy, and never occupied the imagination in any way of the people.

After reading Reinaud's work I must own that I hold still to my own view, but whether after reading Reinaud others will hold it with me is quite another matter.

TRAVELS OF

APOLLONIUS OF TYANA.

THE

INDIAN TRAVELS OF APOLLONIUS OF TYANA.

PHILOSTRATUS, in his life of Apollonius Tyanensis,[1] has given an account of that philosopher's visit to India. And as he professes to have drawn his materials from the note-book of Damis, Apollonius's fellow-traveller and friend; as moreover he professes to have edited that note-book much as Hawkesworth edited the journals of Cook, we may fairly assume that he has given an original and authentic account of India—and indeed the only one that has come down to us from the olden world in a complete state. Again, as Apollonius was the only Greek who up to his time had visited India for other purposes than those of war, negotiation, or commerce; as he visited it to make himself acquainted with its rites, discipline, and doctrines; and as he travelled unencumbered by a retinue, and was welcomed by its kings, and was with Damis for four months the

[1] For another account of Apollonius, by the aid of Satan a miracle worker and maker of talismans, τελεσματα, but without mention of his Indian travels, see from Domninos (Malalas, Chron. B. x, pp. 263-4, Bonn ed., and Cedrenus, who refers to Philostratus, Hist. i, p. 431).

guest of its Brahmins; he and Damis with him had every opportunity of familiar intercourse with all classes of its population, and of thus acquiring much and accurate information on matters beyond the reach of ordinary travellers. Philostratus's account then is full of promise; and I propose to give a condensed translation of it, and afterwards to examine into its authority and value.

Towards the close of the first half century of our era, Apollonius, then upwards of forty years of age[2] and resident at Antioch, set out to visit India, its Brahmins and Sramans (Γερμανες), taking with him two family slaves to act apparently as his secretaries.[3] At Nineveh, he met with and was joined by Damis, a native of the place, who recommended himself to his notice by a practical knowledge of the road to Babylon, and an acquaintance with the Persian, Armenian and Cadusian languages. Together they journey on to Babylon, but warned by a dream first turn aside to visit Sissia and those Eretrians, whom Darius five hundred years before had settled there, and whom they find still speaking Greek, and still as they heard using Greek letters,[4] and

[2] Yet he speaks of himself as a young man, προσηκειν γαρ νεῳ ανδρι αποδημειν—I. B. 18 c; and in Domninos he dies in his thirty-fourth year.—Malalas, u. s.

[3] I presume this from their qualifications; the one is a good, the other a quick penman: μετα δυοιν θεραποντοιν, οἵπερ αυτῳ πατρικω ηστην, ὁ μεν ες ταχος γραφων, ὁ δ' ες καλλος. *ib.*

[4] Herodotus, vi, 119, cotemporary with the sons of the exiles, tells of these Eretrians and of their use of the Greek language—nothing improbable—but Philostratus intimates that when Apollonius visited them some four hundred years afterwards, they

still dwelling near that wondrous petroleum well so carefully described by Herodotus.

After a stay at Babylon of eighteen months, Apollonius, his friend and attendants, in the beginning of summer proceed for India on camels and with a guide furnished by the Parthian king Bardanes. Of their route we know only that it lay through a rich and pleasant country, and that the villages they traversed hurried to do them honour and to supply their wants;

still continued to use the Greek language and character. Is this credible? The scattered Jews have not forgotten Hebrew. The Germans, whom Theodoric in the sixth century located in the mountains of the Vicentino, and who are known as the "Sette Communi," are to this day Germans; and the French refugees who, after the edict of Nantes, settled at Friedrichsdorf in Hesse Homburg, are still French. But these fragments of nations lived in their own villages and married only among themselves; and the Jews, if unlike them, they have in a certain sense mixed with the peoples among whom they have settled, yet they like them have only married with their own race; and they have besides a sacred book written in a sacred language, the study of which is imperative and necessary to their happiness here and hereafter. But these Eretrians when they reached Susa were reduced, so writes Philostratus, to four hundred men and but ten women. Not more then than ten of their families spoke Greek as their mother tongue. Of the remaining three hundred and ninety men, all who married must have married native women, and their children spoke Persian certainly and possibly Greek—but with every succeeding generation more Persian and less Greek—till after a few generations Greek must have been all but forgotten. And that this was so does not history by its very silence show? Or how is it that from the age of Herodotus to that of Apollonius we never hear the voice of these Eretrians save in these pages? And how is it that though so near to Babylon they escaped the notice of Alexander and his historians, who, the one so signally punished, and the other so carefully recorded the punishment of the perfidious and self-exiled Branchidæ?—Strabo, B. xi, xii, c. 49.

for a gold plate[5] on their leading camel announced them guests of the king. We then hear of them enjoying the perfumed air[6] at the foot of Caucasus, the mountain range which, while it separates India from Media, extends by one of its branches to the Red Sea.[7] Of this Caucasus, they heard from the barbarians myths like those of the Greek. They were told of Prometheus and Hercules, not the Theban, and of the eagle; some pointed to a cavern, others to the mountain's two peaks, a stadium apart, as the place where Prometheus was bound; and his chains, though of what made it is not easy to guess,[8] still hung, Damis says, from the rocks. His memory too is still dear to the mountaineers, who for his sake still pursue the eagle with hate; and now lay snares for it, and now with fiery javelins destroy its nest.[9] On the mountain they find the people already

5 So Marco Polo relates that the monks sent by Kublai Khan on an embassy to the Pope, receive "une table d'or en laquel se contenoit ke les trois messages en toutes les pars qu'il alaissent lor deust estre donnée toutes les messions que lor bazongnoit et chevalz et homes por lor escodre de une terre a l'autre."—P. 6, Ed. Société Géographique.

6 So Burnes describes the plain of Peshawar, "thyme and violets perfumed the air," (Bokhara, ii, 70). At Muchnee "a sweet aromatic smell was exhaled from the grass and plants." (*ib.*, 101.)

7 Wilford says "the Indian ocean is called Arunoda, or the Red Sea, being reddened by the reflection of the solar beams from that side of Meru of the same colour." (As. Res., viii, p. 320, 8vo.)

8 *Και δεσμα δ Δαμις ανηφθαι των πετρων λεγει, ου ραδια συμβαλλειν την ὑλην.*—II. B. 3 c.

9 The same tale is in Arrian and Strabo. Wilford thus accounts for it: not far from Banyam is the den of Garuda, the bird-god; he devoured some servants of Maha Deva, and this drew upon him the resentment of that irascible deity, whose servants are called Pramat'has. As. Res. vi, 312-3, corrected by viii, 259, and Radja Taranjini, i, p. 414.

inclined to black,[10] and the men four cubits high: on the other side the Indus the men reached five cubits.[11] On their way to the river, as they were going along in the bright moonshine, they fell in with an Empusa, who now in this form now in that followed after them; until Apollonius, and at his instigation his companions, attacked it with scoffs and jeers, the only safeguard against it, and it fled away jabbering.[12]

As they approached the summit of the mountain,—the dwelling of the Gods as their guide told them,—they found the road so steep that they were obliged to go on foot. On the other side, in the country between Caucasus and the Cophen,[13] they met men riding on elephants, but they were only elephant herdsmen; others on dromedaries, which can run 1000 stadia in a day without rest.[14] Here an Indian on a dromedary rode up to them and asked their guide whither they

10 Strabo, xv, I, § 13, Arrian, Indica, c. vi.

11 Onesicritus, Frag. Hist. Alex. Didot, p. 55, § 25. Lord Cornwallis (Correspondence) remarks on the great height of the Bengal Sepoys; Sir C. Napier (Life) thinks our infantry average two inches below them, but cover more ground. Tall men, therefore; but five cubits!

12 At the foot of the Indus and Cabool river...an ignis fatuus shows itself every evening.—Burnes, II, p. 68. And consult Masoudi's account of the goule and the mode in which the Arabs rid themselves of it.—Les Prairies d'or, III, p. 314, tr. de la Société Asiatique.

13 Cophen, *i. e.* Cabool. Caucasus Grâvakâsas, the bright rock mountain, Bohlen, Das Alte Indien, I, p. 12. "Scythæ...Caucasum montem Groucasum, h. e., nive candidum appellavere."—Plin. Hist. Nat., vi, 19.

14 Elphinstone says, "An elderly minister of the Raja of Bikaneer...had just come on a camel one hundred and seventy-five miles in three days." (Caubul, Introduction, p. 230, I, v.) Sir C. Napier mentions a march of eighty or ninety miles by his camel corps without a halt (Life of Sir C. H. Napier, II, 418), and has

were going; and when he was told the object of their journey he told it again to the herdsmen, who shouted for joy, called to them to come near, and gave them wine and honey, both got from the palm; and also slices of lion and panther flesh, just killed.[15] They accepted everything but the flesh, and rode onward in an easterly direction.

At a fountain they sat down to dine; and, in the course of conversation, Apollonius observed that they had met many Indians singing, dancing, and rolling about drunk with palm wine:[16] and that the Indian money was of orichalcum and bronze—purely Indian, and not stamped like the Roman and Median coins.[17]

They crossed the Cophen, here not very broad or

no doubt with riding camels of marching two hundred miles in forty-eight hours.—III, 78.

15 An exaggeration of a remark of Arrian's probably: Σιτοφαγοι δε...Ινδοι εισιν, όσοι γε μη ορειοι αυτων· ουτοι δε τα θηρεια κρεα σιτεονται ("Indica," xvii, § 5), e.g. "bear's flesh and anything else they can get" (Elphinstone of Caufiristaun, *ib.*, II, 434), "they all eat flesh half raw" (*ib.*, 438). Sir C. Malet in a letter to Forbes tells of a lion killed by him near Cambay. "The oil of the lion was extracted by stewing the flesh when cut up with a quantity of spices: the meat was white and of a delicate appearance, and was eaten by the hunters."—Orient. Mem., II, p. 182, 8vo. Sir H. Holland, in his Remains, speaks of having tasted "filet de lion" in Algeria, but of it as coarse and unpleasant.

16 Of the same mountaineers, Elphinstone: "they drink wine to excess" (*ib.*) And see from the Karnaparva an account of the people of the Panjab, their irreverence, drunkenness, and dissoluteness, to be matched however in our moral and Christian London (Slokas, 11-13; in the Appendix to vol. i of Raj. Taran., 562). Ælian, i, 61, speaks of the Indian drinking bouts; Pliny of the wine: "Reliquos vinum, ut Indos, palmis exprimere" (Hist. Nat., vi, 32): the Vishnu Purana of wine from the Kadamba tree.—P. 571, note 2.

17 The Indian money is: ὑλη κεκομψευμενη, metal refined, prepared;

deep, themselves in boats, their camels on foot, and now entered a country subject to a king. Here they saw Mount Nysa; it rises up to a peak, like Tmolus[18] in Lydia. It is cultivated, and its ascent has thus been made practicable. On its summit they found a moderate sized temple of Bacchus; this temple was a circular plot of ground, enclosed by a hedgerow of laurels, vines, and ivy,[19] all of which had been planted by Bacchus himself, and had so grown and intertwined their branches together as to form a roof and walls impervious to the wind and rain. In the interior Bacchus had placed his own statue—in form an Indian youth, but of white stone. About and around it lay crooked knives, baskets and wine-vats in gold and silver, as if ready for the vintage. Aye, and the cities at the foot of the mountain hear and join in his orgies, and Nysa itself quakes with them.

About Bacchus,[20] Philostratus goes on to say—whether

and the Roman *κεχαραγμενη*, stamped. In Menu's time gold and silver coins were probably unknown, for he gives (viii, 131) "the names of copper, silver, and gold weights commonly used among men," *Ὑλη κεκομψευμενη*, probably; but when Apollonius visited India we know that money, gold and silver coins, were current, issued by the Indo-Greek and Indo-Scythic kings, *vide* Lassen, "Baktrische Könige," *passim*.

18 Nishadha, probably to the south of Meru (Vishnu Purana, 167). Arrian similarly connects Tmolus with Nysa.—Exped. Alex., v, 1.

19 Laurels and ivy Alexander finds on Meru; vines too by implication (Arrian, Exped., v, ii, § 6), but vines on which the grapes do not ripen (Strabo, xv, § 8). Burnes says that in Cabool the vines are so plentiful that the grapes are given for three months in the year to cattle (*ut sup.*, ii, 131. *See* also Wilson's Ariana Antiq., p. 193).

20 Chares, Hist. Alex., p. 117, § 13, one of the historians of Alex-

speaking in his own person or from the journal of Damis I know not—Greeks and Hindus are not agreed; for the former assert that the Theban Bacchus with his bacchanals conquered and overran India, and they cite, among other proofs, a discus of Indian silver in the treasury at Delphi, with this inscription: "Bacchus, Jove and Semele's son, from India to the Delphian Apollo." But of the latter, the Indians of the Caucasus believe that he was an Assyrian stranger, not unacquainted however with him of Thebes; while those of the Indus and Ganges declare that he was the son of the Indus,[21] and that the Theban Bacchus was his disciple and imitator, though he called himself the son of Jove, and pretended to have been born of Jove's thigh,[22] *μηρος*, Meros, a mountain near to Nysa. They add, that in honour of his Indian prototype, he planted Nysa with vines brought from Thebes, and on Nysa the Greek historians assert that Alexander celebrated the Bacchic orgies,[23] but the mountaineers will have it that Alex-

ander, speaks of an Indian god, Σοροαδειος, Sanscrit, Suradevas (von Bohlen), Suryadéva, the Sun God (Schlegel, Ind. Bib., i, 250); which being interpreted is οινοποιος, the wine maker; but the Vishnu Purana knows of no wine god, only of a wine goddess (Varuna, *vide*, pp. 76, 571, 4to. ed.) In general, however, Bacchus may be identified with Siva, and Hercules with Vishnu and Krishna.

21 For the Indo-Bacchus myth, *see* Arrian, v, i, who receives it with hesitation; and Strabo, xv, I, 9, who rejects it; Lassen, Ind. Alt., II, 133; von Bohlen, *ut sup.*, I, 142; and Schwanbeck on Megasthenes, "Frag. Hist.," II, 420, Didot.

22 "Aroushi fille de Manou fut l'épouse de ce sage. Elle conçut de lui ce fameux Aaurva qui vint au monde en perçant la cuisse de son père."—Mahabharata, i, 278; Fauche, tr.

23 According to Arrian, *ut sup.*, and II, 5, it was Meru that Alexander ascended, and on Meru that he feasted and sacrificed to Bacchus.

ander, notwithstanding his love of glory and of antiquity, never ascended the mountain, but satisfied himself with prayer and sacrifice at its foot. He so feared lest the sight of the vines should raise in his soldiers, long accustomed to water, a longing for wine and the ease and pleasures of home.

The rock Aornus,[24] though at no great distance from Nysa, Damis says they did not visit, as it was somewhat out of their way. He heard however that it had been taken by Alexander, and was fifteen stadia in height; and that it was called Aornus, not because no bird could fly over it, but because there was a chasm on its summit which drew down to it all birds, much like the Parthenon at Athens, and several places in Phrygia and Lydia.[25]

On their way to the Indus, they fell in with a lad about thirteen years old riding an elephant and urging him on with a crooked rod, which he thrust into him like an anchor. On the Indus itself they watched a herd of about thirty elephants, whom some huntsmen were pursuing.[26] Apollonius admired the sagacity the elephants displayed in crossing the river; the smallest and lightest led the way, the mothers followed holding

[24] Strabo, xv, L. i, § 8. Aornus; Awara, Awarana, a stockade.—Wilson, Ariana Antiqua, p. 192; but Renas according to v. Bohlen, and Rani-garh according to Lassen, Indische Alterthums: 140, note 7.

[25] *See* Eustathius Com. in Dionys., p. 403, II Geog. Min. According to one of his authorities, the lake Lycophron like the lake Aornus was impassable to birds because of its noisome exhalations.

[26] Just in the same locality (*see* Arrian, IV, xxx, 7) Alexander first sees a troop of elephants, and afterwards joins in an elephant hunt.

up their cubs with their tusks and trunks, while the largest brought up the rear. He spoke of their docility; their love for their keeper, how they would eat out of his hand like dogs, coax him with their trunks, and, as he had seen among the nomads, open wide their mouths for him to thrust his head down their throats. He told too, how during the night they would bewail their slavery, not with their usual roar, but with piteous moans; and how, out of respect for man, they would at his approach stay their wailing; and he referred their docility and ready obedience more to their own self-command and tractable nature, than to the skill or power of their guide and rider. From the people they heard that elephants were found in the marsh, the mountain, and the plain. According to the Indians,[27] the marsh elephant is stupid and idle; its teeth are few and black, and often porous or knotted, and will not bear the knife. The mountain elephants are treacherous and malignant, and, save for their own ends, little attached to man; their teeth are small, but tolerably white, and not hard to work. The elephants of the plain are useful animals, tractable and imitative; they may be taught to write, and to dance and jump to the sound of the pipe;[28] their teeth are very long and white and may be easily cut to any shapes. The Indians use the elephant in war; they fight from it in turrets, large enough for ten or fifteen archers or spearmen; and they say that it will itself

[27] All this was borrowed probably from Juba, but is so put as to seem to rest on Hindu authority; for Ælian, § 4; xiii, II, 1, of the kinds of elephants.—*τους μεν εκ των ελων αλισκομενους ανοητους ἡγουνται Ινδοι.*

[28] Confer Porphyry de Abstinentia, III, 15; died A.D. 305.

join in the fight, holding and throwing the spear with its trunk as with a hand. The Indian elephant is of a large size, as much larger than the Lybian as this than the Nisæan horse. It lives to a great age, and Apollonius saw one in Taxila which had fought against Alexander about three hundred and fifty years before, and which Alexander had honoured with the name of Ajax. On its tusks were golden bracelets, with this inscription: "Ajax to the sun, from Alexander, the son of Jove." The people were accustomed to anoint it with unguents, and ornament it with garlands.[29]

When about to cross the Indus, their Babylonian guide, who was unacquainted with the river, presented to the Satrap of the Indus a letter from Bardanes. And the Satrap, out of regard to the king, though no officer of his, supplied them with his own barge for themselves, boats for their camels, and a guide to the Hydraotis. He also wrote to his sovereign, to beg him that, in his treatment of this Greek and truly divine man, he would emulate the generosity of Bardanes.

Where they crossed, the Indus was forty stadia in breadth.[30] It takes its rise in the Caucasus;[31] and, from

[29] Pliny (viii, v) describes the elephant as crossing rivers in the same way; he speaks of their wonderful self-respect, "mirus pudor," and of one called Ajax; Arrian (Indica, c. 14 and 15) of their grief at being captured, of their attachment to their keepers, their love of music, and their long life extending though to but two hundred years (Onesicritus gives them three hundred, and sometimes five hundred years.—Strabo, xv); Ælian (xiii, § 9) and Pliny (viii) state that they carry three warriors only, and are much larger than the African. The division into marsh and plain, etc., I suspect is from Juba.

[30] Ctesias, 488, says the Indus is forty stadia where narrowest.

its very fountain, is larger (μειζω αυτοθεν) than any other river in Asia.[32] In its course it receives many navigable rivers. Like the Nile[33] it overflows the country, and deposits a fertilizing mud, which, as in Egypt, prepares the land for the husbandman. It abounds, like the Nile, with sea-horses and crocodiles,[34] as they themselves witnessed in crossing it (κομιζομενοι δε δια του Ινδου); and it produces, too, the same flowers. In India the winter is warm, the summer stifling; but the heat, providentially, is moderated by frequent rains. The natives told him, that when the season for the rise of the river is at hand, the king sacrifices on its banks black bulls and horses (black among them, because of their complexion, being the nobler colour), and after the sacrifice throws into the river a gold measure like a corn measure,—why, the people themselves knew not; but probably, as Apollonius conjectured, for an abundant harvest, or for such a moderate[35] rise of the river as would benefit the land.

See Lassen, *ut sup.*, II, 637, who accounts for Ctesias's exaggeration (his reasons do not apply to Damis), and Wilson's Notes on the Indica of Ctesias, who excuses it (p. 13).

[31] "Indus...in jugo...Caucasi montis...effusus...undeviginti accipit amnes...*nusquam latior quinquaginta stadiis.*"—Pliny, Hist. Nat., vi, 23.

[32] So Ctesias, so Ibn Batuta: "the Scinde is the greatest river in the world, and overflows during the hot weather just as the Nile does; and at this time they sow the land." Burnes, I think, shows that it carries a greater body of water than the Ganges.

[33] Strabo, xv. § 16.

[34] Eratosthenes gives it the same animals as the Nile, except the sea-horse; Onesicritus the sea-horse also.—Strabo, u. s., 13.

[35] Sir C. Napier attributed a fever which prostrated his army and the natives to an extraordinary rise of the Indus.—Quarterly Review, October 1858, p. 499.

The Indus passed, their new guide led them straight to Taxila,[36] where was the palace of the Indian king. The people here wore cotton, the produce of the country, and sandals made of the fibre or bark of the papyrus[37] (*υποδηματα βυβλου*), and a leather cap when it rained. The better classes were clad in byssus, a stuff with which Apollonius, who affected a sombre colour in his dress, was much pleased. This byssus grows on a tree, like the poplar in its stem, but with leaves like the willow; it is exported into Egypt for sacred uses.

Taxila[38] was about the size of Nineveh, walled like a Greek city, and was the residence of a sovereign who ruled over what of old was the kingdom of Porus. Just outside the walls[39] was a temple of near a hundred feet, of porphyry[40] (*λιθου κογχυλιατου*), and in it a shrine,

[36] See Aristobulus, Account of the Progress of Alexander.—Strabo, u. s., § 17.

[37] Arrian's Indica: "Their dress is of cotton, their sandals of leather;" but Herodotus gives the Egyptian priests, *ὑποδηματα βυβλινα*.—II, 37.

[38] Wilford (As. Res., viii, 349) speaks of Tacshaila and its ruins; Wilson identifies Taxila with Taksha-sila of the Hindus between the Indus and Hydaspes, in the vicinity of Manikyala (Ar. Ant., 196, Elphinstone, ed. I, 130). Arrian celebrates its size and wealth the largest city between the Indus and the Hydaspes.—V, 8, Exp. Alex.

[39] Ram Raz (Architecture of the Hindus, p. 2), of the temples of Vishnu and Siva, says that the latter should be without the village. Hiouen-Thsang (I, 151), describes Taxila, and speaks of a stupa and convent outside the walls, built by Asoka.

[40] The tope of Manikyala described by Elphinstone is a hundred (150) paces in circumference, and seventy feet high (Ari. Ant., 31). Lassen (II, 514, com. 1181) speaks of the influence of Greek art on Indian architecture; but adds, that the Indians built with brick. They may, however, have faced their buildings with stone; and

small considering the size of the temple and its many columns, but still very beautiful. Round the shrine were hung pictures on copper tablets, representing the feats of Alexander and Porus. The elephants, horses, soldiers, and armour, were portrayed in a mosaic[41] of orichalcum, silver, gold, and oxydised copper (*μελανι χαλκῳ*); the spears, javelins, and swords in iron; but the several metals were all worked into one another with so nice a gradation of tints, that the pictures they formed, in correctness of drawing, vivacity of expression, and truthfulness of perspective,[42] reminded one of the productions of Zeuxis, Polygnotus and Euphranor. They told too of the noble character of Porus, for it was not till after the death of Alexander that he placed them in the temple,—and this, though they represented Alexander as a conqueror, and himself as conquered and wounded, and receiving from Alexander the kingdom of India.

In this temple they wait until the king can be apprised of their arrival. Apollonius whiles away the time with a conversation upon painting, in the course of which he remarks that colour is not necessary to a picture; that an Indian drawn in chalk would be known as an Indian and black of colour, by his somewhat flat nose, his crisp hair, his large jaws, and wild

the *λιθος κογχυλιατης* may have been of that porphyry, or red marble, used in the tombs at Tattah.—Life of Sir C. Napier, iv, 38.

[41] Lassen (513-14) states, on Sinhalese authority, that the Hindus were skilled in mosaics; and (II, 426-7) he describes a casket, the figures on which he supposes were of a mosaic of precious stones.

[42] *Το ευσχιον το εμπνουν και το εσεχον τε και εξεχον.*

eyes.[43] While they are thus talking, a messenger and interpreter arrive from the king, with a permit for them to enter the city, and to stay in it three days, beyond which time no strangers are allowed in Taxila.

They are taken to the palace. They found the city divided by narrow streets, well-arranged, and reminding them of Athens. From the streets, the houses seemed of only one story, but they all had an underground floor.[44] They saw the Temple of the Sun, and in it statues of Alexander and Porus, the one gold, the other of bronze (μελανι χαλκῳ); its walls were of red marble, but glittering with gold; the image of the god was of pearls,[45] having, as is usual with the barbarians in sacred things, a symbolical meaning.

The palace was distinguished by no extraordinary magnificence, and was just like the house of any citizen of the better class. There were no sentinels or body-guards and but few servants about, and perhaps three or four persons who were waiting to talk with the king. The same simplicity was observable in the courts, halls, waiting and inner rooms; and it pleased Apollonius more than all the pomp of Babylon. When admitted to the king's presence, Apollonius, through the interpreter, addressed the king as a philosopher, and com-

[43] Arrian, Indica, vi, and compare with it Vishnu Purana, note 4, p. 100, where is a description of the barbarous races of India.

[44] Lassen, *ut sup.*, 514. The underground floor, Elphinstone says, even the poor have at Peshawur.—Caubul, Introduc., p. 74.

[45] "On représente le soleil la face rouge...ses membres sont prononcés, il porte des pendants à ses oreilles. Un collier de perles lui descend du cou sur la poitrine."—Reinaud, Mem. sur l'Inde, p. 121. "Albyrouny rapporte que de son temps il y avoit un temple érigé au soleil, avec une statue."—pp. 97, 98, 99.

plimented him on his moderation. The king, Phraotes, in answer, said that he was moderate because his wants were few, and that as he was wealthy, he employed his wealth in doing good to his friends and in subsidizing the barbarians, his neighbours, to prevent them from themselves ravaging, or allowing other barbarians to ravage his territories. Here one of his courtiers offered to crown him with a jewelled mitre, but he refused it, as well because all pomp was hateful to him, as because of Apollonius's presence.

Apollonius inquired into his mode of life. The king told him that he drank but little wine, as much as he usually poured out in libation to the sun; that he hunted for exercise,[46] and gave away what he killed; that, for himself, he lived on vegetables and herbs, and the head and fruit of the palm, and other fruits[47] which he cultivated with his own hands. With this account of his kingly tastes and occupations Apollonius was delighted, and he frequently looked at Damis. They now talked together a long time about the road to the Brahmans; and when they had done, the king ordered the Babylonian guide to be treated with the hospitality wont to be shown to travellers from Babylon, and the satrap guide to be sent back home with the usual travelling allowance. Then taking Apollonius by the hand,

[46] V. Strabo, of the Mysicani, *ib.*, 34. "But drinking, dice, women and hunting, let the king consider as the four most pernicious vices."—Menu, vii, 50.

[47] Arrian, Indica, xi, c. § 8. So Nacir Eddin of Delhi, "copiat des exemplaires du livre illustre, les vendait, et se nourrissait avec le prix qu'il en retirait."—Ibn Batoutah, 169, iii, tr. d. l. Soc. Asiatique.

and ordering the interpreter to leave them, Phraotes asked him, in Greek, to receive him, the king, as a table companion. Apollonius, surprised, inquired why he had not spoken Greek from the first. "Because", answered the king, "I would not seem bold, or to forget that I am, after all, only a barbarian; but your kindness, and the pleasure you take in my conversation, have got the better of me, and I can no longer conceal myself from you. And how I became thus acquainted with Greek I will presently show you at large." "But why," again asked Apollonius, "instead of inviting me, did you beg me to invite you to dinner?" "Because," said the king, "I look on you as the better man; for wisdom is above royalty (*το γαρ βασιλικωτερον σοφια εχει*).[48] So saying, he led him to the place where he was accustomed to bathe.[49] This was a garden,[50] about a stadium long, with a swimming bath of cold running water in the middle of it, and on each side an exercising ground. Here he practised the discus and the javelin, Greek fashion,[51] and then, when tired, jumped into the water, and exercised himself with swimming. After

[48] The old Stoic maxim: "Solus sapiens rex." Olearius in Philost.

[49] Hiouen Thsang, I, 70, 71, describes the nice cleanliness of the Indians, but confines the washing before meat to the hands.

[50] Confer Ælian's description of the garden of the Indian kings, xiii, c. 18, de Nat. Animal.

[51] Menu of the kingly duties: "Having consulted with his ministers,...having used exercise becoming a warrior, and having bathed, let the king enter at noon his private apartments for the purpose of taking food" (vii, 216). But Strabo (xv, i, 51) says, the Indians use friction rather than gymnastic exercises.

the bath they went to dinner, crowned with garlands,[52] as is usual with the Indians when they feast in the king's palace.

Of the dinner Damis has given a detailed account. The king, and about five of his family with him, lay on a low couch; the other guests sat on stools. The table was like an altar, about as high as a man's knee; it was in the middle of the room, round, and as large as would be a circle formed by thirty people with joined hands standing up to dance. It was strewed over with laurel, and a sort of myrtle from which the Indians prepare their unguents, and was set out with fish and birds, the carcases of lions and goats and sows, and with tiger loins[53]—the only part of the tiger they eat, and this because they suppose that at its birth it raises its fore-paws to the rising sun. Each guest, as he wanted anything, got up and went to the table; and taking a bit of this, cutting off a slice of that, he returned to his seat and ate his fill, always eating bread with his meat. When they had had enough, gold and silver bowls, each one large enough for ten guests, were brought in, and from these they drank, stooping down like cattle. In the meanwhile, they were amused by various feats which required no little skill and courage: a javelin was thrown upward, and at the same time a boy leaped at

[52] "Le roi et ses ministres ornent leurs têtes de guirlandes de fleurs."—Hiouen Thsang, p. 70, I, v.

[53] Strabo, quoting Nearchus, better describes the Indians, at least he describes them as we at this day find them: *μηδε γαρ νυσους ειναι πολλας δια την λιτοτητα της διαιτης και την αοινιαν* (xv, 1, 45), their food principally *ορυζαν ροφητην*, rice curry or porridge?—§ 53. See however, n. 17, p. 6, *supra.*

it and tumbled head over heels while in the air, but in such a way that he passed over the javelin as it fell, and with the certainty of being wounded if he did not properly time his somersault; indeed the weapon was carried round, and the guests tested its sharpness. One man also was so good a marksman, that he set up his own son against a board, and then threw his darts, so aiming them that, fixed in the board, they traced out his son's outline.[54]

Damis and the others were much amused with these entertainments; but Apollonius, who was at the king's table, paid little attention to them; and, turning to the king, asked him, how he came to know Greek, and where he acquired his philosophy. The king, smiling, answered, "In old times when a ship put into port, the people used to ask its crew if they were pirates,[55] piracy was then so common. But now, though philosophy is

[54] A Chinese juggler lately performed the same feat in London, and a very small feat compared with that of Baresanes, an Armenian, which Julius Africanus himself witnessed. He shot his arrows with such precision as with them to sketch out on a shield the portrait of the man who had it. See the passage from the κεστοι, quoted by Hilgenfeld (Bardesanes, p. 14, n. 6). This archer, Bardesanes, Hilgenfeld is inclined to think is the same man as the heresiarch Bardesanes; for they were cotemporaries, and both were connected with the court of the Abgari. But one was a learned man and a philosopher, the other skilled in archery—and so skilled, that whatever his natural aptitude, he never could have attained to his wonderful proficiency but by life-long painstaking practice, a devotion to his art only to be met with in him who has to live by it, and quite incompatible with the cultivated tastes and scholarship of his namesake. It would require some very strong evidence to induce me to identify them as one and the same.

[55] Allusion to Thucydides, I.

God's most precious gift to man, the first question you Greeks put to a stranger, even of the lowest rabble, is 'Are you a philosopher?' And in very truth with you Greeks, I speak not of you Apollonius, philosophy is much the same as piracy, for to the many who profess it, it is like an ill-fitting garment which they have stolen, and in which they strut about awkwardly, trailing it on the ground. And like thieves, on whom the fear of justice presses, they hurry to enjoy the present hour, and give themselves up to gluttony, debauchery, and effeminacy; and no wonder, for while your laws punish coiners of bad money, they take no cognizance of the authors and utterers of a false philosophy. Here, on the other hand, philosophy is a high honour, and before we allow any one to study it, we first send him to the home of the Brahmans, who inquire into his character and parentage. He must shew that his progenitors, for three generations, have been without stain or reproach, and that he himself is of pure morals and of a retentive intellect. The character of his progenitors," the king went on to say, "if of living men, was ascertained from witnesses; and if of dead, was known from the public records.[56] For when an Indian died, a legally appointed officer repaired to his house, and inquired into, and set down in writing, his mode of life, and exactly, under the penalty of being declared incapable

[56] Strabo of the Indian city ædiles says a part took note of the birth and deaths, that the birth or death of good or bad men may be known: *μη αφανεις ειεν αἱ κρειτονες και χειρους γοναι και θανατοι* (xv, 1, 51); from Megasthenes, Frag. Hist., II, p. 431, § 37, and consult Bardesanes' account of the *Σαμαναιοι* in l. iv, c. 17, of Porphyry de Abstinentiâ.

of holding any public office. As to the youth himself, they judged him worthy or otherwise from his eyes, eyebrows, and cheeks, which as in a mirror reflect the mind and disposition."

The king then told how his father, the son of a king, had been left very young an orphan; and how during his minority two of his relatives according to Indian custom acted as regents, but with so little regard to law, that some nobles conspired against them, and slew them as they were sacrificing to the Indus, and seized upon the government;—how on this his father, then sixteen years of age, fled to the king beyond the Hydaspes, a greater king than himself, who received him kindly, and offered either to adopt him, or to replace him on his throne; and how, declining this offer, he requested to be sent to the Brahmans; and how the Brahmans educated him; and how in time he married the daughter of the Hydaspian king, and received with her seven villages as pin-money (*εἰς ζώνην*), and had issue one son,—himself, Phraotes. Phraotes told of himself, that he was brought up by his father in the Greek fashion till the age of twelve; that he was then sent to the Brahmans, and treated by them as a son, for "they especially love", he observed, "those who know and speak Greek, as akin to them in mind and disposition"; that his parents died; and that in his nineteenth year, just as, by the advice of the Brahmans, he was beginning to take into his own hands the management of his estates, he was deprived of them by the king, his uncle, and was then supported with four servants by willing contributions from his mother's freedmen (*απελευθερων*).

As however he is one day reading the Heraclidæ, he hears from a friend of his father's, that if he will return home, he may recover his family kingdom, but he must be quick. The tragedy he was reading he accepts as an omen; and he goes on to say:—"When I crossed the Hydraotis, I heard that, of the usurpers, one was already dead, and the other besieged in this very palace; so I hurried on, proclaiming to the villages I passed through who I was, and what were my rights: and the people received me gladly; and declaring I was the very picture of my father and grandfather, they accompanied me, many of them armed with swords and bows, and our numbers increased daily; and when we reached this city, the inhabitants, with torches lit at the altar of the Sun, and singing the praises of my father and grandfather, came out and welcomed me, and brought me hither. But the drone within they walled up,[57] though I begged them not to kill him in that way.

Apollonius then enquired whether the Sophoi of Alexander and these Brahmans were the same people. The king told him they were not; that Alexander's Sophoi were the Oxydracæ,[58] a free and warlike race, but rather dabblers in philosophy than philosophers;[59] that the Brahman country lay between the Hyphasis and the Ganges; and that Alexander never invaded it—not through fear, but dissuaded by the appearance

[57] I prefer Olearius's reading, *τον δε εισω χηφηνα περι, το τειχος ειρξαν*, better suited to the *χηφηνα*.

[53] Strabo, xv, I, 33, connects them with the Malli. Burnes identifies them with the people of Ooch, the Malli with those of Mooltan.—*Ut sup.*, I, p. 99.

[59] *Σοφιαν δε μεταχειρισασθαι, οὐδεν χρηστον εἰδοτας.*—Philost., II, c. 33.

of the sacrificial victims. "And though," said Phraotes, he might it is true have crossed the Hyphasis and occupied the neighbouring lands, yet the stronghold of the Brahmans he never could have taken—no, not though every man in his army had been an Ajax or an Achilles.[60] For these sacred and god-loved men would have driven him back—not with human weapons, but with thunders and lightnings, and tempests, as they had routed the Egyptian Hercules and Bacchus, who thought with united arms to have stormed their fort; and so routed them, that Hercules it is said threw away his golden shield, which, because of its owner's renown and its own embossments,[61] they then set up as an offering in their temple."

While they were thus conversing, music and a song were introduced, on which Apollonius enquired what the festal procession meant. The king explained to him that it was usual with the Indians to sing to the king before he retired to rest, songs of good counsel, wishing him good dreams, and that he may rise in the morning a good man and a wise counsellor for his people[62]. And

[60] So the pseudo-Callisthenes notices the Oxydracæ as speaking Greek, p. 88, and as visited but not conquered by Alexander, p. 99, ed. Muller.

[61] These embossments represented, the king goes on to say, Hercules setting up his pillars at Gades, and driving back the ocean; proof, he asserts, that it was the Egyptian, and not the Theban Hercules, who was at Gades.

[62] Menu, among the vices the king is to shun, names dancing and instrumental music (vii, 47), but afterwards advises that, "in the inmost recesses of his mansion, having been recreated by musical strains, he should take rest early."—vii, 224-5; see, however, As. Res., ix, p. 76.

so talking, they went to bed. The next morning, Apollonius discourses upon sleep and dreams, and the king displays his knowledge of Greek legends. They then separate—the king to transact the business of his kingdom and to decide some law-suits—Apollonius to offer his prayers to the Sun. When they again meet, the king tells Apollonius that the state of the victims had not permitted the Court to sit on that day, and he lays before him a case in dispute—one of treasure-trove, and in land which has just changed hands, the buyer and seller both claiming the treasure. The king is in much perplexity, and states the pleas on both sides; and the suit might have been drawn out to the same length, and become as celebrated as that of the ass and the shadow at Abdera, had not Apollonius come to his assistance. He inquires into the life and character of the litigants; finds that the seller is a bad, and the purchaser a good man; and to the last therefore awards the treasure.

When the three days of their sojourn were expired, and the king learns that their camels from Babylon are worn out, he orders that of his white camels[63] on the Indus, four shall be sent to Bardanes, and four others given to Apollonius, together with provisions and a guide to the Brahmans. He offers him besides gold and jewels and linen garments; the gold Apollonius refuses, but he accepts the linen garments because they are like the old genuine Attic cloak, and he picks out besides one jewel, because of its mystic and divine

[63] Elphinstone (*ut supra*, I, 40) speaks of white camels as rare.

properties. He receives also a letter for Iarchas,[64] to this effect:—"The King Phraotes to the Master Iarchas and the wise men with him, greeting: Apollonius, a very wise man, thinks you wiser than himself, and has travelled hither to learn your doctrine. Send him back knowing all you know. Your lessons will not be lost, for he speaks better, and has a better memory than any man I ever knew. Shew him, Father Iarchas, the throne on which I sat when you gave me the kingdom. His followers are worthy of all praise, if only for submitting to such a man. Farewell."

They leave Taxila, and after two days' journey, reach the plain, where Porus is said to have encountered Alexander. There they saw a triumphal arch serving as a pediment to a statue of Alexander in a four-horse chariot, as he appeared on the Issus. A little farther on, they came upon two other arches, on one of which was Alexander, on the other Porus—the one saluting, the other in an attitude of submission.

Having passed the Hydraotis,[65] they pursued their way through several countries[66] to the Hyphasis. Thirty stadia from the river, they saw: the altars Alexander had built there "To Father Ammon and Brother Hercules, to the Providence Minerva and Olympian Jove, and to the Samo-Thracian Cabiri and the Indian Sun and Brother Apollo:" and also a bronze pillar with this inscription:—"Here Alexander halted." And this

[64] Probably, suggests Wilford, a corruption from Rac'hyas.—As. Res., ix, 41.

[65] Hydraotis, in Strabo Hyarotis, Sanskrit Iravati; Hyphasis, Vipasa.—Vishnu Purana, p. 181.

[66] Strabo gives the number as nine.—xv, I, 3, 33.

pillar Philostratus conjectures was raised by the Indians in joy at the return homeward of Alexander.

In reference to the Hyphasis and its marvels, we are told that it is navigable at its very source, in a plain; but that lower down alternate ridges of rock impede its course, and cause eddies which render navigation impossible. It is about as broad as the Ister, the largest of our European rivers, and the same sort of trees grow upon its banks. From these trees the people obtain an unguent with which if the marriage guests neglect to anoint the bride and bridegroom, the marriage rite is thought informal and not pleasing to Venus. To Venus indeed its groves are dedicated, as also a fish found here only, the peacock, so called from its cærulean crest, spotted scales, and golden tail, which it can open out at its pleasure. In this river is also found a sort of white worm, the property of the king, which is melted into an oil so inflammable, that nothing but glass will hold it. This oil is used in sieges, and when thrown on the battlements, it burns so fiercely, that its fire, so far as yet known, is inextinguishable.[67]

In the marshes they catch wild asses with a horn on their foreheads,[68] with which they fight, bull-fashion. From this horn is made a cup of such virtue that if

[67] This worm is mentioned and described by Ctesias, but he places it in the Indus.—Frag. Ctes., ed. Didot, 27, p. 85.

[68] This ass and its horn, with some slight difference, are also in Ctesias (*ib.*, p. 25). Wilson sees in this horned ass two animals "rolled into one," the gorkhar, or wild horse, found north of the Hindu-Koh, and the rhinoceros, whose horn has to this day in the East a high reputation as an antidote.—Notes on Ctesias, 53 and 49.

any one drinks out of it, he need for that day fear no sickness, nor wounds, nor fire, nor poison. It belongs to the king, who also reserves to himself the right of hunting the ass. Apollonius saw the animal, and admired it; but when Damis asked him if he could believe all that was said of the virtue of the cup, he answered, "Yes, when I see any Indian king immortal."

Here they met with a woman black to her breasts, white from her breasts downwards. She was sacred to the Indian Venus, and to this goddess piebald women are sacred from their birth, as to Apis among the Egyptians. Here they crossed that spur of the Caucasus which stretches down towards the Red Sea; it was full of all sorts of aromatic plants. The headlands produced cinnamon,[69] a shrub very like a young vine (νέοις κλήμασι), and so grateful to goats, that if you hold it in your hands they will follow you and whine after you like dogs. On the cliffs grow the tall, and all other sorts of, frankincense, and pepper-trees. The pepper-tree resembles the ἄγνος both in its leaves and the clustered form of its fruit. It grows on precipices inaccessible to man, but frequented by apes, which, as they gather for them the pepper-fruit, the Indians make much of and protect with arms and dogs against the lion; for the lion will lie in wait for the ape, and eat its flesh as medicine when he is sick, and as food when he is old and no longer able to hunt the stag and wild boar. The pepper harvest is gathered in this way:—Directly under the cliffs where the peppers grow, the

[69] Strabo, xv, I, 22, but in the south of India. I believe it is indigenous to Ceylon, and is not found in India at all.

people dig small trenches into which they throw as something worthless the fruit of the neighbouring trees.[70] The monkeys from the heights watch them, and as soon as it is night, begin like them to tear the clustered fruits from the pepper, and like them to fling it into the trenches. In the morning the people come back and carry off the pepper, which they thus obtain without any labour.

On the other side of the mountain was a large plain —the largest in India, being fifteen days' journey to the Ganges, and eighteeen days' to the Red Sea. It was intersected with dykes running in different directions, and communicating with the Ganges, and serving the double purpose of landmarks and canals for irrigation. The land here is the best in India, black and very productive; its wheat stalks are like reeds,[71] and its beans three times as large as the Egyptian; its sesame and millet are also extraordinarily fine. Here, too,

[70] Strabo (*ib.*, § 29) describes a similar trick, by means of which the people catch the monkeys; and Lane observes, "I have myself seen paintings in ancient Egyptian tombs representing the mode of gathering fruit by means of tame monkeys" (Arab. Nights, III, p. 106, and Wilkinson, An. Egypt., II, 150). But without gainsaying the fact that monkeys may be taught to pick fruit, all I have seen of them confirms Waterton's observation, that the monkey never throws, only lets fall.

[71] Elphinstone, describing this bank of the Hyphasis, tells only of sand-hills, and hard clay, and tufts of grass, and little bushes of rue. Of the right bank, however, he says: "There were so many large and deep watercourses throughout the journey, that, judging from them alone, the country must be highly cultivated."—Introd. Burnes, too, observes of Balkh: "The crops are good, and the wheat stalks grow as high as in England, and do not present *the stunted stubble of India.*"—*Ut sup.*, II, 206.

grow those nuts, which for their rarity and size are, as a sort of curiosity, often found in Greek temples. The grapes of the country however are small, like the Lydian and Mæonian, and with an agreeable bouquet when gathered (*τας δε ἀμπελους.........ποτιμους τε και ανθοσμιας ομου τῳ αποτρυγαν.*) A tree is also found here like the laurel but with a fruit like a large pomegranate, within the husk of which is an apple of the colour of a fine hyacinth, and the very best flavoured fruit they ever ate.[72]

As they came down the mountain, they witnessed a dragon-hunt. India, its marshes, plains, and mountains, are full of dragons.[73] Of these they tell us that the marsh-dragon is thirty cubits long, sluggish, and without a crest; the male very like the female (*αλλ' ειναι ταις δρακαιναις ὁμοιοι*). Its back is black, and it has fewer scales than the other kinds. Homer, when he speaks of the dragon at the fount in Aulis as of blood-red back, describes the marsh-dragon better than the other poets, who make the Nemæan dragon crested; for crested you will hardly find any marsh-dragon.

The plain and hill-dragons are superior to, and larger than, the marsh kind. They move along more swiftly

72 Can this be the purple mangosteen, such as it might be described by those who only knew of it from hearsay?

73 Almost all that is here said of serpents will be found in Pliny (viii, 11, 13); their size, though scarcely so large as those of Philostratus, is noticed by Onesicritus and Nearchus (Frag. Hist. Alex., pp. 50 and 105, Didot); their beards by Ælian (xi, c. 26); the beard and the stone in their heads, with some difference (the stones are *αυτογλυφοι*), by Tzetzes from Poseidippus.—Chil., vii, 653, 669; the magic power of their eyes, by Lucan (vii, 657).

than the swiftest rivers, and nothing can escape them. They are crested; and though in the young the crest is small (μέτριον), when they are full-grown, it rises to a great height. They are of a fiery colour, with serrated backs, and bearded; their necks are erect, and their scales shine like silver. The pupils of their eyes are a fiery stone of wonderful and mystic properties. They are hunted for the sake of their eyes, skin, and teeth. A dragon of this kind will sometimes attack an elephant;[74] both then perish, and are a "find" for the huntsmen. They resemble the largest fish, but are more lithe and active; their teeth are hard as those of the whale.

The mountain dragons are larger than those of the plain, and with a fiercer look; their scales are golden, their beard too, which hangs in clusters; they glide on the earth with a sound as of brass; their fiery crests throw out a light brighter than that of a torch. They overpower the elephant, but become themselves the prey of the Indian. They are killed in this fashion. The Indians spread out before the serpent's hiding-place a scarlet carpet enwrought with golden characters, upon which, should the dragon chance to rest his head, he is charmed to sleep. They then, with incantations,[75] call him out of his hole; and if everything goes well—for often he gets the better of them and their "gramary"

[74] This is said of the Ceylon elephants and serpents in the Chiliads of Tzetzes from Poseidippus, vii, 212.

[75] The snake charmer still exists in India. Bochart (Hierozo., cvi, III, II, v.) gives all the passages in ancient authors bearing on the subject.

—as soon as with outstretched neck he is lulled in magic sleep, they rush on him with hatchets and cut off his head, and extract from it bright-coloured stones,[76] flashing with every hue, and of powers wonderful as those of Gyges' ring. These dragons are also found in the mountains bordering on the Red Sea. They are said to live to an incredible age, but of this nothing sure is known.

At the foot of the mountain was situated Paraka, a very large city. Its inhabitants are, from their youth, trained to hunt the dragon, and it is full of their trophies —the heads of dragons. They eat the hearts and livers, and in this way, as was proved by Apollonius himself,[77] they acquire a knowledge of the language and thoughts of animals.

Proceeding onwards, our travellers hear the sound of a shepherd's pipe,[78] and presently see a herd of white stags grazing. The Indians keep them for their milk,[79] which is very nourishing.

Thence, after a four days' journey through a fertile

76 Moor's Oriental Fragments, pp. 80-5, gives an account of the snake stones, "of a dark hue, though not always of the same colour, and about the size of a tamarind stone", and describes the modes by which the snake charmer compels the snake to disgorge them. The pretensions of the snake charmer are pretty well disposed of by Professor Owen in a paper on snake charming in Blackwood, Feb. 1872.

77 At Ephesus (l. iv, c. 3), where he displayed his knowledge of the language of sparrows.

78 Strabo (*ut sup.*, c. 22) says, they have no musical instruments besides cymbals, drums, and κρόταλοι (rattles, castanets ?).

79 "The milk of any forest beast, except the buffalo, must be carefully shunned."—Menu, v. 11.

and well-cultivated country, they approached the stronghold of the Sophoi; and now their guide ordered his camel to kneel, and jumped down sweating with fear. Then Apollonius knew where they were, and laughed at the Indian and bade him again mount his camel. The fact is, the near neighbourhood of the Sophoi frightened him; and, indeed, the people fear them more than the king; for the king consults them as he would an oracle, and does nothing without their advice and concurrence.[80]

When they had reached a village, not the eighth of a mile from the hill of the Sophoi, and were preparing to put up there, they perceived a young man running towards them. He was the very blackest Indian they had yet seen, with a bright spot, crescent-shaped, between his brows, much such a mark as Menon, the Ethiopian foster-child of the sophist Herod, had in his youth. He bore a golden anchor, which, as symbolical of holding fast, the Indians have made their caduceus.

When the messenger coming up addressed Apollonius in Greek, as the villagers also spoke Greek, his companions were not much surprised; but when he addressed Apollonius by name, they were struck with astonishment, all but Apollonius, who, now full of confidence, looking at Damis, said, "The men we have come to visit are wise indeed; they know the future:" and then turning to the Indian, he asked him what he should do, for he wished to converse with the Sophoi imme-

[80] Vide Hist. Frag. II, 438, on a fragment of Megasthenes and Bardesanes on Brahmans and Samanœans in Porphyry, de Abstinent., l. iv, c. 17, *ad calcem*.

diately. The man answered, "Leave your people here, but come you, just as you are, so they (αὐτοι) request." This "they" seemed to Apollonius quite Pythagorean, and he followed the messenger rejoicing.

The hill of the Sophoi[81] rose sheer up from the plain, and was about as high as the Acropolis at Athens. It was besides fortified by a goodly belt of rock, on which you might trace the impressions of hoofs, and beards, and faces, and what seemed the backs of falling men. And they heard that when Bacchus and Hercules attempted the place, Bacchus ordered his Pans, as able to shake it to its foundation (ἱκανους πρὸς τον σεισμον), to storm it: but thunderstruck by the Sophoi, they fell headlong one upon the other and so left these marks upon the stones. They said also, that about and around this hill a cloud hung within which the Sophoi dwelt visible and invisible[82] at will, and that their stronghold was without gates, so that it could not be called either enclosed or open.

Apollonius and his guide ascended the hill on the south side. He saw a well some twenty-four feet about.[83] Over its mouth hung a dark vapour which rose[84] as the

[81] Ctesias tells of a sacred place in an uninhabited part of the country, which the Indians honour in the name of the sun and the moon; it is fifteen days' journey from the Sardian mountains —του ὄρους της Σαρδους, § 8, p. 81, ed. Didot. See also Reinaud, who mentions that this castle of the Brahmans was known to the Arabs —not improbably through Philostratus.—Mém. de l'Inde, p. 86.

[82] A somewhat similar power is ascribed to the Caraunas by Marco Polo, p. 33, u. s., and is employed to beguile Oswif.—Burnt Nial., c. xii, l. 40.

[83] Οργυιων τετταρων.

[84] "In the morning, vapours or clouds of smoke ascended from

heat of the day increased and at noon gave out all the colours of the rainbow. He was told that here the subsoil was cinnabar (σανδαράχινη γη), and that the water of the well was sacred, and never used, and that all the neighbourhood swore by it. Near this place was a crater, which threw out a lead-coloured flame without smell or smoke, and which bubbled up with a volcanic matter that rose to its brim, but never overflowed: here the Indians purified themselves from all involuntary sins. The well, the Sophoi called the well of the test; the crater, the fire of pardon.[85] Here were also seen two vessels of black stone—the urns of the winds and of the rain;[86] and the one or the other is opened or shut just as wind or rain is wanted or otherwise. Here too they found statues of the most ancient Greek gods, and worshipped in the Greek manner; of the Polian Minerva, and of Bacchus, and of the Delian and Amyclæan Apollo.[87] The Sophoi look upon their stronghold as the very navel of India. They here worship fire ob-

the wells till the atmosphere was sufficiently heated to hide it," between the Ravi and the Chenab —Burnes, II, 38.

85 With the well of the text compare: the test fountain in Ctesias; its water hardens into a cheese-like substance, which when rubbed into a powder and mixed with water, and then administered to suspected criminals, makes them tell all they ever did (§ 14, p. 82): also the water of probation mentioned by Porphyry. With the fire of pardon compare that other water, in some cave temple seemingly, which purified from voluntary and involuntary offences (Porphyry de Styge).

86 Olearius, h. l., suggests that these may have been barometers; and then Damis, like the astronomer in Rasselas, merely confounds the power of foretelling with the power of producing.

87 Ω θαυμαστης φιλοσοφιας δι' ἡν Ινδοι θεους Ελληνικους προσκυνουσι.—Plutarch de Fortunâ Alex. Op. Var., I, p. 585.

tained from the sun's rays, and at noon daily hymn its praise.

Apollonius, in an address to the Egyptians, somewhat enigmatically describes the life of the Sophoi:—"I have seen," he says, "Brahmans who dwell on the earth, and yet not on the earth; in places fortified, and yet without walls; and who possess nothing, and yet all things." According to Damis they used the earth as a couch, but first strewed it with choice grasses: they walked too the air[88]—Damis himself saw them—and this not to excite wonder—all ostentation is abhorrent to their nature,—but in imitation of and as a more fitting service to the sun. He saw too the fire which they drew down from the sun's rays,—and which though it flamed on no altar and was confined by no hearth, took shape and body (σωματοειδες) and floated in mid-air,[89] where spite of the darkness, under the charm of their hymned praises[90] it stayed unchanged. As in the night they worshipped this fire, so in the day they worshipped the sun and besought it to order the seasons for India's good. In this way is to be understood Apollonius's first assertion: "The Brahmans live on the earth, and yet not on the earth." His second, Damis refers to that

[88] Απο της γης ες πηχεις δυο (Philos., III, c. 15), two cubits from the ground, no great height, but—ce n'est que le premier pouce qui coûte.

[89] Sir C. Napier says, of Trukkee, "On reaching the top, where we remained during the night, every man's bayonet had a bright flame on the point. A like appearance had also been observed going from Ooch to Shapoor."—Life, III, 272. May not the night light of the Sophoi be referred to some similar phenomenon?

[90] Compare with c. xv the xxxiii, III.

covering of clouds which they draw over themselves at pleasure, and which no rain can penetrate. His third, to those fountains which bubble up for his Bacchanals when Bacchus shakes the earth and them, and from which the Indians themselves drink and give to others to drink. Well therefore may Apollonius say, that men, who at a moment's notice and without preparation can get whatever they want, possess nothing and yet all things.[91] They wear their hair long,[92] like the old Macedonians, and on their head a white mitre.[93] They go bare-foot; and their coats have no sleeves, and are of wild cotton, of an oily nature, and white as Pamphylian wool, but softer.[94] Of this cotton the sacred vestments are made; and the earth refuses to give it up if

91 Compare with these fountains those of milk, wine, etc., of which Calanus speaks in his interview with Onesicritus (Strabo, *ut sup.*, § 64); and that happy India, a real pays de Cocagne, which Dio Chrysostom ironically describes in Celænis Phrygiæ Orat., xxxv, II, p. 70.

92 Hardy, Eastern Monachism (p. 112), by which it would seem that the Brahmans wear long hair; the Buddhist priest, on the other hand, shaves his head; so also Bardesanes describes the newly-elected Samanæan; *ξυραμενος δε του σωματος τα περιττα λαμβανει στολην απεισι τε προς Σαμαναιους.*—Porphyry, *ut supra.*

93 Still worn by some of the mountain tribes about Cabool. Elphinstone says of the Bikaneers, "they wear loose clothes of white cotton, and a remarkable turban which rises high over the head."—Cabool, I, 18.

94 Hierocles speaks of the Brahman garments as made from a soft and hairy (δερματωδη) filament obtained from stones (asbestos).—Frag. Hist., iv, p. 430. In the Mahawanso among the presents of Asoka to Dewananpiatisso, are "hand-towels cleansed by being passed through the fire," p. 70. Burnes says of the Nawab of Cabool, he "produced some asbestos, here called cotton-stone, found near Jelalabad" (ii, 138); see also Pliny, xix. 4.

any but themselves attempt to gather it. They carry a stick,[95] and wear a ring, both of infinite and magic power.

Apollonius found the Sophoi seated on brazen stools, their chief, Iarchas, on a raised throne of bronze ornamented with golden images. They saluted him with their hands, but Iarchas welcomed him in Greek, asked him for the King's letter, and added, that it wanted a δ. As soon as he had read it, he asked Apollonius, "What do you think of us?" "Oh!" said Apollonius, "the very journey I have undertaken—and I am the first of my countrymen who has undertaken it—answers that question." "In what, then," enquired Iarchas, "do you think us wiser than you?" "I think your views wiser, more divine," answered Apollonius; "and should I find that you know no more than I, this at least I shall have learned—that I have nothing more to learn." "Well," said the Indian, "other people usually ask of those who visit them, whence they come and who they are; but we, as a first proof of our knowledge, show strangers that we know them;" and so saying, he told Apollonius who his father was, who his mother, all that happened to him at Ægæ, and how Damis joined him, and what they had said and done on the journey; and this so distinctly and fluently, that he might have been a companion of their route. Apollonius, greatly astonished, asked him how he knew all this. "In this knowledge," he answered, "you are not wholly wanting, and where you are deficient we will instruct you,[96] for

[95] "The first three classes ought to carry staves."—Menu, i, 45; "the priest's should reach to his hair."—*Ib.*, 46.

[96] When Damis speaks of his knowledge of languages to Apollo-

we think it not well to keep secret what is so worthy of being known, especially from you, Apollonius,—a man of most excellent memory. And Memory, you must know, is of the Gods the one we most honour. "But how do you know my nature?" asked Apollonius. "We," he answered, "see into the very soul, tracing out its qualities by a thousand signs. But as midday is at hand,[97] let us to our devotions, in which you also may,

nius, Apollonius merely observes that he himself understands all languages, and that without having learned them; and more, that he knows not only what men speak, but their secret thoughts (L. I., c. xix). But as in India he is accompanied by, and frequently makes use of an interpreter; this pretension of his has, from the time of Eusebius (in Hieroclem, xiv), been frequently ridiculed as an idle boast. Philostratus, however, was too practised a writer to have left his hero open to such a charge. His faults are of another kind. His facts and statements too often, and with a certain air of design, confirm and illustrate each other: thus, with regard to this very power claimed by Apollonius, observe, that he professes not to speak, but to know all languages and men's thoughts—a difference intelligible to all who are familiar with the alleged facts of mesmerism; and look at him in his first interview with Phraotes; watch him listening to, and understanding the talk of the king and the sages, and only then asking Iarchas to interpret for him when he would himself speak. Observe, also, that Iarchas admits only to a certain extent the power of Apollonius, and remember his surprise when he finds that Phraotes knows and speaks Greek.

[97] "At sunrise, at noon, and at sunset, let the Brahman go to the waters and bathe."—Menu, vi, 22. "Sunrise and sunset are the hours when, having made his ablution, he repeats the text which he ought to repeat."—ii, 222. From the Vishnu Purana, however, it seems the Richas (the hymns of the Rig-veda) shine in the *morning*, the prayers of the Yajush at *noon*, and portions of the Saman in the *afternoon*.—p. 235. Bardesanes, *ut supra*, *τον τοινυν χρονον της ημερας καὶ της νυκτος τον πλειστον εις ὑμνους των θεων απενειμαν καὶ ευχας.*

if you will, take part." They then adjourned to the bath, a spring like that of Dircæ in Bœotia as Damis says who afterwards saw Dircæ. They first took off their clothes, and then anointed their heads with an unguent which made their bodies run down with sweat, and so jumped into the water. After they had well bathed they put garlands on their heads and proceeded to the temple, intent on their hymn. There standing round in a circle with Iarchas as their leader they beat the ground with their staves, till bellying like a wave it sent them up into the air about two cubits; and then they sang a hymn, very like the Pæan of Sophocles sung at Athens to Æsculapius. When they had again come down to the earth and had performed their sacred duties, Iarchas called the youth with the anchor, and bade him take care of Apollonius's companions; and he in a shorter space of time than the swiftest birds, was gone and was back again, and told Iarchas,—"I have taken care of them."

Apollonius was then placed on the throne of Phraotes, and Iarchas bade him question them on any matter he pleased, for he was now among men who knew all things. Apollonius therefore asked, as though it was of all knowledge the most difficult, "Whether the Sophoi knew themselves?" But Iarchas answered quite contrary to his expectation, that they knew all things, because they first knew themselves. That, without this first and elementary knowledge, no one could be admitted to their philosophy. Apollonius, remembering his conversation with Phraotes and the examination they had been obliged to undergo, assented to this, more especially as he felt the truth of the observation in himself. He then asked "What opinion they held of themselves?" and was told, "that they held themselves to be gods, because they were good men." Apollonius then enquired about the soul, and, when he heard that they held the opinions of Pythagoras, he further asked, whether, as Pythagoras remembered himself as Euphorbus, so Iarchas could speak of some one of his previous lives, either as Greek or Trojan, or other man? Iarchas, first reproving the Greeks for the reverence they pay to the Trojan heroes and to Achilles as the greatest of them, to the neglect of better men, Greek, Egyptian, and Indian, related: how years long ago he had been one Ganges king of the Indian people, to whom the Ethiopians then Indians were subject: how this Ganges, ten cubits in stature and the most comely of men, built many cities and drove back the Scythians who invaded his territories: and how, though robbed of his wife by the then king of Phraotes's country, he had unlike Achilles kept sacred his alliance with him: how too he had rendered his father the Ganges[99] river propitious to India, by inducing it to keep within its banks and to divert its course to the Red Sea:[1] how, notwithstanding all this, the Ethiopians murdered him, and were driven by the hate of the In-

[98] This is a favourite idea of Philostratus, *i.e.* the Heroica, II, v, 677, ed. Olearii, fol.

[99] The Ganges is a goddess.—Vishnu Purana.

[1] Wilford refers this to the legend of Bhagiratha, "who led the Ganges to the ocean, tracing with the wheels of his chariot two furrows, which were to be the limits of her encroachments."—As. Res., viii, 298.

dians and the now sterile earth and the abortive births of their wives to leave their native land: and how, pursued by his ghost, and still suffering the same ills, they wandered from place to place, till having at length punished his murderers they settled in that part of Africa from them called Ethiopia. He told too, how Ganges had thrust seven adamantine swords deep into the ground in some unknown spot, and how when the gods without indicating it ordered that on that spot a sacrifice should be offered, he then a child of four years old immediately pointed it out.[2] But ceasing to speak of himself, he directed Apollonius's attention to a youth of about twenty, and he described him as patient under all suffering and by nature especially fitted for philosophy, but beyond measure averse to it; and his aversion was attributed to the ill treatment and injustice he had received from Ulysses and Homer in a former life. He had been Palamedes.

While they were thus talking, a messenger announced the king's approach and that he would arrive towards evening, and came to consult with them on his private affairs. Iarchas answered that he should be welcome, and that he would leave them a better man for having known "this Greek." He then resumed his conversation with Apollonius, and asked him to tell something of his previous existence. Apollonius excuses himself, because as it was undistinguished he did not care to remember it. "But surely," observed Iarchas, "to be

[2] So the sword of Mars found by a shepherd and presented to Attila constituted him "totius mundi principem."—Jornandes, xxxv.

the pilot of an Egyptian ship is no such ignoble occupation, and a pilot I see you once were." "True," replied Apollonius, "but an office which should be on a par with that of the statesman or the general has by the fault of sailors themselves become contemptible and degraded. Besides my very best act in that life no one deemed worthy even of praise." "And what was that?" asked Iarchas. "Was it the doubling with slackened sail Malea and Sunium, or the carefully observing the course of the winds, or the carrying your ship over the reefs and swell of the Eubœan coast?" "Well," said Apollonius, "if I must speak of my sailor life, I will tell you of something I did then which I think was wise and honest. In those days pirates infested the Phœnician Sea. And some of their spies knowing that my ship was richly laden came to me and sounded me, and asked me what would be my share of the freight. I told them a thousand drachmas, for we were four pilots. 'And what sort of a home have you?' they asked. 'A hut on Pharos, where Proteus used to live,'[3] I answered. 'Well,' they went on, 'would you like to change the sea for land—a hut for a house—to receive ten times the pay you look for, and rid yourself at the same time of the thousand ills of the tempestuous sea?' 'Aye, that I would,' I said. They then told me who they were, and offered me ten thousand drachmas, and promised that neither myself nor any of my crew should suffer harm

[3] Homer, Odys., iv, 355, and frequently alluded to in Byzantine writers as νησον την λεγομενην Πρωτεως. Pharos ubi Proteus cum Phocarum gregibus diversatum Homerus fabulatur inflatius.—Amin. Marcell., xx, 16, 10.

if I gave them an opportunity of taking my ship. So we agreed that I should set sail in the night, but lie-to under the promontory; and that the pirates, who were at anchor on the other side, should then run out and seize my ship and cargo. All this took place in a temple, and I made them swear to fulfil their promises; while I agreed on my part to do as they wished. But instead of lying-to I made sail for the open sea and so got off." "And this," observed Iarchas, "you think an act of justice?" "Yes," said Apollonius, "and of humanity; for to save the lives of my men, and the property of my employers, and to be above a bribe, though a sailor, I hold to be a proof of many virtues."

Iarchas smiled, and remarked: "You, Greeks, seem to think that not to do wrong is to be just. Only the other day, an Egyptian told us of the Roman proconsuls: how, though knowing nothing of the people they were to govern, they entered their provinces with naked axes; and of the people: how they praised their governors if they only were not venal, just like slave-dealers who to vaunt their wares warrant that their Carians are not thieves! Your poets too scarcely allow you to be just and good. For Minos the most cruel of men and who with his fleets enslaved the neighbouring peoples, they honour with the sceptre of justice as the judge of the dead. But Tantalus, a good man, who made his friends partakers of immortality, they deprive of food and drink." And he pointed to a statue on the left inscribed "Tantalus." It was four cubits high, and of a man of about fifty, dressed in the Argolic fashion with a Thessalian chlamys. He was drinking from a cup as large as would suffice for a thirsty man, and a pure draught bubbled up in it without overflowing.

Their conversation was here interrupted by the noise and tumult in the village occasioned by the king's arrival; and Iarchas angrily observed, "Had it been Phraotes, not the mysteries had been more quiet." Apollonius, seeing no preparations made, inquired whether they intended offering the king a banquet? "Aye, and a rich one, for we have plenty of everything here," they said, "and he is a gross feeder. But we allow no animal food, only sweetmeats, roots, and fruits such as India and the season afford. But here he comes." The king, glittering with gold and jewels, now approached. Damis was not present at this interview, for he spent the whole of the day in the village, but Apollonius gave him an account of it which he wrote in his diary. He says that the king approached with outstretched hands as a suppliant, and that the sages from their seats nodded as if granting his petition, at which he rejoiced greatly as at the oracle of a god; but of his son and brother they took no more notice than of the slaves who accompanied him. Iarchas then rose and asked him if he would eat. The king assented, and four tripods like those in Homer's Olympus rolled themselves in, followed by bronze cup-bearers. The earth strewed itself with grass, softer than any couch; and sweets and bread, fruits and vegetables, all excellently well prepared, moved up and down in order before the guests. Of the tripods two flowed with wine, two with water hot and cold. The cups, each large enough for four thirsty souls, and the wine-coolers, were each one of a single stone, and of a stone in Greece so precious as to be set in rings and necklaces. The bronze cup-bearers poured out the wine and water in due proportions, as usual in drinking bouts.[4] They all lay down to the feast, the king with the rest, for no place of honour was assigned him.

In the course of the dinner Iarchas said to the king, "I pledge you the health of this man," pointing to Apollonius, and with his hand signifying that he was a just and divine man. On this the king observed, "I understand that he, and some others who have put up in the village, are friends of Phraotes." "You understand rightly," said Iarchas, "for even here he is Phraotes' guest." "But what are his pursuits?" asked the king. "Those of Phraotes," answered Iarchas. "Worthless guest worthless pursuits! they prevent even Phraotes from becoming a man indeed," said the king. "Speak more modestly of philosophy and Phraotes," observed Iarchas,—"this language does not become your age." Here Apollonius, through Iarchas, inquired of the king "what advantage he derived from not being a philosopher?" "This, that I possess all virtue and am one with the sun," answered the king. Apollonius: "You would not think thus if you were a philosopher." The king: "Well friend as you are a philosopher, tell us what you think of yourself." Apollonius: "That I am a good man so long as I am a philosopher." The king: "By the sun, you come here full of Phraotes." Apollonius: "Thank heaven then,

[4] So Marco Polo's description of the feasts of the great Khan, borrowed probably from Apollonius, c. lxxv, pp. 71-9, French ed.

that I have not travelled in vain; and if you could see Phraotes, you would say he was full of me. He wished to write to you about me, but when he told me that you were a good man, I bade him not take that trouble, for I had brought no letter to him." When the king heard that Phraotes had spoken well of him, he was pacified and forgot his suspicions; and in a gentle tone said: "Welcome, best friend." "Welcome you," said Apollonius, "one would think you had but just come in." "What brought you to this place?" asked the king. "The Gods and these wise men," answered Apollonius. "But tell me stranger, what do the Greeks say of me?" he next inquired. "Just what you say of them," said Apollonius. "But that is just nothing," he replied. "I will tell them so, and they will crown you at the Olympic games," Apollonius observed. Then turning to Iarchas: "Let us leave this drunken fool to himself. But why pray do you pay no attention to his son and brother, and do not admit them to your table?" "Because," answered Iarchas, "they may one day rule, and by slighting them we teach them not to slight others." Apollonius then perceiving that the number of the Sophoi was eighteen, observed to Iarchas that it was not a square number, nor indeed a number at all honoured or distinguished. Iarchas in answer, told him that they paid no attention to number, but esteemed virtue only; he added, that the college when his grandfather entered it consisted of eighty-seven Sophoi, and that his grandfather then found himself its youngest, and eventually in the one hundred and thirtieth[5] year

[5] Ibn Batuta speaks of Hindus 120, 130, and 140 years of age.

of his age, its only surviving member; that no eligible candidate having in all that time offered himself for admission, he remained four years without a colleague: and that when he then received from the Egyptians congratulations on his alone occupying the seat of wisdom, he begged them not to reproach India with the small number of its wise men. Iarchas then went on to blame the Elians, in that as he had heard from the Egyptians, they elected the Olympic dikasts by lot, and thus left to chance what should be the reward of merit; and that they always elected the same number,—never more, never less; and that they thus sometimes excluded good men and sometimes were obliged to choose bad ones. Better, he said, it had been if the Elians had allowed the number of the dikasts to vary with circumstances, but had always required in them the same qualifications.

The king here rudely interrupted them, and expressed his dislike of the Greeks, and spoke of the Athenians as the slaves of Xerxes; Apollonius turning to him asked if he had any slaves of his own; "Twenty thousand," he answered, "and born in my house."[6] "Well, then," said Apollonius (always through Iarchas), "as you do not run away from them, but they from you, so Xerxes fled like a worthless slave from before the Athenians when he had been conquered at Salamis."

Burnes of one at Cabul of 114, apparently with all his faculties about him.—II, 109.

[6] According to Megasthenes, ειναι δε καὶ τοδε μεγα εν τῃ Ινδων γῃ παντας Ινδους ειναὶ ελευθερους.—Arrian, Indica, xi. ουδε Ινδοις αλλος δουλος εστι. Onesicritus limits this to the subjects of Musicanus. —Strabo, *ut sup.*, § 54.

"But surely," observed the king, "Xerxes, with his own hands set fire to Athens?" "Yes," said Apollonius, "but how fearful was his punishment! He became a fugitive before those whom he had hoped to destroy; and in his very flight was most unhappy: for had he died by the hands of the Greeks, what a tomb would they not have built for him! what games not instituted in his memory!—as knowing that they honoured themselves when they honoured those whom they had subdued." On this the king burst into tears, and excused himself, and attributed his prejudices against the Greeks to the tales and falsehoods of Egyptian travellers, who while they boasted of their nation as wise and holy and author of those laws relating to sacrifices and mysteries which obtain in Greece, described the Greeks as men of unsound judgement, the scum of men, συγκλυδας, insolent and lawless, romancers, and miracle-mongers, poor, and parading their poverty not as something honourable but as an excuse for theft. "But now," he went on to say, "that I know them to be full of goodness and honour, I hold them as my friends, and as my friends praise them and wish them all the good I can. I will no longer give credit to these Egyptians." Iarchas here observed that though he had long seen that the Egyptians had the ear of the king, he had said nothing but waited till the king should meet with such a counsellor as Apollonius. Now however that you are better taught, let us", he concluded, "drink together the loving-cup of Tantalus and then to sleep: for we have business to transact to-night. I will however as occasion offers indoctrinate you in

Grecian learning, the fullest in the world. And so stooping to the cup he first drank and then handed it to the other guests; and there was enough for all, for it bubbled up as if from a fountain.

They lay down to rest, and arose at midnight, and aloft in the air hymned the praises of the sun's ray. The Sophoi then gave private audience to the king. Next morning early, after the sacred rites, the king, for the law forbade his remaining more than one day at the college, retired to the village and vainly pressed Apollonius to visit him there. The Sophoi then sent for Damis, whom they admitted as a guest. The conversation now began; and Iarchas discoursed on the world: how it is composed of five elements—water, fire, air, earth, and æther;[7] and how they are all co-ordinate, but that from æther the Gods, from air mortals, are generated; how moreover the world is an animal and hermaphrodite; and how as hermaphrodite it reproduces by itself and of itself all creatures; and how as intelligent it provides for their wants, and with scorching heats punishes their wrong-doing. And this world Iarchas further likened to one of those Egyptian ships[8] which navigate the

7 Megasthenes (Strabo, *ut sup.*, § 59) gives pretty nearly the same account of the Brahminical doctrines, that the world has a beginning, and will have an end; that God, its ruler and creator, pervades it; and that besides the four elements there is a fifth, æther; and Alexander Polyhistor asserts that Pythagoras was a disciple of the Brahmans; Frag. Hist., III, § 238, p. 239, and p. 241 mentions æther as one of the Pythagorean elements. Also Aristotle de Mundo, II, from a note to Mas'údis Meadows of Gold, Or. Tr. Fund, p. 179.

8 The boat among the Hindus is one of the types of the earth. —Wilford, As. Res., viii, 274; Von Bohlen quotes this passage to

Red Sea. "By an old law, no galley is allowed there; but only vessels round fore and aft (στογγυλοι), fitted for trade. Well, these vessels the Egyptians have enlarged by building up their sides, and fitting them with several cabins;[9] and they have manned them with pilots at the prow, seamen for the masts and sails, and marines as a guard against the barbarians; and over and above them all have set one pilot who rules and directs the rest. So in the world there is the first God, its creator; next him, the gods who rule its several parts—sung by the poets, as gods of rivers, groves, and streams: gods above the earth, and gods under the earth; and perchance too below the earth, but distinct from it, is a place terrible and deadly." Here, unable to contain himself, Damis cried out, in admiration: "Never could I have believed that any Indian was so thoroughly conversant with the Greek language, and could speak it with such fluency and elegance!"

A messenger now announced and introduced several Indian suppliants—a child possessed, a lame and blind man, etc.,—all of whom were cured.

Iarchas further initiated Apollonius, but not Damis, in astrology and divination and in those sacrifices and invocations in which the gods delight. He spoke of the divining power as raising man to an equality with the Delphian Apollo, and as requiring a pure heart and

prove that the Hindus had the knowledge of one God.—Das Alte Indien, i, 152.

9 See Ibn Batoutah's description of a Chinese boat, iv, 92-3, and 350, and 64, pp. Of the ships employed in the Indian trade, Pliny "Omnibus annis navigatur sagittariorum cohortibus impositis, etenim Piratæ noxime impestant."—Hist. Nat., vi, 26.

a stainless life, and as therefore readily apprehensible by the ætherial soul of Apollonius. He extolled it as a source of immense good to mankind, and referred to it the physician's art—for was not Æsculapius the son of Apollo? and was it not through his oracles that he discovered the several remedies for diseases, herbs for wounds, etc.?

Then turning, in a pleasant way, to Damis,—"And you Assyrian," he said, "do you never foresee anything—you, the companion of such a man?" "Yes, by Jove," answered Damis, "matters that concern myself; for when I first met with this Apollonius, he seemed to me a man full of wisdom and gravity and modesty and patience; and for his memory and great learning and love of learning I looked upon him as a sort of Dæmon; and I thought that if I kept with him, that instead of a simple and ignorant man I should become wise,—learned instead of a barbarian; and that if I followed him and studied with him I should see the Indians and see you; and that through his means I should live with the Greeks, a Greek. As to you then, you are occupied with great things, and think Delphi and Dodona or what you will. As for me, when Damis predicts he predicts for himself only like an old witch." At these words all the Sophoi laughed.

Apollonius enquired about the Martichora,[10] an animal the size of a lion, four-footed, with the head of a man, its tail long with thorns for hairs which it shoots out at those who pursue it;—about the golden foun-

[10] Ctesias, p. 80, § 7; Didot.

tain[11] too; and the men who use their feet for umbrellas, the sciapods.[12] Of the golden fountain and Martichora Iarchas had never heard; but he told Apollonius of the Pentarba and showed him the stone and its effects. It is a wonderful gem about the size of a man's thumb-nail and is found in the earth at a depth of four fathoms; but though it makes the ground to swell and crack, it can only be got at by the use of certain ceremonies and incantations. It is of a fiery colour and of extraordinary brilliancy, and of such power, that thrown into a stream it draws to it[13] and gathers round it all precious stones within a certain considerable range.[14] The pigmies he said lived on the other side of the Ganges and under ground; but the Sciapods and Longheads were mere inventions of Scylax. He described also the gold-digging griffins; that they were sacred to the Sun (his chariot is represented as drawn by them[15]) about the size of lions,[16] but stronger because winged; that their

[11] *Id.*, p. 73, § 4. Wilson, Notes on Ctesias, explains and accounts for these myths.

[12] *Id.*, § 104 and 84. Among the people of India, from Hindu authority quoted by Wilford, are the Ecapada, one-footed. "Monosceli singulis cruribus, eosdemque Sciapodas vocari," from Pliny (*ib.*) From Wilson's Notes, the one-footed and the Sciapods should be two different races.

[13] Something like this was that jewel by the aid of which Tchagkuna recovered that other jewel which he had thrown into the water.—Radjatarangini, tr. d. Troyer, II, p. 147.

[14] Strabo from Megasthenes, *ib.*, § 56. Ctesias also mentions it.

[15] In the Vishnu Purana: "The seven horses of the sun's car are the metres of the Vedas," p. 218. Sculptured or painted horses always.

[16] Ctesias, p. 82, § 12, and p. 95, § 70. Wilson (Ariana Antiqua) has shown from the Mahabharata, (Mahabharata, 1859-60, Slok., Fauche's tr. II, p. 53), that this story has an Indian foundation. "Those tribes between Meru and Mandura verily presented in

wings were a reddish membrane, and hence their flight was low and spiral; that they overpowered lions, elephants, and dragons; and that the tiger alone because of his swiftness was their equal in fight. He told of the Phœnix, the one of his kind, born of the sun's rays and shining with gold, and that his five hundred years of life were spent in India; and he confirmed the Egyptian account of this bird—that singing his own dirge he consumed himself in his aromatic nest at the fountains of the Nile. Similarly also swans it is said sing themselves to death, and have been heard by those who are very quick of ear.

They remained four months with the Sophoi. When they took their departure, Iarchas gave Apollonius seven rings named after the seven planets; these rings he ever afterwards wore each in its turn on its name-day. The Sophoi provided him and his party with camels and a guide, and accompanied them on the road; and prophesying that Apollonius would even during his life attain the honours of divinity they took leave of him, and many times looking back as in grief at parting with such a man returned to their college. Apollonius and his companions, with the Ganges on their right the Hyphasis on their left (*sic*), travelled down towards the sea-coast, *a ten days' journey*, and on their road they saw many birds and wild oxen, asses and lions, panthers

lumps of a drona weight, that gold which is dug up by Pippilikas (ants), and which is therefore called 'Pippilika ant-gold'." (P. 135, note). See also A Journey to Lake Mánasaróvara, by Moorcroft, who speaks of a sort of marmot in the gold country which Schwanbeck supposes to be the original of this ant.—As. Res., xii, 442. This myth was not unknown to the Arabs.—Gildemeister Script. Arab. de Rebus Indicis, p. 221.

and tigers, and a species of ape different from those that frequent the pepper-groves, black, hairy, and dog-faced, and like little men. And so conversing as their custom was of what they saw, they reached the coast, where they found a small factory and passage-boats of a Tuscan build and the sea of a very dark colour. Here Apollonius sent back the camels with this letter to Iarchas:—

"To Iarchas and the other Sophoi from Apollonius, greeting: I came to you by land, with your aid I return by sea, and might have returned through the air[17]—such is the wisdom you have imparted to me. Even among the Greeks I shall not forget these things, and shall still hold commerce with you—or I have indeed vainly drunk of the cup of Tantalus.[18] Farewell, ye best philosophers."

Apollonius then embarked, and set sail with a fair and gentle breeze. He admired the Hyphasis, which at its mouth narrow and rocky hurries through beetling cliffs into the sea with some danger to those who hug the land. He saw too the mouth of the Indus, and Patala, a city built on an island formed by the Indus, where Alexander collected his fleet. And Damis con-

17 Easy and pleasant as this mode of travel is thought to be, Apollonius had recourse to it but once—on that memorable occasion when about mid-day he disappeared from before the tribunal of Domitian, and the same evening met Damis at Dicæarchia, Puteoli, Vit. Apol. Philostr., viii, xc.

18 Philostratus, v, 1, has another letter purporting to be written by Apollonius to Iarchas. He shows us too Apollonius occasionally and always reverentially speaking of Iarchas and Phraotes, and Porphyry, *περι Στυγος*, quotes a letter of Apollonius in which he swears *μα το Τανταλιον ὑδωρ*—from Stabœus.—In Olearius, note c. 51, III, L. Philost.

firms what Orthagoras has related of the Red Sea—that the Great Bear is not there visible; that at noon there is no shadow; and that the stars hold a different position in the heavens.

He speaks of Byblus with its large mussels, and of Pagala of the Oritæ where the rocks and the sands are of copper; of the city Stobera and its inhabitants the Ichthyophagi, who clothe themselves in fish-skins and feed their cattle on fish; of the Carmani, an Indian race and civilized, who of the fish they catch keep only what they can eat, and throw the rest living back into the sea; and of Balara where they anchored, a mart for myrrh and palms. He tells too of the mode in which the people get their pearls. In this sea which is very deep the white-shelled oyster is fat, but naturally produces no pearls. When however the weather is very calm and the sea smooth and made still smoother by pouring oil upon it, the Indian diver equipped as a sponge-cutter with the addition of an iron plate and a box of myrrh goes down to hunt for oysters. As soon as he has found one he seats himself beside it, and with his myrrh stupefies it and makes it open its shell. The moment it does this, he strikes it with a skewer and receives on his iron plate cut into shapes the ichor which is discharged from its wound. In these shapes the ichor hardens, and the pearls thus made differ in nothing from real pearl.[19] This sea he adds is full of monsters, from which the

[19] Is this an indistinct and garbled account of the Chinese mode of making pearls described in a late Journal of the Society? Tzetzes says that two origins are ascribed to pearls. Some assert that they are the produce of lightning, others that they are χειροποιητους; and he then describes the *modus operandi*, which is that in our text, and probably borrowed from it.—Chiliad., xi, p. 375; 472 L.

sailors protect themselves by bells[20] at the poop and prow. Thus sailing, they at last reach the Euphrates, and so up to Babylon, and again meet Bardanes.

In reviewing this account of India, our first enquiry is into the authority on which it rests. Damis was the companion of Apollonius, so Philostratus and not impossibly public rumour affirmed. Damis wrote a journal, and though no scholar was according to Philostratus as capable as any man of correctly noting down what he saw and heard.[21] But Damis died, and his journal, if journal he kept and such a journal ever existed, lay buried with him for upwards of a century, till one of his family presented it to the Empress Julia Domna the wife of Severus, curious in such matters. But in what state?—untouched?—with no additions to suit the Empress's taste? Who shall tell? Again, the Empress did not order this journal to be published, but gave it to Philostratus a sophist and a rhetorician, with instructions to re-write and edit it; and so re-written and edited he at length published it, but not till after the death of his patroness, the Empress. Weighing then these circumstances all open to grave suspicion,

[20] Nearchus drives these same fish away, *ταις σαλπιγξιν*.—Strabo, xv, II, 12, p. 617, as was still done in Strabo's time.—*ib.*, p. 138, Didot ed. The Arabs similarly. In the Voyages Arabes (tr. Reinaud) of a monster fish in their seas, we are told, "La nuit les equipages font sonner des cloches semblables aux cloches des chrétiens, c'est enfin d'empêcher ce poisson de s'appuyer sur le navire et de le submerger."—I, p. 2.

[21] *Διατριβην αναγραψαι, και ὁ, τι ηκουσεν η ειδεν ανατυπωσαι—σφοδρα ικανος ην, και επετεδευε τουτο αριστα ανθρωπων.*—i, c. 19.

every one must admit that the journal of Damis gives no authority to Philostratus's work; but that this last, and more especially the books which relate to India, may give authority to the journal and history. By their contents then they must be judged.

That Apollonius should pay little attention to, and not very accurately describe, external objects might be expected. One can understand that, occupied with the soul and the gods, he should toil up the Hindu-kush without one remark on its snow-covered peaks—one plaint on the difficulties and dangers of its ascent.[22] But how explain these lengthy descriptions of animals and natural wonders that never had existence? If you put forward Damis—of the earth, earthy, the Sancho Panza of this Quixote—an eager and credulous listener, you have still to show how it is, that these descriptions so exactly tally with those of Ctesias and the historians of Alexander; how it is they are never original, except to add to our list of errors or to exaggerate errors already existing. Thus on Caucasus, more fortunate than the soldiers of Alexander, he not only hears of Prometheus but sees his chains. He climbs Mount Nysa, and has to tell of Bacchus and his orgies, and they are now no longer the inventions of flattery as Eratosthenes so shrewdly suspected, for Damis there found his temple and his statue. Similarly in general terms Seleucus

[22] Dangers which not even Hiouen-Thsang was indifferent to; but Apollonius's indifference we may account for by an observation of Cicero: "In India, qui sapientes habentur, nudi ætatem agunt, et Caucasi nives hyemalemque vim perferunt sine dolore."—Tusc. Quæst., lib. v.

Nicator and Onesicritus had vaunted the long life of elephants; but in Taxila Damis admired the elephant of Porus and on its golden bracelets read its name and age. Copying Ctesias, he speaks of the Indus as forty stadia broad where narrowest;[23] of giant Indians five cubits high; of worms with an inextinguishable oil; of winged griffins, but instead of large as wolves he makes them as large as lions; and of the swift one-horned ass and the jewel Pantarbas, both of which he and Apollonius saw. Again Onesicritus knew by hearsay of serpents the pets of Aposeisares,[24] of eighty and a hundred and forty cubits. Damis had been present at a dragon-hunt and had seen dragons' heads hanging as trophies in the streets of Paraka. Surely such information, not put forward as mere reports but solemnly vouched for, can never have come from a man who had really visited India, or they came from one of as little authority as Mendez Pinto, when he gives an account of his expedition to and a description of the imperial tombs of China.[25]

But, it will be said, these wonders were the common stock in trade of Indian travellers; every man believed in them, and every man who went to India and wrote of India, was ashamed of not seeing at least as much as

[23] Philostratus scarcely so strong, *το γαρ πλωιμον αυτου τοσουτον*, its breadth at the ferry where people usually cross.—II, 17 and 18.

[24] One of the Ptolemies could boast a similar pet, but it was only thirty-five cubits long, *τριαχονταπενταπηχυν*.—Tzetzes, Ch. III, Hist. 113.

[25] Pinto narrates what he saw—Damis like—and not, that he had heard something like what he narrates. *See* Masoudi, p. 313, Eng. tr.

his predecessors. Leaving then these common-places, examine Damis where he is original, or nearly so. To him we owe the porphyry temple and the metal mosaics at Taxila; to him, that spur of Caucasus, stretching down from the Indian side of the Hyphasis to the Indian Ocean; to him, its pepper-forests, and its monkeys, so useful in gathering the pepper-harvests. Through him we know of the groves sacred to Venus, and the unguent so necessary to an Indian marriage. He alone tells of the wondrous hill; its crater-fire of pardon, its rain-cask, and its brimming-cup of Tantalus; and though of wind-bags and of self-acting tripods Homer had already written, and though of a well of the test Ctesias had vaguely heard and its qualities Bardesanes has described, Damis gives them local habitation, has seen them all.

With the Sophoi Damis lived four months in closest intimacy, and yet from his description of them, who shall say, who and what they were? To the powers he ascribes to them both Buddhists and Brahmans pretend. But while their mode of election determined by ancestral and personal character points them out as Buddhists, their name, their long hair, their worship of the sun, declare them Brahmans.[26] But Buddhist or Brahman, at their feet after a long and weary travel Apollonius sits a disciple, and they instruct him—in doctrines and opinions which were current at Athens. In the very heart of India he finds its sages[27] though "inland far

[26] Bardesanes, who knew of Brahmans and Buddhists only from report, has given a very clear and intelligible account of both. I have already referred to it.—Porphyry, iv, 17.

[27] That a Greek kingdom with Greeks as its rulers, could not have

they be", well acquainted with Greek geography and the navigation of the Grecian seas, worshipping Greek gods, speaking Greek, thinking Greek,—more Greek than Indian. Absurd and impossible as this description seems to us, our Damis, if I judge him rightly, was not the man to advance what the Greek mind was wholly unprepared to receive. Accordingly, long ago Clitarchus and the historians of Alexander had announced an Indo-Greek Bacchus; to him Megasthenes added a Hercules; and more recently Plutarch had proclaimed, I know not on what authority, that the Indians were worshippers of the Greek gods;[28] vague rumours therefore of such a worship were not improbably current, and Damis's journal merely confirmed them. Again Nicolaus Damascenus[29] was the first who spoke of the Greek language in connection with India. He states, that when at Antioch Epidaphne (22 B.C.) he met with some Indian ambassadors on their way to Augustus Cæsar, and that their letter of credentials was in Greek. Diodorus,[30] quoting Iambulus, speaks of the king of Palibothra as a lover of Greeks. Plutarch (end of the first century), though

existed, bordering on India and in India for upwards of a century, without some influence on the Hindu mind, what we now see going on in India assures us; but that that influence was very limited we may gather from the very examples which its most strenuous supporter adduces to prove it.—Reinaud, Mem. sur l'Inde, pp. 333, 347, 362, 363.

[28] *Vide supra,* note 6.

[29] Frag. Hist., § 91, 4. 419, Didot's ed.

[30] Iambulus was brought *ες πολιν Παλιβοθραν...οντος δε φιλλελληνος του βασιλεως.*—Diod. Sic., Bib. Hist., II. 60. Diodorus and Damascenus were cotemporaries and flourished in the latter half of the century B.C., and the earliest part of the first century.

he does not name the Indians, in enumerating the great deeds of Alexander narrates that by his means Asia was civilised and Homer read there, and that the children[31] of Persians, Susians, and Gedrosians sang the tragedies of Euripides and Sophocles. Dio Chrysostom,[32] cotemporary with Plutarch and a friend of Apollonius, in a panegyric upon Homer insists upon his wide-spread reputation; that he lived in the memory not only of Greeks but of many of the barbarians; "for his poems it is said are sung by the Indians, who have translated them into their own language; so that a people who do not contemplate the same stars as ourselves, in whose heaven our polar star is not visible,—are not unacquainted with the grief of Priam and the tears and wailings of Hecuba and Andromache and the courage of Achilles and Hector." Ælian, of about the same age as Philostratus, tells us that not only the Indians but the kings of Persia also have translated and sung the poems of Homer, "if one may credit those who write on these matters."[33] On such vague authority, coupled doubtless with the fact that an Indo-Greek kingdom had formerly existed and had at one time extended to the Jumna, and that barbaric kings so honoured Greece that on their coins they entitled themselves Philhellene,[34] Damis built up this part of his romance, which flattered Greek prejudices and soothed Greek vanity and was willingly received by that influential and edu-

[31] Και Περσων και Σουσιανων και Γεδρωσιων παιδες τας Ευριπιδου και Σοφοκλεους τραγωδιας ηδον, *ut supra*.

[32] De Homero Oratio, LIII, 277; II, Reiske.

[33] Variæ Hist., L. xii, c. 48.

[34] Bayer Reg. Græc. Bactriani Hist., p. 117.

cated class to whom it was addressed, and who were struggling to give new life and energy to the perishing religion of Greece.

Of Damis's geography I can only say that it reminds me of a fairy tale. As soon as he leaves the well-known scene of Alexander's exploits, he crosses mountains unknown to any map, and then describes an immense plain of fifteen days' journey to the Ganges and eighteen days to the Red Sea, but which he himself travels over in fourteen days; for in four days he reaches the hill of the Sophoi, and thence in ten days arrives at the one mouth of the Hyphasis. Who shall explain these discrepancies, account for these mistakes, and fix localities thus vaguely described?

Reviewing the whole work of Philostratus, it seems to me that Apollonius either pretended or was believed to have travelled through, and made some stay in India, but that very possibly he did not really visit it; and that if he did visit it, our Damis never accompanied him, but fabricated the journal Philostratus speaks of, for it contains some facts, from books written upon India and tales[36] current about India which he easily collected at that great mart for Indian commodities and resort for Indian merchants—Alexandria.

[36] Traceable to the same sources as those from which Dio Chrysostom obtained his stories about India. In his oration to the people of Alexandria, he speaks of Bactrians, Scythians, Persians, and a few Indians (Ινδων τινας), as frequenting their city (*Ib.*, I, p. 672); and as authority for his Indian tale to the Celæni, he gives: *τινες των αφικνουμενων εφασαν· αφικνουνται δε ου πολλοι τινες εμποριας ἑνεκεν. οὑτοι δε επιμιγνυνται τοις προς θαλαττῃ· τουτο δε ατιμον εστεν Ινδων το γενος, οἱ τε αλλοι ψεγουσιν αυτους.*—II, 72, p. 3.

ON THE

INDIAN EMBASSY TO AUGUSTUS.

ON

THE INDIAN EMBASSY TO AUGUSTUS.

NICOLAUS DAMASCENUS, in a fragment preserved by Strabo,[1] relates that at Antioch Epidaphne he fell in with three Indian ambassadors, then on their way to the court of Augustus. They were, as their letter showed, the survivors of a larger embassy, to the other members of which the length of the journey principally had proved fatal.[2] Their letter was written on parchment (διφθερα)[3] and in the name of Porus and in Greek.

[1] Geograph. India, l. xv, c. I, 73, also Damasceni, Frag. 91; Frag. Hist. Græc., iii, v, p. 419, Didot.

[2] Οὓς εκ μεν της επιστολης πλειους δηλουσθαι, σωθηναι δε τρεις μονους οὓς ιδειν φησι, τους δ'αλλους ὑπο μηκους των ὁδων διαφθαρηναι το πλεον. *Ut supra.* Similarly of the six or seven hundred sent by Kublai Khan with the Polos to conduct his daughter to the Prince of Persia only eight reached their destination. "Et sachiez sans faille que quand ils entrerent en mer, ils furent bien vi cent personnes sans les mariniers. Tous morurent, qu'il n'en eschapa que viii." Marco Polo, c. xxiii, 30, p. 1, ed. Pauthier; all but eighteen, ed. Soc. Geog. Six hundred of the crew died, of the three ambassadors only one survived, whilst of the women only one died.—Ed. Marsden, p. 24.

[3] Ετι δε και το κατ' εμε, πολλοι των βαρβαρων ες...διφθερας γραφουσι. Herodotus, v, 58. As materials used for writing on in India, Reinaud, Mem. sur l'Inde, p. 305, mentions barks of trees in the north and palm leaves in the south. Heeren, Hist. Res., II, 107, on the authority of Paolino, adds to these cotton, Dr. Rost's rice

F

It set forth that Porus, though lord over six hundred kings, much valued the friendship of, and was ready to open his dominions to, Cæsar, and to assist him on all just and lawful occasions.[4] The presents they brought with them were in the charge of eight well-anointed slaves naked all but their girdles, and consisted of a youth whose arms had been amputated at the shoulders in childhood, a sort of Hermes, some large vipers, a snake ten cubits long, a river tortoise of four cubits, and a partridge somewhat larger than a vulture. With the ambassadors was that Indian, who burned himself at Athens—not to escape from present ills, but because, hitherto successful in everything he had undertaken, he now feared, lest any longer life should bring him misery and disappointment; and so smiling, naked and perfumed, he leaped into the burning pile. On his tomb was placed this inscription:—

"Here lies Zarmanochegas, of Bargosa, who according to the ancestral custom of the Hindus gave himself immortality."[5]

In this narrative, the king of kings Porus, the Greek

paper; while Hiouen Thsang intimates that in his time the Tâla leaf was generally used. "Les feuilles des Tâla (Borassus flabelliformis) sont longues, larges, et d'une couleur luisante. Dans tous les Royaumes de l'Inde il n'y a personne qui n'en recueille pour écrire," iii, v, p. 148. On the whole I very much doubt if the Hindus ever wrote on parchment or any prepared skin. Dr. Rost, librarian of the India House, knows of no Hindu parchment MSS.; and of no MSS. more than five hundred years old.

[4] Και ετοιμος ειη διοδον τε παρεχειν, ὁπη βουλεται, και συμπραττειν ὁσα καλως εχει. *Ut supra.*

[5] Ζαρμανοχηγας Ινδος απο Βαργοσης κατα τα πατρια Ινδων εθη ἑαυτον απαθανατισας κειται. MS.

letter, the beggarly presents better suited to a juggler's booth than to the court of a great sovereign, strike us with surprise; and we ask whether an Indian, or what purported to be an Indian Embassy, and such an embassy as described by Damascenus, ever presented itself to Augustus, and by whom and from what part of India it could have been sent?

To this Indian Embassy, Horace, a cotemporary, in more than one ode, exultingly and with some little exaggeration alludes;[6] and to it Strabo almost a cotempo-

[6] Carmen Seculare, 55, 56 (written about 17 B.C.); Ode 14, L. iv, (13 B.C.), and Ode 12, L. i (22 B.C. according to Bentley, 19 B.C. according to Donatus) where he speaks of "Subjectos......Seres et Indos." Who the Seres were I do not know; Reinaud, however, will have them to be the Chinese. Indeed, in a series of papers on the Relations between Rome and India, the first of which appeared in the Journal Asiatique for March, 1863, and the whole of which have been subsequently published in a separate form, he argues that between the two countries considerable political and commercial intercourse existed already in the reign of Augustus. And in support of his view he cites from Tibullus, Propertius, Virgil, Horace, etc., passages which with one exception are so general that they surely are but as Sibylline prophecies or poetic aspirations. The one exception I allude to is the 3 El., B. iv, of Propertius, which purports to be the letter of a wife Arethusa to her husband Lycotas, a soldier, whose continued absence she deplores.

> Te modo viderunt *iteratos* Bactra per ortus
> Te modo munito Sericus hostis equo,
> Hybernique Getæ pictoque Britannia curru,
> Ustus et Eoo decolor Indus equo.

But as the armies of Augustus never passed the Euphrates, it cannot have been as a Roman soldier that Lycotas traversed and retraversed Bactria, and surely than that Lycotas, as Reinaud suggests, was an ambassador from Antony to Kanischka, it is easier to suppose that he was a mercenary Greek, who had fought in the armies of the Parthian kings, and whose adventures had been noised in Rome; and easiest of all to look on the letter as without

rary a second time refers,[7] when in opening his account of India he laments the scantiness of his materials; that so few Greeks, and those but ignorant traders and incapable of any just observation, had reached the Ganges; and that from India but one embassy to Augustus from one place and from one king Pandion or Porus had visited Europe. Of later writers who mention it, Florus (A.D. 110, 17) states that the ambassadors were four years on the road, and that their presents were of elephants, pearls, and precious stones":[8] and Suetonius (A.D. 120, 30) attributes it to the fame of Augustus' moderation and virtues, which allured Indians and Scythians to seek his alliance and that of the Roman people.[9] Dio Cassius (A.D. 194) speaks of it at length; he tells, that "at Samos (B.C. 22, 20) many embassies came to Augustus, and that the Indians, having before proclaimed, then and there concluded, a treaty of alliance

any foundation in fact, as purely imaginary as the subject Indians and the Seric cavalry, and on Lycotas as the representative of the Roman armies, and their achievements past and to come, a delicate flattery of the courtly Propertius.

7 *Ut supra*, 4, c. Και οἱ νυν δε εξ Αιγυπτιου πλεοντες εμποριкοι τῳ Νειλῳ και τῳ Αραβιῳ κολπῳ μεχρι της Ινδικης σπανιοι μεν και περιπλευκασι μεχρι του Γαγγου, και οὑτοι δ' ιδιωται και ουδεν προς ἱστοριαν των τοπων χρησιμοι, κᾳκειθεν δ' αφ' ἑνος τοπου και παρ' ἑνος βασιλεως Πανδιονος και αλλου (η κατ' αλλους, Groskurd) Πωρου, ηκεν ὡς Καισαρα τον Σεβαστον δωρα και πρεσβεια και ὁ κατακαυσας ἑαυτον Αθηνησι σοφιστης Ινδος, καθαπερ ὁ Καλανος Αλεξαιδρῳ την τοιαυτην θεαν επιδειξαμενος.

8 Hist. Rom., iv, c. 12, ad calcem "Indi cum gemmis et margaritis elephantes quoque inter munera trahentes nihil magis quam longinquitatem viæ imputabant quam quadriennio impleverant."

9 Augustus, c. 21. "Qua virtutis moderationisque fama, Indos etiam ac Scythas auditu modo cognitos pellexit ad amicitiam suam populique Romani ultro per legatos petendam."

with him;[10] that among their gifts were tigers now seen for the first time by Romans and even Greeks, and a youth without arms like a statue of Hermes, but as expert with his feet as other people with their hands, for with them he could bend a bow, throw a javelin, and play the trumpet." Dio then goes on to say that "one of the Indians, Zarmaros, whether because he was of the Sophists and therefore out of emulation, or whether because he was old and it was the custom of his country, or whether as a show for the Athenians and Augustus who had gone to Athens, expressed his determination of putting an end to his existence. And having been first initiated in the mysteries of the two Gods[11] held out of their due course for the initiation of Augustus, he afterwards threw himself into the burning pile." Hieronymus (A.D. 380) in his translation of the Canon

[10] Hist. Rom., L. 9, 58, p. ii, Bekker A. V. 734. B.C. 18. Augustus being then in Samos, Παμπολλαι δη πρεσβειαι προς αυτον αφικοντο, και οἱ Ινδοι προκηρυκευσαμενοι προτερον φιλιαν τοδε εσπεισαντο, δωρα πεμψαντες αλλα τε και τιγρεις, πρωτον τοτε τοις Ρωμαιοις, νομιζω δ' ὁτι και τοις Ελλησιν, οφθεισας· και τι και μειρακιον οἱ ανευ ωμων, οἱους τους Ἑρμας ὁρωμεν, εδωκαν· και μεντοι τοιουτον ὁν εκεινο ες παντα τοις ποσιν ἁτε και χερσιν εχρητο, τοξον τε αυτοις ενετεινε και βελη ηφιει και εσαλπιζεν...γραφω γαρ λεγομενα...εἱς δ' ουν των Ινδων Ζαρμαρος...ειτε και ες επιδειξιν του δε Αυγυστου και των Αθηναιων (και γαρ εκεισεν ηλθεν) αποθανειν εθελησας εμυηθη τε τα τοιν θεοιν, των μυστηριων καιπερ ουκ εν τῳ καθηκοντι καιρῳ, ὡς φασι, δια τον Αυγυστον και αυτον μεμυημενον γενομενων, και πυρι ἑαυτον ζωντα εξεδωκεν.

[11] Suetonius, without going into detail, casually confirms this initiation of Augustus at Athens, "Namque Athenis initiatus, &c.," Aug. c. 93. But allowing that Augustus was initiated at Athens at this time, it does not follow that this Hindu was initiated with him, though such an initiation would be no impossible proceeding in a Buddhist priest.

Chronicon of Eusebius[12] just notices an Indian Embassy to Augustus,[13] but places it in the third year of the 188th Olympiad, or B.C. 26. And Orosius, a native of Tarragona (early part of the 5th century) relates,[14] that "an Indian and a Scythian Embassy traversed the whole world, and found Cæsar at Tarragona, in Spain;" and with some rhetorical flourish, then observes, "that just as in Babylon Alexander received deputations from Spain and the Gauls, so now Augustus in the furthest

[12] I have not cited Eusebius, because, in Maius' and Zohrab's edition of his Canon Chronicon founded on an old Armenian version, there is no allusion whatever to our embassy. I observe also that Scaliger's edition makes the same double and confused mention of it, and in the very same words that does George the Syncell's Chronographia, from which Scaliger largely borrowed. Knowing then how Scaliger made up his edition of the Canon Chron., I suspect that even supposing a notice of our embassy in the original work, and this is doubtful (Maius' Pref., xviii), such a notice could not well have existed in the shape in which it now appears. For Georgius and Scaliger's Canon Chronicon under the one hundred and eighty-eighth Olymp., state, *τοτε και Πανδιων ὁ των Ινδων βασιλευς επεκηρυκευσατο φιλος Αυγυστου γενεσθαι (και συμμαχος)*; then going back to the hundred and eighty-fifth Ol. (40-36 B.C.), each tells of the death of Antony and the capture of Lepidus, and how Augustus then became sole emperor, and how the Alexandrians compute the years of Augustus, and then adds *Πανδιων ὁ των Ινδων βασιλευς φιλος Αυγυστου και συμμαχος πρεσβευεται.* Georg. Syncellus Byzant. Hist. Niebuhr, 588-9, *ib.*

[13] Indi ab Augusto amicitiam postularunt, 188th Olym. (Migne ed.)

[14] Interea Cæsarem apud Tarraconem citerioris Hispaniæ urbem legati Indorum et Scytharum toto orbe transmisso tandem ibi invenerunt, ultra quod quærere non possent, refuderuntque in Cæsarem Alexandri Magni gloriam; quem sicut Hispanorum Gallorumque legatio in medio Oriente apud Babylonem contemplatione pacis adiit, ita hunc apud Hispaniam in Occidentis ultimo supplex cum gentilitio munere eous Indus et Scytha boreus oravit. —Orosius, Hist. vi, c. xii.

west was approached with gifts by suppliant Indian and Scythian Ambassadors." From these authorities, I think we may safely conclude, that an Indian Embassy, or what purported to be an Indian Embassy, was received by Augustus.

But while we allow that our authorities are applicable to or certainly not irreconcilable with Damascenus' embassy which Augustus received at Samos, 22-20 B.C.; we cannot but observe that St. Jerome's is referred to the year 26 B.C. and that Orosius brings it to Tarragona, whither Augustus had gone 27 B.C., and where he was detained till 24 B.C. by the Cantabrian war. Hence a difficulty, which Casaubon and others have endeavoured to remove by assuming two Indian Embassies; the one at Tarragona to treat of peace, the other at Samos to ratify the peace agreed upon. But—not to mention that this preliminary embassy is unknown to the earlier writers,[15] who all so exult in the so-called second embassy that they scarcely would have failed to notice the first—I would first remark that no author whatever speaks of two Indian Embassies. And I would secondly refer to the ambassadorial letter of which Damascenus has preserved the contents, and in which we find no allusion to any previous contract or agreement between the two sovereigns, but simply an offer on the part of the Hindu prince to open his country to the subjects

[15] I do not overlook the προκηρυκευσαμενοι προτερον φιλιαν τοτε εσπεισαντο of Dio Cassius. But is it, looking at the context, possible to conceive that those προκηρυκευσαμενοι were other than those who τοτε εσπεισαντο, and who were at Antioch 22 B.C. and who then probably gave notice of their mission by herald?

and citizens of Rome in the person of Cæsar. Surely then, than this embroglio of embassies which come to sue for peace where war was impossible, it is more natural to suppose that Jerome a careless writer[16] misdated his embassy; and that Orosius, a friend and pupil of Jerome,[17] finding that the date in Jerome tallied with Cæsar's expedition to Spain, seized the opportunity both of illustrating his native town and of instituting a comparison between Augustus and Alexander the Great. I think we may rest content with one embassy.

But is Damascenus' account of this embassy a trustworthy and faithful account? Strabo evidently gives credit to it, and to some extent confirms it by stating that the Hermes he himself had seen (*ὁν και ἡμεις ειδομεν*); and in another place, while he attributes our embassy to a Pandion rather than a Porus, he still connects it with the Indian who burned himself at Athens.[18] Plutarch (A.D. 100, 10) in noticing the self-cremation of Calanus Alexander's Gymnosophist adds, that many years afterwards at Athens another Indian in the suite of Augustus similarly put an end to his life, and that his monument is still known as the Indian's tomb.[19] Horace, Florus, and Suetonius, give indeed another character and other objects to the

16 "Propter festinationem quam ipse in Chronici præfatione fatetur."—Maius, Can. Chron. Præf. xix.

17 Smith's Dict. of Greek and Rom. Biog., Art. Orosius.

18 Vide supra, note 7.

19 *Τουτο πολλοις ετεσιν ὑστερον αλλος Ινδος εν Αθηναις Καισαρι συνων εποιησεν και δεικνυται μεχρι νυν το μνημειον Ινδου καλουμενον.* Alexandri vita, vitæ iii, p. 1290.

embassy, but write too loosely to be authorities for any fact not reconcilable with the narrative of Damascenus. With that narrative Dio Cassius, too, in the main agrees; but as he specifies tigers, a truly royal gift,[20] and unknown to Damascenus, as among the Indian presents, he gives us an opportunity of testing his and Damascenus' accuracy. For he affirms that the tigers of the embassy were the first ever seen by Romans. Now Suetonius mentions it as a trait of Augustus, that he was ever so ready to gratify the people with the sight of rare or otherwise remarkable animals, that he would exhibit them "extra ordinem," out of due course and on ordinary days, and that in this way he exhibited a tiger on the stage.[21] And Pliny states that "a tame tiger" (and other than tame tigers our ambassadors would scarcely carry about with them) "was shown in Rome for the first time at the consecration of the Theatre of Marcellus (the in scenâ of Suetonius) in the Nones of May and during the consulships of Q. Tubero and Fabius Maximus,[22] or in the year 11 B.C., i.e. nine years after the date of our embassy, hardly, therefore,

[20] Suleiman Aga when sent by the Pasha of Bagdad to the Governor-General of India takes as presents five horses and four lions.—Castlereagh Dispatches, v, 193.

[21] "Solebat etiam citra spectaculorum dies, si quando quid novitatum dignumque cognitu advectum esset, id extra ordinem quolibet loco publicare: ut rhinocerotem apud septa, tigrim in scenâ, anguem quinquaginta cubitorum pro Comitio."—Augustus, c. 43.

[22] Augustus Q. Tuberone, Paulo Maximo coss. iv. Nonas Maias Theatro Marcelli dedicatione tigrim primus omnium Romæ ostendit in caveâ mansuefactum: Divus vero Claudius simul quatuor.—Plin. Hist. Nat., viii, 25. How common afterwards!—v. Martial, viii, l. 26, Ep.

a tiger presented by it. The evidence of Dio Cassius on this point is then, to say the least of it, unsupported, and we see no reason to believe that tigers were among the Indian gifts. We thus find the account of Damascenus confirmed in several particulars, and in none satisfactorily impugned. We accept the Indian Sophist, we accept the Hermes, we accept the beggarly presents, and because we accept so much we accept also the Greek letter, and the Pandyan or Puru, king of kings; for we believe, as Strabo also evidently believed, that what Damascenus wrote, he wrote from his own knowledge. But how then explain what is so at variance with our established notions?

Lassen[23] in that great Encyclopædia of Hindu literature the "Indische Alterthumskunde", evidently struck by the good faith of Damascenus' narrative, has endeavoured to smooth down the difficulties attached to it. The six hundred subject kings he sets down to evident exaggeration, but he identifies the Porus of the embassy with the Paurava king, who at the beginning of our æra on the death of Kadphises II founded an independent kingdom in the Western Punjâb. This Prince he observes was a serpent-worshipper, and as a serpent-worshipper would naturally look upon the sacred reptile as a fit offering to a brother sovereign. He accounts: for the presents, by suggesting that the more valuable of them the ambassadors had sold on the road: and for the Greek letter, by supposing that it was obtained from some Greek scribe, and substituted for the royal credentials.[24]

[23] Indische Alterthumskunde, 59, 60, p. iii.

[24] Surely the Greek legends on Indian coins, where the sove-

This explanation, however ingenious, is scarcely satisfactory. For,

1st. Even supposing that our ambassadors had procured a Greek version[25] of the royal letter, yet as Damascenus expressly states that their letter was in Greek, not translated, it follows that they must have suppressed the original and substituted for it what may or may not have been a translation, *i.e.*, we must suppose them guilty of the gravest crime which can be laid to the charge of ambassadors, the falsification of their credentials.

2ndly. Allowing our Porus to have been a serpent-worshipper, was he therefore likely to approach an unknown ally with one of his pet gods, and such a god! as an offering?[26] I have never heard that the old Egyptian Pharaohs, in reciprocating civilities with any

reign's name, which could not have been copied from any existing die, is found with its proper inflexions, as e. g. on the coins of Azes 50 B.C. ΒΑΣΙΛΕΩΖ ΒΑΣΙΛΕΩΝ ΜΕΓΑΛΟΥ ΑΖΟΥ (Wilson's Ariana Antiqua, 325), would indicate that in the north-west provinces of India the Greek language was not utterly forgotten: and if we could believe that our embassy came from the Punjâb, we would take it for granted that its Greek letter was composed there.

[25] Rubruquis, A.D. 1250, thus speaks of the royal letter which he delivered to the Tartar king: "Afterwards I delivered unto him your Majesty's letters with the translation thereof into the Arabike and Syriake languages. For I caused them to be translated at Acori into the character and dialect of both the rude tongues."—Hakluyt, I, 117. But the Buddhist priest who brings a letter, A.D. 982, from an Indian King to the Chinese Emperor delivers it, and the Emperor orders it to be translated.—Faits concernant l'Inde, tr. du Chinois, Pauthier, p. 73.

[26] Yet Hadrian consecrated an Indian serpent in the Olympion at Athens, *δρακοντα απο Ινδιας κομισθεντα ανεθηκεν*.—Dio Cassius. Xiphilinus II, p. 329, Bekker.

neighbouring king, ever presented him with some well-grown crocodile, or a case of beetles with their appropriate garniture. But let the serpent pass. You have still to account for the vipers and the tortoise. And if you allege in apology that these were but the dregs and refuse of a once richly freighted embassy, and that all that was of value, the pearls and spices, had been sold: then as it could only have been sold under the pressure of want, you have to show that under the circumstances the pressure of want was probable.[27] Now, though the journey before our ambassadors was long and perhaps dangerous, it was over no strange and untrodden country, but along the most ancient route in the world,[28] frequented by caravans, with many stopping-places well known and at ascertained distances;[29] it is scarcely credible then that they should set out otherwise than provided against all contingencies, as well provided at least as the merchants whom they probably accompanied, and scarcely credible that they should have actually suffered from want. But may not the troubles which then harassed the Parthian Empire have delayed their

[27] The French expedition from Saigon to Shangai left June 5th, 1866, reached Yunnan Dec. 23rd, 1867, and Shangai June 12th, 1868. They took two years, but were detained at Bossal on the Lower Laos four months. At Yunnan they arrived exhausted and in absolute want,—instruments, books, every thing had to be abandoned. At Tonghenan their chief died. But the route was an unexplored one.—Saturday Review, Nov. 21, 1868, p. 683.

[28] Arrian speaks of a λεωφορος ὁδος, extending evidently, from the context, in the direction of India through Bactria.—Exped. Alexand., iii, L. c. 21.

[29] V. Mansiones Parthicæ Isidori Characeni. Geograph. Minor iv, Didot ed., and a short account of another route for goods in Pliny, Hist. Nat., vi, xix.

progress, lengthened their journey, and thus increased its expenses? Yes, but as those troubles were now of long standing, they appear surely rather as a reason against the setting out of the embassy than as one for its miserable plight on arrival.

3rdly. The Paurava Prince to whom Lassen would ascribe this embassy, obtained his throne only after the death of Kadphises II, and in the beginning of our æra. And as Kadphises conquered India, more properly the Punjâb and Kabulistan, according to Lassen himself about 24 B.C. and died about 10 B.C.,[30] and as our embassy met Augustus at Samos 22, 20 B.C., it very evidently could not be the embassy of the Paurava Prince. And it could hardly have represented either Kadphises or the King whom Kadphises dethroned; because it is improbable that Kadphises in any transaction with a foreign sovereign would appear disguised under a Hindu name; and very improbable that either the king who had just conquered a kingdom, or the king who was on the point of losing one, should occupy himself with embassies not of a political but of a purely commercial character, and for an object which the very countries that separated him from Rome rendered impossible.

30 Lassen ut supra, ii, p. 411, corrected by note 8, p. 813. "Kadphises wahrscheinlich Indien 24 v. Christi G. eroberte und etwa 14 Jahren nachher starb." Wilson, Ariana Antiqua places him, however, "not earlier than the commencement of the Christian æra", and seems to have misunderstood Lassen when he adds that "Lassen proposes the end of the first century as the term of the kingdom of Kadphises," p. 353. As to the extent of his dominions, Lassen *ib.* p. 818, observes "Seine Beinahme, Beherrscher der Erde, macht Ansprüche auf ein ausgedehntes Reich. Diese Ansprüche müssen auf Kabulistan und das Punjâb beschränkt werden."

But how then account for all that surprises us in this embassy?

What do we gather from Damascenus' narrative?

I. He met our ambassadors at Antioch Epidaphne. Now Antioch Epidaphne is so situated that it is just as probable they arrived there on the road to Greece from the western coast of the Indian Peninsula, either by way of the Red Sea and Alexandria or the Persian Gulf and the Euphrates, as by the mid-Asiatic route and from the Punjâb.

II. Damascenus speaks of a native of Bargosa as accompanying or attached to the embassy, and though he states that the ambassadorial letter was written in the name of Porus, Strabo rather attributes it to a Pandion: and as Barygaza is a trading town at the mouth of the Nerbudda on the Indian coast, and Pandya a kingdom extending along the Western shores of the Indian Peninsula, to the Western coast of India I conclude with Strabo that the embassy probably belongs.

III. This native of Bargosa or Barygaza, Sanscrit Varikatcha (Julien), is described as a Hindu, and bears a name Zarmanos Chegan, Sanscrit çramanakarja,[31] *i.e.*, Teacher of the Shamans, which points him out as of the Buddhist faith and a priest, and as his death proves a priest earnest in his faith. His companions then were probably Hindus also, and perhaps Buddhists and the representatives of a Hindu and possibly a Buddhist prince.

[31] Lassen ut supra iii, p. 60. Just in the same way I conclude that Calanus who followed Alexander and burned himself in Persia was a Buddhist as well from his willingness to leave his home and his death as from his conversation with Onesicritus.—Strabo, xv.

IV. The wretched presents—the Greek letter—the sort of doubt which hangs over the name and country of the prince, are all indicative not of the sovereign of a great kingdom, but of the petty raja of some commercial town or insignificant district.

V. The presents not unsuited to the tastes of Augustus, and the Greek letter and its purely commercial tone, indicate that our embassy was planned and organized by Greek traders, and more for Greek than Hindu interests.

VI. This embassy is conceivable only under the supposition that, if it forwarded the interests of the Greeks who planned it, it also benefited the Hindu prince who was induced to lend it his name.

But who was this Prince? who these Greeks? and what their common interests? The prince and his residence we are unable to identify. There is nothing in the reptiles of the presents, larger indeed in Guzerat[32] but common to the whole western coast of India, which can enable us to fix on the locale of the embassy. If we turn to the name of the prince, we find that he is a Porus in the ambassadorial letter, but had become Pandion when Strabo wrote[33] and the Peninsula was better

[32] For the serpents of Guzerat see Forbes, Oriental Memoirs, i, 480; for the partridges of the Nerbudda, the black kind are striking from their beauty, none remarkable for their size, *id.*, 501. Might the partridge of the embassy, large as a hawk, have been the jungle fowl which Forbes describes as having something of the plumage of the partridge?

[33] As the kingdom of Pandya according to the Periplus Erith. Anony. is the S. Deccan and extends from Nelkunda, Nelisuram, to Komar, Cape Comorin (§ 54, 58, Didot ed.), we see how with the

known. A Puru of the Punjâb we have seen that in all probability he was not; and I do not understand how he could well have been a Pandyan; because Pandya was a great and powerful sovereign and of the Saiva faith,[34] the most bigoted of the Hindu forms of religion, and was not likely therefore either to have initiated a commercial alliance with a foreign state, or to have initiated it by such an embassy as ours. D'Anville suggests that he was a Rana of Ougein who claimed a descent from Porus.[35] But surely a descent from Porus real or pretended, is not in itself sufficient to identify our prince, unless it can be shown that like the Pandyans and the Guptas he attached to his own name that of his ancestors, used it as a family name and in all public documents styled himself son of Puru. Besides, it seems to me that Ougein is too far inland to have already come into direct contact with Greek traders, and to have known anything of Augustus and the Roman Empire. To recur then to our narrative, it records the name of one Indian town, Bargosa or Barygaza.[36] And in the

increase in the direct trade the name Pandion should become better known at Alexandria than that of Porus, and at length take its place.

34 The prevailing form of the Hindu religion in the south of the Peninsula was at the commencement of the Christian era and some time before it, most probably that of Siva. Hist. Sketch of Pandya.—Wilson, Journal Roy. As. Soc. iii, p. 204.

35 Vincent's Commerce of the Antients, ii, 407. It is perhaps as well to state, that from a Note of Wilson's in his sketch of Pandya, it seems that the Aarivansa and Agni Purana make Pandya of the line of Puru; but that as he is not so specified in the Vishnu Purana, Wilson is of opinion that "his insertion is the work of more recent authorities."—Journal Roy. As. Soc. iii, No. 1 note.

36 Barygaza was the port of Ougein and may have belonged to

neighbourhood of Barygaza, and indeed throughout the Northern part of the Peninsula, statues and temples of Buddha are still seen, which indicate that there formerly Buddhism was certainly recognised, perhaps flourished, and was on the ascendant.[37] Barygaza besides situated at the mouth of a great river was when the Periplus was written a place of considerable trade, the great and legal mart[38] for the commerce of the West, a city therefore which would probably avail itself with eagerness of any opportunity for assuring its friendly relations with its great customer, Rome; and to it I should be inclined to refer our embassy. But when we remember that Damascenus miscalls it, and that Strabo copies and does not correct him and never himself notices the place, we may well doubt whether in the times we are speaking of it was frequented by Greeks, or better known to them than the other commercial ports on the same part of the coast.[39] And except

it, Ενι δε αυτῃ (Inest huic regioni) και εξ ανατολης πολις λεγομενη Οζηνη εν ῇ και τα βασιλεια προτερον ην, αφ ἧς παντα——εις Βαρυγαζα καταφερεται, § 48.

[37] Forbes in the plates to his Oriental Memoirs, gives a statue of Buddha (he calls it of Paravant) which he saw at Cambay, and of Buddhist figures on columns at Salsette. Hiouen Thsang, in noticing the state of Buddhism in Barygaza and Ougein, speaks of it as on the decline, iii, 154, as flourishing in Guzèrat, *ib.*, 165, and in the Konkan, *ib.*, 147.

[38] Not always so. The Periplus tells us that Καλλιενα (hodie Calliani non longe a Bombay distans) επι των Σαραγονου του πρεσβυτερου χρονων εμποριον γενομενον. μετα γαρ το κατασχειν αυτην Σανδανην εκωλυθη επι πολυ, και γαρ τα εκ τυχης εις τουτους τους τοπους εισβαλλοντα πλοια Ἑλληνικα μετα φυλακης εις Βαρυγαζα εισαγεται. § 52 with the note.

[39] See preceding note.

that one of its citizens was in the ambassadorial suite, I do not think it can show any special claim to our embassy.

Who our Greeks were we may more accurately determine. After the destruction of the Persian Empire, the two great Western marts for the produce of India were Palmyra and Alexandria. But with regard to Palmyra—

I. Its distance from the Peninsula of India was too short, and the route through the Persian Gulf and up the Euphrates too direct to admit of a journey so long, that from the mere time it occupied as hinted by Damascenus several of the ambassadors should have died on the road.

II. Palmyra at this period still retained its national character and civilization and was essentially a Syrian republic. It had not yet merged into that Græco-Roman city which it became after the time of Trajan, and which its ruins and the legends on its coins and the names of some of its citizens illustrate.[40] Greek and Roman residents it no doubt admitted, but they could have been neither numerous enough nor powerful enough to have organised and forwarded our embassy.

III. Palmyra, situated in the desert some eighty miles from the Euphrates, was pre-eminently an inland

[40] For this account of Palmyra I have consulted Pliny, Hist. Nat., v, 21; Gibbon's Roman Empire, c. xi, vol. i; Heeren's Manual of Ant. Hist., pp. 348, 57; the Art. Zenobia, Smith's Gk. and Rom. Biog. Dict., and the Articles Palmyra by Flügel, and Paläographie, iv, by Gesenius, in Ersch. und Grüber's Encyclopedie.

town. Its citizens and resident strangers were merchants, warehousemen, carriers, agents, but they assuredly were not seafaring men; they possessed no ships, and received the produce of India through the Arabs, whose vessels delivered it at Sura or Thapsacus on the Euphrates whence it was brought on camels to Palmyra. They neither had nor could have any direct intercourse with India, and without such an intercourse our embassy is not conceivable.

IV. Palmyra is not likely to have encouraged any Indian embassy to the Roman Emperor. It was a free city.[41] Its inhabitants had not forgotten the designs of Antony and the dangers they had but lately escaped,[42] and it is not probable that they would now of their own free will call Roman attention to their wealth, and place the Indians from whom they derived it in direct communication with their own best customers. Through Palmyra this embassy could not have made its way to Augustus.

We turn now to the Greeks of Alexandria. Alexandria with a population made up of about every nation under the sun was essentially a Greek city. It

[41] Palmyra—velut terris exempta a rerum naturâ *privatâ sorte*, inter duo imperia summa, Romanorum Parthorumque, et prima in discordia semper utrumque cura. Plin. ut supra—privatâ sorte, sui juris.

[42] Antony sent out a body of cavalry to surprise and plunder Palmyra, *μικρα μεν επικαλων αυτοις, ὁτι Ρωμαιων και Παρθυαιων οντες εφοριοι, ες ἑκατερους επιδεξιως ειχον, εμποροι γαρ οντες κομιζουσι μεν εκ Περσων τα Ινδικα τῃ Αραβιᾳ διατιθενται δ' εν τῃ Ρωμαιων.*—Appian de Bell. Civ., v, ix. Appian attributes this expedition to a desire for plunder only. I suspect it was rather undertaken in the interests of Alexandria.

carried on a large, profitable and increasing trade with the East.[43] And though at the period of our embassy its merchants seldom ventured beyond the Arab Ports of Cane and Aden,[44] where they traded for the products and manufactures of India, they nevertheless occasionally sailed for the Indian Seas, and made their way even to the Ganges. And as they then interfered with the Arab monopoly, they saw themselves every where jealously watched and opposed by the Arabs, every where treated as interlopers, and had every where to encounter the persecutions of an excited populace.[45] Only in some of the smaller and therefore neglected ports, could they find opportunity and permission to trade. And then how eagerly would they lay before the authorities the advantages of a direct trade! They would show them the prices asked and obtained by the Arabs for Hindu and Greek commodities, and point out how of the profits the Arabs carried away the lion's share. And if they fell in with some Rajah of the Buddhist faith—a faith without the prejudices of race, proselytising, catholic—and not averse to travel, they surely would easily persuade him, as in after times the Rajah of Ceylon was persuaded, to further and attempt

[43] Strabo states that in the time of the Ptolemies, some twenty ships only (xvii, L. i, c. 130) ventured to cross the Indian seas, but that the trade had so greatly increased that he himself saw at Myos Hormos one hundred and twenty ships destined for India, L. ii, v, c. 12 §.

[44] Vincent's Commerce of the Antients, ii, 53, and Periplus, c. 27.

[45] Just as the Arabs stirred up the populace of Calecut against the Portuguese on their first attempts at trade in Calecut. Maffei, Hist. India, pp. 49, 52, 114; comp. p. 24.

to assure the direct trade by an embassy, the details of which a small Prince would willingly leave to them.

But besides this commercial interest common to both peoples, the Greeks of Alexandria had an interest of their own in getting up this embassy. In the great civil war but just concluded they had been partisans of Antony, they had fought in his ranks and were the last to yield after his defeat. They had to conciliate the favour of the conqueror. But they were no vulgar flatterers, theirs was not that adulation which repeats ever the same cuckoo note of praise. They studied their man and to his temper and character adapted their tone. To the literary Claudius they devoted a new room in their Museum,[46] and placed his works among their class-books. The theatre-circus-loving Nero they wheedled by hired bands of artistic *claqueurs*.[47] And the usurpation of the plebeian Vespasian they sanctioned by endowing him with miraculous powers.[48]

[46] Denique et Græcas scripsit historias—Quarum caussâ veteri Alexandriæ Museo alterum additum ex ipsius nomine; institutumque ut quotannis in altero Τυρρηνικων liberi, altero Καρχηδονιακων, diebus statutis, velut in auditorio recitarentur.—Suetonii Claud., c. 42.

[47] "Captus autem modulatis Alexandrianorum laudationibus, qui de novo commeatu Neapolim confluxerunt, plures Alexandriâ evocavit."—*Ib.*, Nero, c. 20.

[48] Auctoritas et quasi majestas quædam, ut scilicet inopinato et adhuc novo Principi deerat: hæc quoque accessit. E plebe quidam luminibus orbatus, item alius debili crure, sedentem—adierunt, orantes opem valetudinis, demonstratam a Serapide per quietem. Cum vix fides esset—ideoque ne experiri quidem audiret, hortantibus amicis palam pro concione utrumque tentavit, nec eventus defuit.—*Id.*, Vespasianus, c. 7. Tacitus gives the miracles; but in Tacitus, Vespasian is only mystified. Hist., iv, 81. Dio Cassius, after mentioning the miracles, describes the disappointment of

How now would such a people seek to win over the politic Augustus? They bring to his feet these Indian ambassadors, and thus raise him to a rivalship with Alexander. That he was too wise and far-seeing to be himself deceived is probable enough, but is no valid objection. What cared he that the crown was of copper-gilt and the robes of tinsel, provided that the plaudits were real? The object of the Alexandrians was not to impose on him, but to gain his favour by enabling him to impose on the Roman people; and that they fully succeeded Roman history sufficiently testifies.

In conclusion, I thus explain and account for our embassy. In the Northern half of the Indian Peninsula Greek merchants in their intercourse with a Hindu Raja often press upon his notice the greatness and wealth of their metropolis, and insist upon the advantages which he and his country would derive from more intimate commercial relations with it. They advise an embassy, and offer a passage in their ship for the ambassadors and for such presents as they can conveniently carry and he conveniently send. The Raja is persuaded. In due course the embassy arrives at Alexandria, and for Alexandria only it may have been originally intended. But the Alexandrians alive to their own interests quickly forward it on to Augustus, and give it weight and dignity by affixing to the Greek letter with which they provide it a well-known and time-honoured name. The presents they leave unchanged, aware that the travel-worn ambassadors,

the Alexandrians who expected favour, and only got increased taxation.

whose home is so distant that some of them have died on their way to Cæsar, will impress the imagination more strongly than heaps of barbaric pearl and gold.

While I offer this explanation, I do not pretend that it is entirely satisfactory, "refutation-tight;" enough if it seems to others as to me, less improbable, less open to objection, more simple and more in accordance with the facts given, than others.

ON THE

SECOND INDIAN EMBASSY TO ROME.

ON THE

SECOND INDIAN EMBASSY TO ROME.*

THE second Indian embassy to Rome was the result of an accident. Pliny tells the story thus. A freedman of one Annius Plocamus, while in the Red Sea collecting the tolls and customs farmed of Claudius by his patron, was caught in a gale of wind, driven past Carmania, and on the fifteenth day carried into Hippuros, a port of Ceylon. Here, though his ship with its contents seems to have been seized and confiscated to the king's use,[1] he himself was kindly and hospitably treated. In six months' time he learned the language. Admitted to familiar intercourse with the king,[2] in answer to his questions to told him of Rome

* Pliny, Nat. Hist., vi. 24.

[1] Not expressly stated in the text, but surmised from an expression subsequently used, "denarii in captivâ pecuniâ."—Pliny, Hist. Nat., vi, l, c 24.

[2] So Sopater, and the Aditulani, his companions, A.D. 500, on their arrival in Ceylon are carried by the chiefs and custom-house officers to the king, as was the custom: *κατα το εθος οἱ αρχοντες και οἱ τελωναι δεξαμενοι τουτους αποφερουσι προς τον βασιλεα.* Cosmas Indicop.; Montfaucon, N. Coll.; Patrum, i, p. 338. So of Sinbad when found stranded on Ceylon, "the people talked together, and said 'We must take him with us, and present him to our king.'"—Lane's Arabian Nights, p. 70, iii. Of this custom, however, I find no trace whatever in the travels of Fa-hian, early part of fifth century, or of Hiouen Thsang, seventh century.

and of Cæsar. In these conversations and from some denarii which had been found in the Roman ship, and which from the heads upon them had evidently been coined at different times and by different persons, and which nevertheless were all of the same weight,[3] the Sinhalese monarch learned to appreciate Roman justice. He became desirous of entering into alliance with Rome, and for that purpose sent thither one Rachias with three other ambassadors from whom as he intimates Pliny[4] derived that fuller and more accurate information with respect to Ceylon which he has embodied in his Natural History.

They stated that in Taprobane were five hundred towns:[5] that in the south was situated Palisæmundus,

[3] The next time we hear of Romans at the Sinhalese Court, Roman money then, as now, played its part. It seems that when Sopater was presented, a Persian Ambassador was presented with him. The Sinhalese monarch, after the first salutations, asked whose was the most powerful sovereign. The Persian hurried on to assert the wealth and superiority of the great king. Sopater appealed to the coins of both people. The Roman money, and Sopater had only choice pieces with him, was of gold, bright, well rounded, and of (a musical ring ?) λαμπρον, ευμορφον, ευροϊζον; the Persian was of small pieces of silver. The king examines the coins, and decides in favour of the Romans, who he declares are a wise, illustrious, and powerful people.—Cosmas in loc. cit. In another place, p. 148, he speaks of the excellence and universal use of Roman money.

[4] "Hactenus a priscis memorata: nobis diligentior notitia .. Contigit legatis etiam ex insu la advectis...Ex iis cognitum".—Pliny, u. s.

[5] "An evident exaggeration", says Lassen, "but one fostered by the native books". Thus the Rajavalli (Tennent's Ceylon, i, 422) gives in A.D. 1301 to Ceylon 1,400,000 villages; but as the same work states that Dutugamini built "900,000 houses of earth, and

the capital,[6] with its harbour and royal residence of two hundred thousand inhabitants:[7] that inland was a lake, Megisba, three hundred and seventy-five miles round, and studded here and there with grass islands; and that from this lake two rivers issued, of which the one took a northerly course and was called the Cydara, while the other, the Palisæmundus, flowed by the city of that name, and fell into the sea in three streams—the broadest fifteen, the narrowest five stadia across. They said that Cape Coliacum was the point of land nearest to India, that four days'[8] sail from it was the Sun

8,000,000 houses which were covered with tiles."—(Upham, Sacred Books of Ceylon, p. 222, iii), and this, though some fifty years after a forest still existed at the gates of Anarajapura (Mahawanso, p. 203), the authority is of no great weight. I am inclined to think with Hamilton, that the population of Ceylon was never greater than at present.—Geog. Desc. of Hindostan, ii, 469.

[6] Cosmas, sixth century, places the great mart and harbour in the south. Of the two kings of the island, he says "ὁ εἱs εχων τον ὑακινθον, και ἑτερος το μερος το αλλο εν ᾡ εστι το εμποριον και ὁ λιμην· μεγα δε εστι και των εκεισεν εμποριον, *ib.* 337. Here Sopater probably landed. Fa-hian, early part of the fifth century, and Hiouen Thsang on the other hand, celebrate the capital of the Hyacinthine king; Fa-hian, p. 334, its streets and public buildings and fine houses; Hiouen Thsang its viharas and their wonders, ii, 143-4. Marco Polo, thirteenth century, describes the hyacinthine stone: "Et si a le roy de ceste isle, un rubis le plus bel et le plus gros qui soit en monde; et vous disay comment il est fait. Il est long bien une grant paume, et bien gros tant comme est gros le bras d'un homme. Il est la plus resplendissant chose du monde à veoir; et n'a nulle tache. Il est vermeil comme feu."—p. 586, ed. Pauthier.

[7] "Portum contra meridiem appositum oppido Palisæmundo, omnium ibi clarissimo et regiam cc. mille plebis."—Pliny, i, l, c.

[8] Hiouen Thsang relates, that when he first heard of Ceylon, he heard also that to reach it from India no long sea voyage was necessary, but then one "pendant laquelle les vents contraires, les

Island[9] in mid-channel, and that the sea there was very green and full of trees,[10] the tops of which were often broken off by the rudders of passing ships. They admitted that with them the moon was only visible from the eighth to the sixteenth day; and while they wondered at our Great Bear and Pleiades as constellations of another heaven, they boasted of their Canopus, a great and brilliant star. But what of all things most astonished[11] them was that their shadows fell in the direction of our and not their hemisphere, and that the sun with us rose on the left and set on the right hand, just the contrary of what took place with them. They calculated that that side of their island which lies opposite to the south-east coast of India was ten thou-

flots impétueux et Yakshas demons vous exposeraient à mille dangers. Il vaut mieux partir de la pointe sud-est de l'Inde méridionale; de cette manière on peut y arriver par eaux dans l'espace de trois jours."—Vie et Ouvrages de Hiouen Thsang, tr. Julien, p. 183. In the time of Ibn Batuta, 1334, between Bakala "on the coast of Ceylon and the Malabar districts, Coromandel coast, there is a voyage of one day and one night."—Travels, p. 184.

[9] Identified by Tennent with the Island of Delft.—Ceylon, ii, 550; by Vincent with Manaar or Ramana-Koll, Periplus, ii, 492.

[10] So also Megasthenes describes the Indian seas, "*Μεγασθενην δε τον τα Ινδικα γεγραφοτα ἱστορειν εν τῃ κατα την Ινδικην θαλαττῃ δενδρα φυεσθαι.*"—Frag. Hist. Græc., ii, p. 413, 1755. The sea in these parts is described as very green and full of coral, and "on the purity of the water and on the coral groves which rise in the clear blue depths," Sir Emerson Tennent (*ut supra*, p. 555) dwells with delight.

[11] "Septentriones...*mirabantur*...sed maxime *mirum* iis...umbras suas in nostrum cælum cadere." This "mirabantur" and "mirum iis" Windt observes, would lead one to suppose that Pliny had himself received this information direct from the interpreter.—Windt, Ceylon, p. 103.

sand stadia, or about twelve hundred and fifty miles, in length.[12] They told also of the Seræ,[13] who dwelt beyond the Montes Emodi, and whom the father of Rachias had visited, and who would trade with and show themselves to their people; they described them as tall, red-haired,[14] blue eyed, rough-voiced, and with

[12] Onesicritus, *ου διορισας μηκος ουδε πλατος*, without stating whether he refers them to its length or breadth, estimates Ceylon, says Strabo (xv, I, § 15) at five thousand stadia, or six hnndred and twenty-miles. Vincent, however, is of opinion that these five thousand stadia were intended by Onesicritus as the measure, not of either the length or breadth of the island, but of its circumference, six hundred and sixty miles, which they not very inaccurately represent. But how then get over the fact that Onesicritus places Ceylon at twenty days sail from the continent? besides, we we have no evidence—I put aside that of Solinus (Polyhist., c. 53) —that he ever visited it, and he must, therefore, like Eratosthenes, have derived his knowledge of it from the Hindoos, whose fabulous accounts of its size obtained so late as the days of Marco Polo (Vincent, *ut supra*, p. 499), and spread even to China: "Son etendue du nord en sud est d'environ two thousand lis," *i. e.*, five hundred miles.

[13] In his fiftieth chapter Solinus, borrowing from Pliny (vi, 20), notices the leading customs of the Seres—and as they are the same as those here given to the Seræ, and as the names of the peoples are similar, he evidently identifies them, for in his chapter on Taprobane (53) he omits as superfluous all mention of the Seræ and their customs, but shows their neighbourhood to Ceylon by observing that its inhabitants "cernunt latus Sericum de montium suorum jugis."

[14] Solinus u. s. applies this description to the Sinhalese themselves, and attributes the red hair to a dye, "crines fuco imbuunt." I have followed my text and given it to the Seræ—thus distinguishing them from the Seres of Pliny, whom, if Chinese, this description will scarcely suit—for they, the Chinese, call themselves the "Blackheads" (Morrison's tr. from the Chinese Official Reports, p. 28, note), and of them black hair is so decided a characteristic that Remusat somewhere concludes that the Japanese, because

no intelligible language. In other respects their accounts tallied with those of our own merchants; as that, *e.g.*, in trading with the Seræ, the merchant crossed over to the further bank of one of their rivers, and, having there laid out his merchandise, retired. The Seræ then came forward, and placed opposite it such and so much of their goods as they deemed it worth, and these goods, if the trader was satisfied, he took away, and the bargain was concluded.[15]

In Ceylon gold and silver are prized, marble variegated like the shell of the tortoise and gems and pearls are much esteemed; slavery is unknown;[16] and

their hair is not black but rather of a deep brown blue, must be of a different race.

[15] So Joinville (As. Res., 484, ii) describes the veddah of Ceylon: "When he wants an iron tool or a lance...he places in the night before the door of a smith some money or game, together with a model of what he requires. In a day or two he returns and finds the instrument he has demanded." *See* also Knox, Hist. Relations, pt. II, c. i, p. 123; Ribeyro, quoted by Tennent, ii, p. 593; and Tennent's Ceylon, ii, p. 437, where the subject is exhausted. Matouanlin, *ut supra*, p. 42, ascribes this mode of barter to the demons, the primæval inhabitants of Ceylon: "Ils ne laissaient pas voir leurs corps, et montraient au moyen de pierres précieuses le prix que pouvaient valoir les marchandises," and borrows its account probably from Fa-hian, who writes: "Quand le tems de ce commerce était venu, les genies et les demons ne paraissaient pas, mais ils mettaient en avant des choses précieuses," p. 332. Similar modes of barter, as prevailing on the Libyan shore, are described by Herodotus, l. iv, c. 196; in Sasus on the African coast, by Indicopleustes, *ut supra*, p. 139; and in the interior of Africa in the present day, by Speke (Adventures among the Somali, June or July number of Blackwood, 1860).

[16] So Arrian, of India, c. x: "Ειναι δε και τοδε μεγα εν τῃ Ινδων γῃ, παντας Ινδους ειναι ελευθερους, ουδε τινα δουλον ειναι Ινδον...Λακεδαιμονιοις

no man sleeps either after daybreak or during the day.[17] The houses are low;[18] the price of corn never varies;[19] and there are neither courts of law nor law-suits. Hercules is the patron god of the island. The government is an elective monarchy, and the king is chosen by the people for his age and clemency, but he must be childless; and should a child be born to him after his election he is obliged to abdicate, lest the crown should become hereditary.[20] He is assisted by a council of thirty also chosen by popular suffrage, which, but only by the vote of an absolute majority, has the power of death; against its sentence however there is an appeal to the people, who then appoint seventy judges specially to try the case. If these set aside the judgment of the council its members are for ever deprived of their rank and publicly disgraced. For his faults the king may be

μεν γε οἱ Ἑλωτες δουλοι εισιν...Ινδοισι δε ουδε αλλος δουλος εστι, μητοιγε Ινδων τις.

[17] Not probable. *See* Tennent's description of mid-day, ii, pp. 255-6.

[18] So Ælian, evidently from Eratosthenes, says the houses are of wood and reeds, *στεγας δε εχουσιν εκ ξυλων δε πεποιημενας ηδη δε και δονακων.*—De Nat. Animal., L. xvi, c. xvii.

[19] "Depuis l'origine de ce royaume," says Fa-hian, "il n'y a jamais eu de famine, de disette, de calamités, ni de troubles."—Foe-koue-ke, p. 334; Hiouen Thsang similarly speaks of its abundant harvests, ii, p. 125.

[20] Stronger in Solinus, *ut supra,* "In regis electione non nobilitas prævalet sed suffragium universorum," and afterwards, in reference to his having children, "etiam si rex maximam præferat æquitatem nolunt se tantum licere." There is, however, in the Appendix to Taylor's Oriental MSS., p. 47, a long list of Sinhalese kings, though belonging to a later age, who all seem to have died childless.

punished and with death. All avoid him and converse with him, and thus though no man kills him he dies of inanition. The king wears a robe much like that given to Bacchus; the people dress Arab fashion. They are industrious cultivators of the soil, and have all fruits in abundance, except grapes. They spend their festal days in the chase, and prefer that of the elephant and tiger.[21] They take great pleasure in fishing, especially for turtle, which are so large that the shell of one is a house for a family.[22] They count a hundred years as but a moderate life for a man. Thus much has been learned and ascertained concerning Taprobane.

To fix the precise date of this embassy is impossible. But because it was an embassy accredited and presented to Claudius, it must have taken place during his reign, *i.e.* some time between A.D. 41 and 54. And

[21] Ælian speaks of the size of the Sinhalese elephants, and how they are hunted by the people of the interior, and are transported to the continent in big ships and are sold to the king of Calinga, *ut supra*, c. cxviii. Tigers were however unknown in Ceylon, though Knox says, "there was a black tygre catched and brought to the king...there being no more either before or since heard of in that land," I. c. vi, p. 40; Ptolemy, VII §, gives tigers to Ceylon; Lassen, Ind. Alterthumskunde, thinks leopards were meant, I., p. 198, note 1; *see* also Hist. of Ceylon by Philalethes, c. xliii; and Ellis, of the leopards in Africa, "which are called tigers," Madagascar, p. 223.

[22] Ælian, *ut supra*, c. xvii, tells of these enormous turtles, how that the shell is fifteen cubits and makes a roof which quite keeps off the sun's heat and the rain's wet, and is better than any tile. Let me add, that among other sea monsters which according to the same authority frequent the Sinhalese coast we find the original mermaid, but without her beautiful hair, *και γυναικων οψιν εχουσιν, αίσπερ αντι πλοκαμων ακανθαι προσηρτηνται*, l. xvi, c. xviii, § 30.

because it is not mentioned, nor in any way alluded to, by Pomponius Mela, we conclude that it reached Rome subsequently to the publication of his Geography, which appeared certainly after A.D. 43, and probably before A.D. 47.[23] And moreover because it is unrecorded by any political writer, because it is in fact known to us only from this account of Pliny[24] and his copyist Solinus (A.D. 400), we presume that it reached Rome when other and more interesting events, Messalina's violent death or the daring intrigues of Agrippina, engrossed men's minds, during the latter and more troubled years of Claudius' life; and that it left Ceylon in the reign of Chandra Muka Siwa[25] who according to the Mahawanso ascended the throne A.D. 44 and died A.D. 52.

The Roman galley was carried into Hippuros. Hippuros has been identified with the Ophir of Solomon, and is in fact, according to Bochart,[26] Ophir disguised

[23] After 43 A.D., because he notices the triumph of Claudius for his expedition to Britain: "Quippe tamdiu clausam (Britanniam) aperit, ecce principum maximus...qui propriarum rerum fidem ut bello affectavit, ita triumpho declaraturus portat."—Geog., III, vi, § 35. And before 47 A.D., because he nowhere alludes to the great discovery of Hippalus.

[24] It is not impossible that Pliny may have derived his information directly from the ambassadors, as he returned to Rome from Germany, A.D. 52.—Smith, Greek and Roman Biographical Dict., art. Pliny.

[25] *Vide* Mahawanso's List of Kings in the Appendix, lxii; and Tennent's Ceylon, i, p. 321.

[26] Geographia Sacra, Phaleg lib. II, c. xxvii; and Chanaan, lib. I, c. xlvi, p. 691, though indeed he believes in two Ophirs, this one and another in Arabia.

by the pronunciation of uneducated Greek sailors. And if Hippuros be Ophir, Galle may very well be Tarshish, as Sir Emerson Tennent seems inclined to believe.[27] But as Ophir and Tarshish are intimately associated with the trade in gold and silver;[28] and as gold and silver can scarcely be said to be products of Ceylon,[29] it follows that Ophir and Tarshish, if Sinhalese ports, must have been ports carrying on a great trade not only with Phœnicia, but with other and gold-producing or gold-exporting countries, and a trade of a magnitude and a character which presupposes a certain, and even considerable, civilisation. But, according to the Sinhalese books, it was not until the conquest of Wijayo,[30] B.C. 543, some four hundred years after

27 Ceylon, Preface to 3rd edit., pp. xx, xxi, and p. 102, II, and also note 1, p. 554, v. I.

28 "And king Solomon made a navy of ships in Ezion-geber" (1 Kings, ix, 26). "And he (Jehoshaphat) joined himself with him (Ahaziah) to make ships to go to Tarshish" (2 Chron. xx, 36). "For the king had at sea a navy of Tarshish...once in three years came the navy of Tarshish bringing gold and silver, ivory, apes, and peacocks" (1 Kings, x, 22). From these passages it would seem as if Tarshish were a great mart, all the commerce of which was carried on by the ships of those nations who traded with it. But as Psalm xl, written subsequently to David's time (v. 9), gives ships also to Tarshish: "Thou breakest the ships of Tarshish with an east wind," and Ezekiel, B.C. 588, "the ships of Tarshish did sing of thee in thy markets" (xxvii, 25), it seems that with its great trade it did in the course of years itself possess them, unless indeed ships of Tarshish mean great ships merely.

29 "Gold is found in minute particles......but the quantity has been too trivial to reward the search......its occurrence......as well as that of silver and copper is recorded in the Mahawanso as a miraculous manifestation."—Tennent, Ceylon, p. 29, I, v.

30 "This prince, named Wijayo, who had then attained the

the building of Solomon's temple and about forty years after Ezekiel had celebrated the fleets of Tarshish, that Ceylon was opened to the influence of civilisation. Before that time its inhabitants were, as their descendants the Veddahs still are,[31] a barbarous and unimprovable race, to whom all commerce was hateful, and who were not likely therefore to have founded Ophir and Tarshish.

But may not Ophir and Tarshish though Sinhalese ports have been founded and colonised by some other people? But what people? That the people were not Phœnicians the terms in which our Scripture speaks of them sufficiently indicate; and that they could not have been either northern Hindus or Tamils we conclude, in the one case from the otherwise inexplicable silence of the Mahawanso, and in the other from its account of the Tamil invasions and their results.[32] But what is it that we do know of Ophir and Tarshish? Of Ophir, that it exported largely, and raw produce only, gold and precious woods and stones; of Tarshish that the fleets which traded with it from the West sailed from a port in the Red Sea, that the voyage out and home took up three years, and that the return cargoes were of gold and silver, ivory, apes and peacocks. It seems moreover that ivory, apes and peacocks are indigenous to India and that the words used in

wisdom of experience, landed in the division Tambapanni, of this land Lanka, on the day that the successors of former Buddhas reclined in the arbor of the two delightful sal-trees to attain nibbanam."—B.C. 543, A. B. 1, Mahawanso, p. 47, Turnour's tr.

31 Tennent's Ceylon. On the Veddahs, p. 437, II, v.

32 *Vide* Tennent, Ceylon. On the Sinhalese Chronicles, pp. 397, 413, I. v.

Hebrew to designate them are not Hebrew but Tamil words.[33] But in the great mart of Tarshish where merchants from the east and west were wont to congregate, what more natural than that there the productions peculiar to any country should retain their natural name, which they as naturally carried away with them to their new habitat? And we conclude that these Tamil words point to a trade between Tarshish and Southern India and induce us to look to Southern India for Ophir, but do not help us to identify Tarshish.

Hippuros: Lassen identifies it with the headland at the southern extremity of the Arippo-aar, called Kudramale,[34] the Horse-mount, of which Hippuros is but the Greek equivalent.[35] Simple and natural as this identification is, I should have preferred one based on phonetic grounds. For among the towns on the Malabar coast I find that Ptolemy[36] places a Hippocura. I observe also that some few divine or descriptive names[37] ex-

[33] *Id.*, II, 102. Sandal wood. Almug trees, Sans. mocha, with Arab. art. al. Peacocks, Heb. Tukeyim, Malabar, Togei. Ape, Heb. Koph: Sans. and Malabar, Kapi: Greek, Κηπος and Κηβος: (Gesenius, Ophir, Ersch und Gruber, Ency.) Assyrian, Gupi, Lenormant, Zeitschrift f. Ægypt. Sprache, p. 24.

[34] The name, as accounted for in a Hindu Hist. of Ceylon, translated in the 24th vol. of the Asiatic Journal, seems to be not a descriptive but a mythic name. "A certain chitty setting out for the purpose of pearl fishing drifted near a mountain, which he called Coodiremale," p. 53, in honour probably of the horse-faced princess (mentioned *ib.*, p. 16) who, bathing in one of the wells there, lost her horse face.

[35] Lassen's Indische Alterthumskunde, iii, p. 217; and his de Taprobane Insulâ Veteribus cognitâ, p. 22.

[36] Geographia, lib. vii, c. i, p. 168.

[37] Thus Indra becomes Zeus, Siva Dionysos, Lassen, *ib.*, iii, p. 219. And (*ib.*, p. 6) where he enumerates the towns and harbours on the coast, and observes on the Greek names by which they

cepted, Greek traders did not translate but merely adapted the native names to their own pronunciation and idiom. And I am not a little surprised that this freedman who so correctly renders the compound Kudramale should according to Lassen's own showing seem quite unaware that Rachias, a simple word and in common use, is not a name but a title and one borne by the members of the royal family.[38] But whether Kudramale or some other port, Hippuros was probably situated in the north of Ceylon; because to the north of Ceylon a vessel cruising off the Persian gulf and caught in a northerly gale and driven southward till it fell in with the spring or south-west monsoon would by the winds and currents be naturally driven.

"Taprobane," Sanscrit "Tâmraparní," Pali "Tâmbapanni,"[39] the *red leaf.* Thus Wijayo the first Hindu

were known, as Naustathmos, Byzantion, Triglyphon, he adduces but one Theophila—now Surdhaur, Sans. Surâdara, *i. e.,* God-worshipping—which is possibly the Greek translation of a Hindu name. Of descriptive names we have the Panjaub "Pentapotamoi," Tadmor "Palmyra," etc.

[38] "Da dieser Name am passendsten durch Râgan könig erklärt wird, und dieses Wort auch für Männer aus dem königlichen Geschlichte gebraucht werden kann, so gehörte Rachias wohl zur familie des königs und wir erfahren somit nicht seinen Eigennamen," *ib.*, iii, p. 61. *See,* however, Tennent, Ceylon, vol. i, p. 556, note 2, who suggests that "Rachias" may be "Rackha," a name of some renown in Sinhalese annals.

[39] Lassen de Taprobane, pp. 6, 8; but from "Tamra," *red,* and "pân'i," *a hand,* according to the Mahawanso, a derivation which Lassen rejects as ungrammatical, but which the Mahawanso, p. 50, confirms, by telling that when Wijayo and his men "had landed, supporting themselves on the palms of their hands pressed on the ground, they sat down. Hence to them the name Tambapannyo, copper-palmed," and to the wilderness the name of Tambapanni, and afterwards to the country.

settler called that part of Ceylon where he landed, and the city which he afterwards built. This name in the course of time was applied to the whole island; and as it is the only name known to the companions of Alexander, and is the name by which Ceylon is designated in the inscriptions of Asoka,[40] it must early have supplanted even among the Hindus the old mythological one of Lanka. Subsequently, when our ambassadors lived and when the Periplus was written, it seems to have become obsolete, and to have been superseded by that of Palæsimundus or rather Palæsimoundou[41] which itself yielded to Salike, Serendiva,[42]—the Serendib of

[40] Lassen de Tap., p. 9, and Wilson's tr. of the Kapur di Giri Inscription (p. 169, XII, J. Roy. As. Soc.), with his observations, p. 167, on the identification of Tamrapani.

[41] *Εις πελαγος εκκειται προς αυτην την δυσιν νησος λεγομενη Παλαισιμουνδου παρα δε τοις αρχαιοις αυτων Ταπροβανη* (Scrip. Mar. Eryth., c. 61, p. 301, I, v, Geog. Græc. Minores, ed. Müller), perhaps so called after the best known capital; for Marsden observes that by a mistake not unusual, the name of a principal town is sometimes substituted for that of the country.

[42] Ptolemy, A.D. 160, *Ταπροβανη ἥτις εκαλειτο παλαι Σιμουνδου, νυν δε Σαλικη. και οἱ κατεχοντες αυτην κοινως Σαλαι.*—Geog., l, VII, c. iv. But Marcianus, early part of the fifth century, who borrowed largely from Ptolemy, thus: *Ταπροβανη νησος προτερον μεν εκαλειτο Παλαισιμουνδου νυν δε Σαλικη.*—Perip. Maris Ext., I, c. 35. Ammianus Marcellinus, A.D. 361, on Julian's accession: "Legationes undique concurrebant, nationibus Indicis certatim cum donis optimates mittentibus...abusque Divis et *Serendivis*, xxii, L, c. 7. §. 10. Sopater, in Cosmos Indicopleustes, who visited the island about A.D. 500: *Ἡ νησος, ἡ μεγαλη παρα μεν Ινδοις καλουμενη Σιελεδιβα, παρα δε Ἑλλησι Ταπροβανη.*—Montfaucon, Nov. Coll. Patrum, i, p. 366. The Relations Arabes, Reinaud, ninth century: "La dernière de ces Iles est Serendyb...c'est la principale de toutes," I, v, p. 6. This Salike is formed, according to Lassen (de Tap., p. 16), from Sihala, the Pali form of Sinhala, the home of lions, with sometimes

the Arabs—Séelediba, which are but various forms of the Pali Sihala, with the addition in some cases of "dipa" or "diba," *an island.*[43]

Palisæmundus, the capital of the island, and which probably gave the island its name, is described as a sea-port situated in the south, and on a river of the same name which communicated with the sea by three mouths. This Palisæmundus Vossius identifies with Galle,[44] Lassen, and he is followed by Tennent in his map according to Pliny and Ptolemy, with Anarajapura.[45] But Anarajapura, though seated on the banks of a river of some magnitude and a capital and a great city which must have been known to and could scarcely have been left unnoticed by our ambassadors, is an inland town[46]

the addition of "dipa" or "diba," *an island.* By the Chinese, Ceylon is called the kingdom of lions. For the connection of Salike with Sihala, *see* Bournouf, la Geogr. ancienne de Ceylan, N. J. Asiatique for 1857, xv, pp. 104-7.

43 Immediately after it has told of the origin of the name Tamrapanni, the Mahawanso goes on to say that the descendants of Sihabu were called Sihala (lion slayers), and that this Lanka having been conquered by a Sihalo obtained the name of Sihala, p. 80, Turnour tr. And the Bhánavára embodies in the following verses several of the names of Ceylon.

Oja-dipo, Vara-dipo, Manda-dipo, cha tada' ahu,'
Lanka-dipo cha pannati Tambapanniti ñ'ayeti.
D'Alwis's Descriptive Catalogue, p. 138.

44 "Portus Insulæ...esse ad meridiem. Quis dubitet quin iste sit quem Galle vulgo nominant."—Vossius, Observationes ad Pomponium Melam, p. 572.

45 De Taprobane, etc., p. 13.

46 It is the chief of the inland towns, the *πολεις μεσογειοι* of Ptolemy, and by him designated as *βασιλειον*, the royal residence, while Maagrammon is the metropolis, *ut supra.* Of Anarajapura, *see* also a description in Knox's Hist. Relation, p. 11.

and not even a river port, and is besides in the northern and not the southern half of the island. It answers, then, in no way to the description of Palisæmundus; Galle, on the other hand, has a fine harbour, and is in the southern extremity of the island, and is, says Tennent, "by far the most venerable emporium of foreign trade now existing in the universe," but then it is without a river, and we have no evidence that it was ever a royal city.

Of the name Palisæmundus or Palisæmoundou we may observe:

I. That only in the Natural History of Pliny and the so-called Periplus of Arrian is it an actual living name. Some century later it is noticed by Ptolemy, but as a name which the island had once borne, and which had fallen into disuse.

II. That though it was communicated to Pliny by our ambassadors, themselves Sinhalese, and though it is given by the author of the Periplus, a Græco-Egyptian merchant, as the name by which Ceylon was known in those Hindu, and perhaps Arab, ports where he traded; yet is it a name which we are unable to connect in any way with the inhabitants or language of the island, and of all the island names, the one of which neither Hindu nor Sinhalese Histories, so far as yet ascertained, have preserved the memory.

III. That as it has no signification in Greek or Latin, it is probably a native or Hindu name adapted to a western pronunciation. Indeed, though not very successfully, it has been explained by or identified with certain eastern words or names by several scholars, beginning with Vossius,[47] and in our own time by Burnouf, Lassen, and Windt, and with seemingly no better success than their predecessors. First, Windt,[48] bearing in mind the legend of the Ramayana, wide-spread in the east, traces it to the seafolk of Limarike, and finds in Palâci-mund its original—Palaci, Gnome, Mund, capital—Gnomes-capital, a name of reproach, and not likely, therefore, to find a place in the Sinhalese annals. How is it, then, that we know the name not merely through the seafaring author of the Periplus, but through Pliny[49] also, here the mouthpiece of Sinhalese ambassadors, men, as their statements show, no way likely to depreciate their country? Secondly, Lassen,[50] occupied with the splendours and glories of Sinhalese Buddhism, the learning, power, and mighty works of its priests and kings, identifies Palæsimoundou with Pali-simanta, the head of the Holy Law, a religious title which might have been conferred on or assumed by any Buddhist city. But then how account for the fact that this city's chroniclers—for the city is Anarajapura according to Lassen—who must have rejoiced in, did not perpetuate, this appellation so honourable to themselves and their country, do not even seem aware of it? But putting aside

47 Vossius in Pomp. Melam, ed. Gronovii, p. 569, 1854.

48 Windt, Insel Ceylon, p. 96. published 1854.

49 Pliny, and the author of the Periplus—somewhat later, *see* the accounts of Hippalus, § 57—I regard as nearly cotemporaries, both for the reasons adduced by Vincent, Ant. Com., II, and Müller's Prolegomena to the Periplus; and I think the very fact that they are the only writers who know of Palisæmundus as a living name—obsolete in Ptolemy's time (A. D. 170), is an evidence that Dodwell's date is erroneous.

50 De Taprobane Insulâ, p. 15.

all general objections, Professor Goldstücker objects to Lassen's *Pali*simanta, because the "*Pali*" does not in sound fairly represent the Παλαι, and because the sense lent to it is contrary to everything known of Pali and Sanscrit names. And thirdly, Burnouf, in an admirable essay on the ancient geography of Ceylon, suggests from the Sinhalese, Palal-sumana-diva, the island of the vast mountain Sumana, as phonetically not ill-representing Palisæmundus, but as he cannot find such a name given to the island by any native historian, he suggests but to reject it.

But if Palisæmundus be Galle or any other town on the south coast, is there not hope that we may still possibly come upon some indication of the name? The only chronicles of Ceylon that we have at hand are those of the northern kingdom, composed in the monasteries, and by the priests, of Anarajapura. But of Galle we know next to nothing. The very kingdom of which we presume it the capital, Rohuna, almost independent, is itself very seldom noticed in the Mahawanso, and then briefly and only when the necessities of the northern king drove him there for protection or assistance. And yet the country "from Galle to Hambangtotte, colonised at an early period by the followers of Wijayo and their descendants, had", says Sir E. Tennent, "neither intercourse nor commixture with the Malabars. Their temples were asylums for the studious; and to the present

[51] Burnouf, *u. s.*, 96. For the various names given to Ceylon, and the explanations variously given to them, *see* Vincent, *u. s.*, II, pp. 413-4; and more fully and for all that has been guessed about Palisæmundus.—Burnouf, *u. s.*, p. 87.

day some of the priests of Matura and Mulgirigalle are accomplished scholars in Sanscrit and Pali, and possess rich collections of Buddhist manuscripts and books".[52] From these manuscripts and books then, some native local chronicle, hitherto inaccessible, but beginning to attract the attention of European scholars,[53] we are not without hope to learn the Sinhalese name, of which Palisæmundus was the Roman echo.[54]

But, as in the second century after Christ and for a short time, the island was known as Palisæmundus, so three centuries before Christ its inhabitants, according to Megasthenes, were called Palæogonoi.[55] For this name Lassen accounts by supposing that Megasthenes was acquainted with the Ramayana[56] which peoples Ceylon with Rakshasas, giants, the sons of the progenitors of the world, "gigantes progenitorum mundi filii", and Nagas, demon snakes, monsters whom he not inaptly designates as Palæogonoi. But surely Megasthenes, by his "incolasque Palæogonos appellari", does not pre-

[52] Ceylon, ii, p. 112.

[53] As we may gather from the Descriptive Catalogue of the able Secretary of the Ceylon Asiatic Society, Mr. D'Alwis.

[54] Mr. J. H. Nelson has made inquiries for me at the College of Madura and elsewhere, but the name Palisæmundus is unknown in the Tamil country. He and Mr. Burnall have suggested several explanations of it, and it seems explicable in so many ways, each with as many reasons against as for it, that we may fairly put it down as inexplicable as the laugh of Gelimer, or the mishap of Welpho.

[55] "Megasthenes flumine dividi, incolasque Palæogonos appellari."—Pliny, *ut sup.*

[56] "Res ita videtur posse expediri, ut dicamus, notum fuisse Megastheni fabulam Indorum, quâ primi insulæ incolæ Raxasæ sive Gigantes progenitorum mundi filii fuisse traduntur."—*ib.* p. 9.

tend to describe the inhabitants *of the island*, but merely to give the name by which they were known, and to give it because it was other than the name of their country. And if he had wished to describe them, would he have chosen a name unknown to the Greek mythology, and which could have conveyed to the Greek mind no clear and definite conception, and this, when there were Titans and giants at hand to whom he might so obviously have likened them? For these and other such reasons Schwanbeck objecting to the explanation of Lassen, contends that we must look to some mispronounced native word for the original of this Palæogonoi, and he finds it in the Sanscrit "Palig'anás", *men of the sacred doctrine.*[57] But as this is an appellation which could scarcely have been given to others than earnest and learned votaries of Buddha, it is surely not applicable to a people who were not even Buddhist till the reign of Asoka,[58] the son and successor of that Chandragupta, in attendance on whom Megasthenes gained his knowledge of India.[59]

57 *Vide* Schwanbeck, on this passage from Megasthenes preserved by Pliny, Frag. Hist. Græc., 412, II.

58 Lassen, Indische Alterthumskunde, ii, 245.

59 "Notat *pâli* ab origine limitem, terminum, finem, atque amplificato apud Buddhistas sensu, regulam doctrinæ sacræ, contextum traditionum legumque."—Lassen, de Tap., p. 15. But Professor Goldstücker, in a letter to me, Nov. 12th, 1871, assures me that pâli has not the signification assigned to it by Lassen; and that g'anâs means not a people but a series, and he adds that the nearest approach he can find to Palæogonoi is *pare* on the other side the river, and *Janas* a people; *Parejanas* a people on the other side the river. It seems to me that the origin of Palæogonoi, as of Palisæmundus, is as yet unexplained.

Our ambassadors describe the situation of the island, and the sea which separates it from the continent, and give some idea of its size, population and fertility and general features. And we cannot but observe that their statements are rarely correct, but rather confirm and even exaggerate the extravagant views then current and which the Greeks had borrowed from the Hindus. They reduce its distance from India about 70 miles, from a twenty to a four days' sail, but increase its length, really of 270 miles, from the 7,000 stadia of Eratosthenes[60] to 10,000 stadia or 1,250 miles. They speak of it as a parallelogram lying with its longest side opposite to the Indian coast, which itself they seem to suppose extended in a line almost parallel to the equator. The villages of Eratosthenes, though they reduce the number from 7,000 to 5,000, they magnify into towns, and to the capital[61] they give 200,000 inhabitants. They tell moreover of a great lake—Ceylon has no lakes[62]—the Megisba,[63] almost an inland sea, and the source of

[60] "Eratosthenes et mensuram prodidit, longitudinis vii M stad., latitudinis v M, nec urbes esse, sed vicos septingentos."—Pliny, *ut supra.*

[61] Literally it is the palace that has this number of inhabitants. "Ac regiam cc mill. plebis," but the text is supposed corrupt, and I take the more probable sense of the passage.

[62] "Nullum in eâ stagnum", says Vossius, "insignis magnitudinis nedum aliquod cujus ambitus habet ccclxxv pass. mill." Ad Pomponium Melam, p. 572.

[63] Megisba. Maha-vapi, *e.g.*, great tank, identified as the Kalawewa tank by Lassen, iii, p. 218, and which he describes as it was after it had been enlarged by Dhatusera, A.D. 459, *vide* Mahawanso, p. 256, and note to p. 11, Index, and not as it was in the time of Pliny.

two rivers, which, as they take the one a northerly and the other a southerly course, necessarily divide the island into two sections and thus occupy the place of the great river commemorated by Megasthenes and identified as the Mahawelli Ganga. Of its fauna they enumerate its elephants, prized and celebrated in the days of Alexander,[64] and the tiger now unknown, and not known ever to have belonged, to Ceylon, but which may be, Lassen thinks, the leopard. Its people they describe as a nation of freemen, wealthy and peaceable, industrious and long-lived, much as the Greeks were wont to describe the Hindus.

In their accounts of the celestial phenomena, with observations which at first startle us, but which on examination prove to be well-founded, we find others not only inaccurate but inexplicable. Thus they asserted that they saw the Pleiades and the Great Bear for the first time, and yet the former is always, and the latter is at most seasons, visible in their heaven. They told too of a moon which showed itself only in its second quarter, though in Ceylon the moon shines and has ever shone just as it shines everywhere. But their surprise that in Europe their shadows fell north, and that the sun rose on the left,[65] the contrary of what took place with them, was natural. For with the Hindus, accord-

64 "Majores, bellicosiores" according to Onesicritus, Pliny l.c. But Hamilton describes them as not so tall as those of Pegu; but in their hardness and strength, added to their docility and freedom from vice and passion, is their superiority.—Hist. Descrip. of Hindustan, ii, p. 491, 4to.

65 Lassen, Ind. Alterthumsk., iii, p. 216; but compare Vincent, Commerce of the Antients, ii, p. 492.

ing to Wilford (Asiatic Res., x, 157), north and left, south and right, are identical; and Sir Emerson Tennent explains their remark, "by the fact of the sun passing overhead in Ceylon in his transit to the northern solstice, instead of hanging about the south as in Italy after acquiring some elevation in the horizon."[66]

They spoke of the laws and constitution of their island. They told of an elected and responsible monarch, who to be eligible must be, and as king must remain, childless, and whose authority was limited and controlled by an elected council, which was itself accountable to the great body of the people. Now I presume that our ambassadors were the real representatives of a real sovereign. But in a strange land when men are called upon to give some account of their native country unknown there, though I can very well understand that they should exaggerate its wealth and power and beauty, and hurry over or suppress its natural and political disadvantages, I believe that in the main their statements will be founded on fact, and that the picture they draw however highly coloured will in its more prominent features bear some resemblance to its original. Further, if either in their enthusiasm or in their desire to conciliate admiration they venture on pure fiction, I conceive that they will necessarily shape their discourse in the one case to their own ideal, in the other to that of their auditors. But of Ceylon, the Ceÿlon of the Mahawanso, where the king and the priests in turn were absolute, and the crown without any strict law of

[66] Ceylon, i, p. 558.

succession was hereditary, and though often forced out of the direct line always confined to one family, it is surely altogether improbable that any native, the ambassador of such a king, should boast of a constitutional monarchy. And at Rome and on their way thither who were the companions of our Sinhalese? During their long voyage they associated on terms of intimacy with the freedman of Plocamus and his crew; they feasted probably with the merchant Greeks of Alexandria; and at Rome they were received and welcomed by the courtiers and freedmen of Claudius. And in this degraded society of this degraded age, where could they have heard even a whisper of liberty, and where have acquired for themselves the idea, and for their country the honour of a responsible sovereign?

How then account for these statements? From the Mahawanso we learn: first, that in the third century B.C. Ceylon was twice invaded[67] by bands of Tamil adventurers, whose chiefs on each occasion after a victorious war put to death the native king, and in his place ruled over the northern districts of the island, the first time for twenty-two, the second for forty-four, years. Secondly, that at the close of the second century B.C., seven adventurers of the same nation landed with a great army at Mahattotthe, marched upon Anarajapura, fought and defeated the king, drove him into the Malaya, and for fourteen years held possession of his capital. And thirdly, that about 50 B.C. Tamils were settled in

[67] Vide Mahawanso, p. 127, for the first invasion, B.C. 257; for the second, p. 128, B.C. 207; and for the third, p. 203, B.C. 103.

the country, and that a Tamil became the favourite of, and was raised to the throne by, the Queen Anula.[68] So far the native chronicles. From a Hindu history of Ceylon, of which there is a translation in the Asiatic Journal,[69] we learn that from an early period the northern extremity of Ceylon was occupied by Tamils; that in the year 3300 of the Kali age a daughter of Pandian attended by sixty bands of Wannies proceeded to Ceylon and was married to its king, and that at his desire her companions went northward and settled at Yaulpanam now Jaffnapatam, and that subsequently other emigrants from the same part of the continent settled

[68] "Anula then forming an attachment for a Damillo, named Watuko...who had formerly been a carpenter in the town."—*Ib.*, p. 209.

[69] *Vide* vol. xxiv, pp. 53, 153. "This happened three thousand three hundred years in the Kali age."...And as "in the year 5173 of the age Kali, the king Sangalee making war with the Portuguese will perish"...and the Portuguese will rule "till the year 5213, after which the Dutch...will govern the kingdom until the year 5795, when on the 6th June the English will come and govern" (p. 155), we are enabled to ascertain the date of the arrival of the princess. For Rajah Singha was finally defeated, and died of his wounds in A.D. 1592, and as from A.K. 3300 to A.K. 5173, there have elapsed 1873 years, it follows that the princess arrived in Ceylon B.C. 281 (the only daughter of Pandya who came to Ceylon, according to the Mahawanso, came the year after Buddha's death, A.D. 543), or some thirty years before the first Tamil invasion. Again, from A.K. 5173 to A.K. 5213, we have an interval of forty years, but, as in fact the Dutch had a fort in Cottiar in 1612, or twenty years after the death of Singha, though they were not finally masters of the island to the exclusion of the Portuguese till A.D. 1658, or sixty-six years after that event, we must take forty years as an average. The date given to the English rule is inexplicable, unless as a mistake 5795 A.K. is put for 1795 A.D.—*See* also Tennent, II, p. 38.

in and occupied the north of the island as far as the Wanny. These Tamils, Sir Emerson Tennent states, were ruled by a dynasty of Rajahs who held their court at Nalloor; and he adds that he considers it "possible that Rachias......who arrived at Rome in the reign of Claudius may have represented not the Sinhalese monarch, but the Rajah of Jaffna."[70] A moment admit that he did, and how would this affect or account for the statements attributed to him? The Tamils were southern Hindus, and as the great temple on the island of Ramiseram indicates, worshippers of Rama, whom Greeks and Romans would probably identify with Hercules. They colonised and were strictly confined to the northern extremity of the island, and up to the time of our embassy they never seem as a nation to have penetrated beyond the Malaya or to have formed any permanent settlement on the southern bank of the Cydara. Our ambassadors then had probably no opportunities of making themselves acquainted with the real size of Ceylon, and they would eagerly accept the gigantic proportions assigned to it by their own Hindu tradition. They would also be ignorant to some extent of the political institutions of the Sinhalese, but scarcely to the extent shown in the narrative of Pliny; and we ask therefore whether this elective and limited monarchy might not have been their own? On their government and political institutions the Mahawanso gives no information. If we study the people themselves, even at this day we find them distinguishable from the Sinhal-

[70] Ceylon, II, p. 539, note 2.

ese by qualities which we are accustomed to look upon as the characteristics of a free people, or at least of a people living under known laws. They are industrious, persevering, intelligent, orderly, provident, and have a keen sense of the rights and advantages of property. In their country you meet with no stupendous ruins of palaces or dagobas or artificial lakes, to attest the selfish magnificence and sometimes the far-seeing wisdom of an absolute sovereign. There the villages and cottages are neat and clean, and the gardens and fields enclosed by carefully made and well-trimmed fences; there to ensure the irrigation and fertility of the land each village built out in the open has its tank, each farm-house its well, the work of its owner's hands or his predecessor's; there you everywhere meet with something that tells of municipal care or individual exertion, but with nothing that is the work of an imperial will aided by imperial resources.[71]

Again the Pandyan chronicles, though they tell of Sera and Sora wars and their results, contain no notice of any Tamil settlements in Ceylon. And of the three Tamil invasions of Ceylon which had occurred previous to our embassy, and which are recorded by the Mahawanso, we find that the first and third were under the leadership the one of two, the other of seven, chieftains. We learn further that of the seven chiefs who conducted this last expedition, two after the capture of Anarajapura re-embarked with their booty for their own country; that of the remaining five one was

[71] Tennent's Ceylon, II, p. 542, etc.

probably chosen as king, but that after a three years' reign he was put to death and supplanted by his minister, who in his turn suffered the same fate by the same means, until at length five kings had occupied the throne, each one of whom was murdered by his minister and successor except the last, and he lost his life and capital to the native Sinhalese monarch.[72] Coupling now the silence of the Pandyan chronicle with the information slight as it is which the Mahawanso affords of the untimely deaths of these Tamil kings, may we not infer that these Tamil invasions and conquests were not national acts, the expression of the national will,[73] but rather the exploits of individual adventurers banded together for a special object, and conducted by leaders whom they had elected, and whom they could depose as easily as they had elected? And after these Tamils had been driven out of Anarajapura and back to their old boundaries, with as the narrative of the Mahawanso presumes no one among them pre-eminent by his wealth, or birth, or authority, is it not probable that after many a continuous struggle among themselves for a power which was no sooner attained than it was overthrown by the jealousy of former equals, after many a revolution and the assassination of many a king, is it not probable that these rival chieftains, if they wished not their country and

[72] Mahawanso, pp. 203-4.

[73] In the geographical description of the Tamil country, Appendix D, II, p. 25, Taylor's Oriental Hist. MSS., Cape Comorin is the furthest southern boundary, and no mention whatever is made of Ceylon as Tamil, or subject to Tamil rule.

themselves utterly to perish, should settle down at length to some form of government not very dissimilar to that described by Pliny on the authority of their ambassador?

But, again, our ambassadors spoke a language which had never before been heard in Rome, and which the freedman of Plocamus alone could interpret, and with which even he was most probably but imperfectly acquainted. What they told then might easily be misrepresented by the ignorance of the translator, or its purport misunderstood when it associated itself in the minds of their audience with some previous knowledge or foregone conclusion. In this way the impossible account of the celestial phenomena of Ceylon may be attributed to ignorance of the language, and the story of the supposed Seres to a misunderstanding, but a misunderstanding which I am unable satisfactorily to explain.

I would ask however why it is that we identify the Seres with the Seras of our text? If they are one and the same people as Pliny thought why here and here only do they appear as Seras? And if Seres, a distant people—would Rachias' father, even though of Tamil extraction and of a more energetic race than the Sinhalese proper, would he have talked of their country as one he was in the habit of visiting, *commeasse?* But if not Seres who are these Seras? It is clear to me that they are Seras not without reason. Pliny or whoever took down the statements of our ambassadors reproduced as nearly as he could the exact names he heard from them. Now the northern boundary of the

Pandyan, the Tamil, kingdom and in frequent relations of peace and war with it is known as "the Great Chera" or Sera[74] country, a country not so distant but that Rachias' father might occasionally have gone to and fro between it and his home, and a country the inhabitants of which would be designated as Seras or Seræ. But with this people, these Seras, Pliny's authority connects a strange fashion of barter, though one in use among several wild races;[75] and if it could be shown that such a race wandered amid the forests and mountains of Chêra our task would be easy, our explanation found. But I can meet with no trace or record of any such race there. In Ceylon itself however we hear of Bedahs or Veddahs who from time immemorial have haunted and still haunt its rocks and coasts and still carry on their small traffic unseeing and unseen, and who are besides so barbarous that even their possession of a language has been doubted.[76] But these are Sinhalese? True, but of them and their singular custom of trade the ambassadors would not improbably speak, and as this very custom was intimately associated in the Roman mind[77] with the Seres, whoever they may

74 Chîra, Nelson's Madura country, III, *pt. passim.* Sera, Taylor's Oriental MSS., Appendix II, p. 26. In re-examining the statements of the ambassadors, I read with Gronovius, "Iidem narravere latus insulæ quod prætenderetur Indiæ x mill. stad. esse ab oriente hyberno ultra montes Emodos."—*i. e.*, that part of these mountains—"quorum promontorium Imaus vocatur."—Pliny, c. xxvi, *ad cal.*

75 *Supra*, note 15, p. 96.

76 Reinaud, Mem. s. l'Inde, p. 345. Tennent's Ceylon, 441, II.

77 Thus Pomponius Mela, III, vii, 10: "Seres intersunt...genus plenum justitiæ, ex commercio, quod rebus in solitudine relictis absens peragit *notissimum.*" And Pliny, vi, 20: "Seres mites

have been, his Roman interlocutor would naturally ask: Did they then know the Seres? And he would tell of the Seras. Hence a confusion probable enough and explicable. But unluckily he also adds a description of this wild race. He gives them large bodies, red hair, blue eyes and a rough voice[78] *i.e.*, he describes a Scythic[79] not a Hindu people and certainly not the Veddahs whose long black matted hair, and large heads and misshapen limbs[80] and miserable appearance attracted the notice and excited the pity of Sir E. Tennent. Of course it may be pointed out that Rachias

quidem, sed et ipsis feris persimiles cœtum reliquorum mortalium fugiunt, commercia expectant."

[78] I find from Pritchard (Nat. Hist. of Man, p. 245), that grey-eyed and red-haired Sinhalese are occasionally to be met with, but these are so few that they can never have stood for Pliny's description of the Seræ; nor can we, as I at first supposed, refer either to the Rakshasas (Ramayana, Fauche tr., vi, 140), the mythic aborigines of Ceylon and the supposed ancestors of the Veddahs, or to the demon masks worn by the Sinhalese in their solemn dances (Kolan Nattannawana, Upham's tr., Or. Tr. Fund), as its originals; for neither have anything in common with, or any possible likeness to, these Seræ.

[79] "Traces of a Scythic descent are to be found among the Kattees of Kattywar at this day."—Letter from Sir G. le G. Jacob, read at the Asiatic Society, February 19th, 1872. From the Periplus, § 38, we learn that they occupied, and that their capital was seated on, the lower Indus, but that they were then subject to the Parthians. We know too that at the commencement of our era they conquered India, but I cannot find that they ever settled in the northern part of the peninsula. If then we suppose Rachias' father sailing to the Indus to meet with those blue-eyed men, we have still to account for their mode of traffic which is not Scythian.

[80] Pritchard, on Dr. Davy's authority, gives a pleasanter account of the Veddahs, but of the village Veddahs probably.

does not speak of his own knowledge, that his memory may be at fault, that his questions confounded one people with another, but after all this the misunderstanding is not accounted for or cleared up.

Finally, if we give this embassy to the Sinhalese proper, then, if our ambassadors were not guilty of absurd and purposeless falsehoods, which is very improbable, they were grossly ignorant of the size and characteristics of their native land—a conclusion which nothing in their history warrants. On the contrary, the frequent retreat of the Court to the Malaya and Rohuna,[81] and the complaint of Gamini,[82] and the tanks and other great works of the native kings, indicate a knowledge of the island, its size, resources, and general features. If on the other hand, we take our ambassadors from the Tamils of Ceylon, we then have a story full of errors it is true, but easily accounted for, and the most extraordinary statement of which, that relating to the Seræ, is capable of possible explanation.

81 Whenever driven from Anarajapura the native king retires to the southern kingdom. Thus after the conquest of Elaro we find him and his queen resident at Mahag'amo.—Mahawanso, p. 134. So the queen Anula on the occasion of the invasion of the seven Damilos flees to the Malaya.—*ib.*, p. 204.

82 "Gamini laid himself on his bed with his hands and feet gathered up. The princess mother inquired: 'My boy why not stretch thyself on thy bed and lie down comfortably?' 'Confined,' replied he, 'by the Damilos beyond the river (Mahawelliganga), and on the other side by the unyielding ocean, how can I lie down with outstretched limbs?'"—*ib.*, p. 136.

ON THE

INDIAN EMBASSIES TO ROME.

ON

THE INDIAN EMBASSIES TO ROME,

FROM THE REIGN OF CLAUDIUS TO THE DEATH OF JUSTINIAN.

AFTER the Sinhalese embassy to Claudius, the Indian embassies to Rome were few and far between. To the death of Justinian, A.D. 565, four only have been noticed and barely noticed by historians. The first, to Trajan,[1] was present with him at the great shows which he offered to the Roman people, A.D. 107. The second, to Antoninus Pius,[2] A.D. 138-161, came to pay homage to his virtues. The third to Julian,[3] though intended Zonaras asserts for Constantius, reached him according to Am-

[1] Προς δε τον Τραιανον ες την Ρωμην ελθοντα πλεισται δσαι πρεσβειαι παρα βαρβαρων αλλως τε και Ινδων αφικοντο· και θεας...εποιησεν εν αἱς θηρια...χιλια και μυρια εσφαγη...ὁτι ὁ Τραιανος τους παρα των βασιλεων αφικνουμενους εν τῳ βουλευτικῳ θεασασθαι εποιει.—Dio Cassius, vol. I, 68, 156; II, p. 313, Bekker.

[2] "Quin etiam Indi Bactriani Hyrcani legatos miserunt justitiâ tanti imperatoris compertâ."—Aurelian Victor, Epit. xvi.

[3] "Perinde timore ejus adventus...legationes undique solito ocius concurrebant...nationibus Indicis certatim cum donis optimates mittentibus ante tempus abusque Divis et Serendivis."—Ammianus Marcellinus, xxii, 7, 277, p. i; but Zonares, Εχρηματιζε δε και πρεσβεσιν εκ διαφορων εθνων σταλεισι προς τον Κωνσταντιον.

mianus Marcellinus, before it was expected, A.D. 361, and included ambassadors from the Divi (Maldives) and the Serendivi (the Sinhalese) who now for the first time appear under their own name and the name by which they were known to the Arabs. And the fourth to Justinian[4] brought him gifts, and was at Constantinople, A.D. 530.

These are but scant memorials of petty diplomatic courtesies, and scattered as they are over nearly five hundred years they do little to illustrate the intercourse between Rome and India, which during the first half of these long centuries reached its highest point of development, while during the last it had so fallen away that in so far as it was direct it may be regarded as extinct. Of that intercourse I now propose to give a rapid sketch.

The discovery of the monsoons, and the distracted state of the Parthian Empire had at the beginning of the second half of the first century, the close of Claudius' reign, driven the whole of the trade between the east and west to the great city of Alexandria.[5] Its people quick-witted but restless of disposition and excitable of temper grew wealthy, and grew insolent as they

[4] Εν αυτῳ δε τῳ χρονῳ (when John of Cappodocia was made Prætorian Exarch, A.D. 530, Smith, Biog. Dict.) και πρεσβυτης Ινδων μετα δωρων κατεπεμφθη εν Κωνσταντινουπολει.—Malalas, p. 477; and a Hindu embassy I gather on comparing it with another African-Indian embassy mentioned, pp. 458-9, *ib.*

[5] Dio Chrysostom, time of Trajan, speaks of it as second only to Rome, πολις δευτερα των υπο τον ἥλιον.—Oratio, xxxii, pp. 669-70; even in the sixth century it was Μεγιστη πολις.—Cosmas Montfaucon, Nova Collectio Patrum, I, 124.

grew wealthy. The person and character of the sovereign was a favourite theme for their ridicule;[6] and on every slight occasion, when not taken up with factious fights among themselves, they rose in tumult against their governors and sometimes even in revolt against the state. The emperors looked upon them with no friendly eye. And it was, perhaps, as much to abate their insolence as to forward the interests of trade, that Hadrian put an end to their monoply, and admitted Palmyra into the commercial system of the Roman Empire.[7] Under his patronage, and that of his successors, the Antonines,[8] who lived much in the east, and followed out, we have every reason to believe, his policy, Pal-

[6] See Hadrian's letter to the Consul Servianus in Flavius Vopiscus: "Genus hominum seditiosissimum, vanissimum, impurissimum: civitas opulenta dives fæcunda...utinam melius esset morata civitas...huic ego cuncta concessi...et in filium Verum multi dixerunt, et de Antinoo quæ dixerunt comperisse te credo." —Augustæ Scriptores, 234, II. Dio Chrysostom speaks of the turbulent sneers, and mocks, and angry hisses with which they greeted both king and private man, *ουκ εδεισα τον υμετερον θρουν, ουδε τον γελωτα, ουδε την οργην, ουδε συριγμους, ουδε τα σκωμματα οἱς παντας εκπληττετε...και ιδιωτην και βασιλεα*, *id.*, p. 664; and that this had estranged the emperors we may gather from p. 687, *εις ὑποψιαν αυτους καθ' ὑμων ηγαγετω.* Also p. 700, Reiske ed. And Ammianus Marcellinus "Sed Alexandria in internis seditionibus diu aspere fatigata."—xxii, § 16, p. 207.

[7] Ersch and Grüber, Encyclopedie, art. Palmyra. Not, however, forgetting that between India and Palmyra trade already existed; for Trajan, having descended the Tigris, *επ' αυτον τον Ωκεανον ελθων...και πλοιον τι ες Ινδιαν πλεον ιδων.*—Cassius, L. 67, c. 28. And through Palmyra probably "That colony of Jews which after the destruction of Jerusalem settled in Cochin, made their way."—Buchanan's Researches; Day's Permaul, pp. 341-53.

[8] Of works treating of India belonging to this period we have—The Periplus of the Erythræan Sea (A.D. 81, 96); Prolog. de Auct.

myra rapidly developed the advantages which it derived from its position on the nearest route to India. It flourished and grew daily in importance. And when Emesa, almost on its frontiers, and on its high road to Antioch and Damascus, gave to Rome Julia Domna, the wife of one Emperor, Severus, and the mother of another, Caracalla, and afterwards two Emperors, Ela-

Perip., p. xcvii, L. Geog. Minor, ed. Didot—a manual of Roman, or rather Egyptian, trade with India; a really original work, the result of the author's own observation and experience as a merchant and supercargo. The Geography of Ptolemy (A.D. 138, 161), the first work which makes the circuit of Ceylon, and names the harbours and headlands on its coast, its rivers, mountains, and towns. The Expedition of Alexander and the Indica of Arrian (A. D. 150, 160), both compilations, but the compilations of a man of sense and critical acuteness—the one made up from the cotemporary histories of Alexander, the other from the narratives of Megasthenes, Eratosthenes, and Nearchus. We have besides notices of India and Indian manners scattered through several of the numerous treatises of Plutarch and the orations of Dion Chrysostom (A.D. 100); but they both draw their information from the common storehouse,—and even in that longer description of India as the true pays de Cocagne which Dion gives in his Oratio in Calenis Phrygiæ, he merely throws together in one piece the various Indian myths which Ctesias and Onesicritus so willingly collected and believed. Among the writers of this age we may also though with some hesitation class Q. Curtius (Smith's Biog. Dict., v. 1), and Dionysius Periegetes (Geog. Hist. Proleg., p. 18, II, Didot). But neither had of himself any knowledge of India; the first merely copied and compiled from the old historians of Alexander, and the second as well in his Bassarika as in his Periegesis is *original* (?) only in so far as he connects the known country of India with the exploits of Bacchus: indeed he says of himself—

ου γαρ μοι βιος εστι μελαιναων επι νηων
ουδε μοι εμποριη πατρωιος, ουδ' επι Γαγγην
ερχομαι, οία τε πολλοι.—vv. 709-11.

gabalus and Alexander: then sated with wealth it began to aspire to other than the arts of commerce; it levied or hired armies; it made conquests and acquired territory; it became a power, and for a moment held with Rome divided empire.[9]

The trade between Rome and India, even under the earlier Antonines, must have been important;[10] for it attracted the attention of the Chinese. Their annals speak of it as carried on principally by sea; they enumerate the commodities as coral, amber, gold, sapphires, mother-of-pearl, perfumes, etc., which it preferred, and allude to the trade frauds and manipulations by which Roman merchants freshened up and flavoured exhausted perfumes[11] for foreign and provincial markets. They speak of Roman merchants in relations of commerce with and visiting Burmah, Tonquin and Cochin China; and what more interests us, they have preserved the memory of an Embassy from the Roman Emperor

[9] See de Odonato XIV, the Duo Gallieni III, the Claudius XII, Trigint. Tyran., Trebellii Pollion., and Aurelian's letter to the senate, excusing the appearance of Zenobia in his triumphal procession. Vopisci, Hist. Aug. Script., and note 9 to c. 32, vii, L. of Eusebius, Eccl. Hist., Heinichen's ed.

[10] Pausanias, a cotemporary of Antoninus Pius and Aurelius, incidentally notices it, but in a way which would lead one to suppose it was insignificant. *οἱ δε ες την Ινδικην εσπλεοντες φορτιων φασιν Ἑλληνικων τους Ινδους αγωγιμα αλλα ανταλλασσεσθαι, νομισμα δε ουκ επιστασθαι, και ταυτα χρυσου τε αφθονου και χαλχου παροντος σφισι.*—III, L. c. xii, § 3.

[11] Rather inferred than expressed. "Ils prennent les composés de plantes medicinales, en extraient les parties succulentes afin d'en composer des pâtes odorantes et ils vendent le residu privé de ses meilleures qualités aux marchands des autres royaumes."—Pauthier, Examen des faits relatifs au Thian-Tchu ou l'Inde, p. 23.

Antun (Marcus Aurelius), which A.D. 166 was received by and offered tribute to the Chinese sovereign, elephants' teeth, rhinoceros' horns and tortoise shells.[12]

But for this embassy there is no Roman authority whatever, and as an embassy paying tribute when Marcus Aurelius was emperor, it is simply impossible. And yet it is so slightly noticed, and so little is made of it, that one cannot put it away as a mere invention of the Chinese historian to magnify his country. Besides, we find that the same writer records the visit some years later of a Roman merchant,[13] one Lun, to the Chinese Court, and speaks of his interviews with the then Chinese Emperor, curious about the songs and manners of other countries, and yet never speaks of him as other or more than a merchant. Surely then we have no reason to assume that the Romans of the so-called embassy had their ambassadorial character thrust upon them, they must have taken it upon themselves for purposes of trade.[14]

[12] "Ce royaume de l'Inde fait un grand commerce à l'occident avec le Ta-thsin, l'Empire Romain ; c'est par la mer surtout."—*Id.*, p. 22. "Les habitans de ce royaume vont très souvent pour leurs relations de commerce jusqu'au Fou-nan, Burmah : au Jiwan, Cochin Chine : au Kie-tchi, le Tonquin."—P. 25. "La neuvième des années Yan-ti de Houan-ti de la dynastie des Han (A.D. 166). Autun roi du Ta-thsin envoya une ambassade pour offrir des presents."—P. 24, and in a note, "Le tribut consistait en dents d'éléphant, etc."

[13] "Le cinquième des années Hoang-wou (A.D. 222-278) un marchand du Ta-thsin...du nom de Thsin-lun, Lun le Romain, vint dans le Tonquin. Le gouverneur l'accompagna près du souverain Chinois. Ce dernier l'interrogea sur les chants, les mœurs de son pays."—*Id.*, p. 25.

[14] Reinaud, l'Empire Romain, et l'Asie Orientale, Jour. Asiat.,

Again, the presents or tribute with which these ambassadors approach the Celestial throne, as they are products not of Italy but of Africa or India, are scarcely the presents with which the Roman would greet a brother Emperor. But on the other hand they are just the sort of commodities which Alexandrian merchants trading to India would gather up on a roving voyage, and which as curious and valuable they would be likely

1863, p. 323, connects with this embassy—for embassy he will have it—a notice concerning silk, introduced *à propos des bottes*, by Pausanias, at the close of B. vi, c. 26, Desc. Græciæ. He there says, that "silk is not the produce of a plant, but that it is obtained from a small animal about twice the size of a beetle, which the Greeks but not the Seres call *σηρ*. This animal is like the tree-spider, and like it has eight legs. The Seres rear it in houses suited to the hot and cold seasons, and it works up a thin thread which it rolls about with its feet (the *beetle*). For four years they feed it with millet, *ελυμος*, and on the fifth give it a greenish reed, which it eats greedily till it bursts. When it is dead, a great quantity of thread is found within its body." I must own that I overlooked or put aside as worthless this account of the silkworm; but Reinaud, with his quick perception and great memory, saw all its importance and remarked, that this is the first notice we have both of silk as an animal product, and of the care taken by the Seres in rearing the silkworm, and I admit that Pausanias in some way or another derived his information from the Romans, who at this time visited China. Let me, however, express my surprise that Pliny, who describes the bombyx of Cos and the thread obtained from its cocoon, and the stuff made from that thread, should have clung to some plant as the origin of silk; but then Pliny was but a reader of books, and perhaps a man of the world—not an observer of nature; and in his account of the bombyx he seems, judging from the notes to the Delphin Pliny, Valpy's, to have borrowed from Aristotle's Hist. Animal. In these notes, speaking of the same Bombyx, Julius Pollux (A.D. 134) is cited as observing that there are some people who say that the Seres collect their silk from other such animals.—Pliny, Hist. Nat., xi, 27, note.

to offer as present or tribute to any potentate they cared to propitiate. I look on this embassy as the fraud of Alexandrian merchants.

But it was during the reigns of Severus, his son Caracalla, and the pseudo-Antonines, that Alexandria and Palmyra were most prosperous, and that Roman intercourse with India was at its height. Then Roman literature gave more of its attention to Indian matters, and did not, as of old, confine itself to quotations from the historians of Alexander or the narratives of the Seleucidian ambassadors, but drew its information from other and independent sources. Then Clemens Alexandrinus (A.D. 192, 217), thus wrote of the Gymnosophists: "They are," he says, "Sarmanai, or Brahmins. Of the Sarmanai, the Allobioi neither dwell in cities nor under a roof, but 'wear a vesture of bark', and live on acorns, and drink water from their hands, and know neither marriage nor the procreation of children. And they are *the* Indians[15] who obey the precepts of Boutta: and him for his exceeding majesty they honour as a god." And in another place, but on the authority of Alexander Polyhistor, he tells of the Brahmans,[16] how

[15] In general rendered "And there are Indians," etc. I subjoin the whole passage:—*Και των Σαρμανων οἱ Αλλοβιοι (Ὑλοβιοι) προσαγορευομενοι, ουτε πολεις οικουσιν, ουτε στεγας εχουσι, δενδρων δε αμφιεννυνται φλοιοις* (Menu, vi, § 16); *και ακροδρυα σιτουνται και ὑδωρ ταις χερσι πινουσιν· ου γαμον, ου παιδοποιΐαν ισασιν, ὡσπερ οἱ νυν Εγκρατηται καλουμενοι. εισι δε των Ινδων οἱ τοις Βουττα πειθομενοι παραγγελμασιν ὃν δι' ὑπερβολην σεμνοτητος εις Θεον τετιμηκασι.*—Stromata, I, 110. I beg attention to the ambiguity of the last paragraph.

[16] *Βραχμανοι ουτε εμψυχον εσθιουσιν, ουτε οινον πινουσιν, αλλ' οἱ μεν αυτων καθ' ἑκαστην ἡμεραν, ὡς ἡμεις, την τροφην προσιενται· ενιοι δ' αυτων, δια τριων ἡμερων ὡς φησιν Αλεξανδρος ὁ Πολυιστωρ εν τοις Ινδικοις· κατα-*

"they neither drink wine nor taste of animal food; how some of them eat daily, others but once in three days;[17] how from their belief in a second birth, παλιγγενεσιαν, they despise death and are indifferent to life; and how they worship Hercules and Pan. He says further that those called Semnoi go naked, and cultivate truth, and foretell the future, and worship a pyramid which is supposed to cover the bones of a god; that neither Gymnosophists nor Semnoi marry, because marriage they look upon as contrary to law and nature, and they therefore keep themselves chaste, so do the Semnoi women who devote themselves to a virgin life. He adds that they observe the heavenly bodies, and through them foretell the future."

The name and precepts of Buddha, and the worship of the pyramid topes, recorded in these passages, are to be found in no other ancient writer whatever. If derived originally from Megasthenes as is supposed, it is strange that they have escaped the notice of Plutarch and

φρονουσι δε θανατου, και παρ' ουδεν ἡγουνται το ζην· πειθονται γαρ ειναι παλιγγενεσιαν. οἱδε σεβουσιν 'Ηρακλεα και Πανα· οἱ καλουμενοι δε Σεμνοι των Ινδων, γυμνοι διαιτωνται τον παντα βιον· οὑτοι την αληθειαν ασκουσι και περι των μελλοντων περιμηνυουσι, και σεβουσι τινα πυραμιδα ὑφ' ἡν οστεα τινος Θεου νομιζουσιν αποκεισθαι. ουτε δε οἱ Γυμνοσοφισται, ουθ' οἱ λεγομενοι Σεμνοι, γυναιξι χρωνται· παρα φυσιν γαρ τουτο και παρανομον δοκουσι· δι' ἡν αιτιαν σφας ἁγνους τηρουσι· παρθενευουσι δε και Σεμναι. δοκουσι παρατηρειν τα ουρανια, και δια της τουτων σημειωσεως των μελλοντων προμαντευεσθαι τινα.—*ib.* iii, 194.

17 In the Prabodhatschandradaja is an allusion to this observance. The scholar asks of his master why the observers of religious rites eat but one meal in three days. "Wenn Essen und Trinken die Hauptaufgabe des Menschen ist...denn warum wird...das Leben... durch Bussübungen...wie in drei Tagen nur ein Mal speisen, gequält?"...Hirzel's Tr., p. 23, and Menu, vi, 18, etc.

Porphyry, curious in such matters; and still more strange that, as characteristic of one of the great religions of India, they should have been passed over by Strabo, Diodorus Siculus, and Arrian, who in their works have embodied his Indica, at least that part of it which treats of the sects and castes of India. But the paragraph with the name of Boutta, at the close of the first citation, is so loosely worded that it is impossible to ascertain whether it refers to the Sarmanai previously mentioned, or to some altogether different sect. It is besides so clumsily introduced, that it reads like an afterthought, a fact thrown in that it may not be lost, or a piece of information which Clemens had obtained from some of those Indians mentioned by Dion as residents at Alexandria,[18] and which he now tacks on to a description notoriously taken from Megasthenes.

Of the second[19] passage, all that refers to the Semnoi

[18] Ad Alexandrinos,—*δρω γαρ ου μονον 'Ελληνας παρ' ὑμιν, ουδ' Ιταλους*, etc., etc., *αλλα και Βακτριους, και Σκυθας, και Περσας, και Ινδων τινας, οἱ συνθεωνται και παρεισιν ἑκαστοτε ὑμιν.*—Orat., xxxii, p. 672, Reiske ed.

[19] The term Sarmanai Germanai as the name of a Hindu sect was first used by Megasthenes (A.D. 302-288), and is found in Strabo and Clemens cited above; that of Samanæoi belongs to Alexander Polyhistor, and is found in Clemens (A.D. 193-217) in the same section and just before the passage relating to the Gymnosophists which I have given in the text: and in Cyril, cont. Julianum iv (A.D. 433), but is in both writers the name of the philosophers or priests of Bactria, and copied from Polyhistor. After Clemens, who lived at the close of the second and beginning of the third century, it is used by Bardesanes (A.D. 217) to designate for the first time, so far as we know, the Buddhist priests of India; by Origen (A.D. 245-249) in the same sense, and lastly by Hieronymus, close of the fourth century (Epist. cont. Jovian, pt.

I am disposed to look upon as an addition of Clemens.[20] For though Alexander Polyhistor was a great reader and voluminous writer, he was a compiler merely, and no more professed originality than does an Encyclopædia. A native too of one of the Greek cities of Asia Minor, he fell upon unhappy times, and was carried away to Rome before mid age a prisoner and a slave, and passed the remainder of his days in Italy. Under these circumstances I do not see how he could have heard or learned any new thing about India, anything

i, tr. ii, xxxix), and expressly borrowed from Bardesanes. But to show that both Clemens and Cyril have been writing from the same authority, I will place their words side by side, observing that Cyril expressly quotes from the Pythagorick symbols of Polyhistor.

Προεστησαν δε αυτης (φιλοσοφιας) Αιγυπτων τε οἱ προφηται και Ασσυριων οἱ Χαλδαιοι, και Γαλατων οἱ Δρυιδαι, και Σαμαναιοι Βακτρων, και Κελτων οἱ φιλοσοφησαντες και Περσων οἱ μαγοι ..Ινδων τε οἱ Γυμνοσοφισται...Σκυθης δε και Ανυχαρσις ην.—Stromat., I.

'Ιστορει γουν Αλεξανδρος ὁ επικλην Πολυιστωρ εν τῳ περι Πυθαγορικων συμβολων...εφιλοσοφησαν και παρ' Αιγυπτιοις οἱ κεκλημενοι προφηται και μην και Ασσυριων Χαλδαιοι, και Γαλατων οἱ Δρυιδαι, και εκ Βακτρων των Περσων Σαμαναιοι, και Κελτων ουκ ολιγοι, και παρα Περσαις οἱ Μαγοι, και παρ' Ινδοις οἱ Γυμνοσοφισται, και αυτος Αναχαρσις παρα Σκυθαις.—Cyril cont. Julian, L. iv, p. 133, ed. Spanheim's (A.D. 375 ?).

20 Bardesanes we examine at length presently. Origen, cont. Celsum, I, 24, speaking of the innate force of words, ὡs τισι χρωνται Αιγυπτιων οἱ σοφοι και των παρα Περσαις μαγων οἱ λογιοι, και των παρ' Ινδοις φιλοσοφουντων βραχμανες η Σαμαναιοι.—Hieronymus, "Bardesanes vir Babylonius in duo dogmata apud Indos Gymnosophistas dividit, quorum alterum appellat Bragmanos, alterum *Samanæos*." *See*, however, Schwanbeck in Müller's Hist. Græc., Frag., p. 437, v. III, and Lassen Ind. Alterthum, v. III, pp. 355-6.

not already contained in books. But look now at Clemens Alexandrinus. He lived in Alexandria, then in frequent communication with India, where Hindus occasionally resorted. He was besides a Christian, and as a Christian he necessarily frequented the society of artisans and merchants, and among them if anywhere had opportunities of meeting either with Hindus or with those who had visited India. But could a man of his acquirements and eager, earnest, and inquiring mind meet with such men, and not draw from them some information relating to India before unknown? His keeping within the well beaten path of old facts would be to me as surprising as Polyhistor's straying from it. Again, in no known fragment of Polyhistor are the Buddhist priests called Semnoi; indeed the term as applied to them is found only in this passage. And I can very well understand Clemens choosing it, because in sound it sufficiently resembles the Tamil Samana,[21] and in sense expresses satisfactorily the ideas attached to an ancient priesthood; and perhaps also because, though unaware of their brotherhood, he thus distinguished the Hindu Buddhist from Polyhistor's Samanæos or Bactrian priest.

Then Philostratus,[22] a cotemporary of Clemens, published his romance of Apollonius of Tyana, and Ælian[23]

21 Pronounced, Mr. J. H. Nelson, C.S., Madras, informs me, as semen, the *e* sounded as in Italian. Boutta too he thinks more closely allied to the Tamil Buttha than the Sanscrit Buddha, though he would hesitate to derive it thence.

22 Philostratus published his Appollonius after the death of the Empress Julia Domna, as he himself states, consequently some time after A.D. 217.—V. Dio Cassius, L. 78, 6, 24.

23 Ælian flourished A.D. 225.

his Variæ Historiæ, in which are many notices of Indian animals and Indian peoples and customs, but from Megasthenes and Ctesias principally.[24] And then too Art employed itself on Indian subjects, as we gather from Callistratus' description of the statue of a drunken and reeling Hindu.[25] Then Dio Cassius wrote his history, lost in its entirety, but of which the fragments and summary by Xiphilinus sufficiently attest the interest he took in all that related to India. Then too Bardesanes,[26] as we learn from the extracts preserved by Porphyry,[27] gave to the world his Indica, the materials for which he obtained he states from one Dandamis or Sandanes, the chief of some unrecorded embassy to the Cæsars, and whom he met it seems at Babylon in the reign of Antoninus of Emesa,[28] Elagabalus (A.D. 218-222). He

[24] To this age also probably belongs the Περιοδος Θωμα, which speaks of Thomas' visit to India, and tells of an Indian king, Goundaphores, whose agent was in the Roman Empire looking out for mechanics, and who may be identified with Gondophares of the Indo-Parthian coins, a cotemporary of the last Arsacidan kings (about A.D. 216) Thilo, Acta St. Thomæ and Wilson, Ariana Antiqua. And to this age we may refer one of the heresies of the Christian Church introduced by and brought απο Σηρων της Παρθιας. --Bunsen Analecta Antenicæna, i, p. 378.

[25] Descript. iv. εις το Ινδου αγαλμα. On the statue of an Indian evidently; and not, On the statue of the Indus, as Lassen renders it.—Ind. Alt., III, 73. Callistratus wrote about A.D. 250.

[26] He speaks also of Indians idolatrous and non-idolatrous in his Book of Fate.

[27] Porphyry, de Abstinentiâ, iv, 17.

[28] Ινδοι οἱ επι της βασιλειας της Αντωνινου του εξ Εμεσων εις την Συριαν Βαρδησανη τῳ εκ της Μεσοποταμιας εις λογους αφικομενοι εξηγησαντο.—Stobæus Physica, i, 54. Gaisford's ed. This reading proposed by Heeren and adopted by Gaisford, necessarily, it seems to me, brings down our embassy to the reign of Elagabalus (A.D. 218-222),

writes, that "the Indian Theosophs, whom the Greeks call Gymnosophists, are divided into two sects, Brahmans and Shamans, Samanæoi. The Brahmans are one family, the descendants of one father and mother, and they inherit their theology as a priesthood. The Shamans on the other hand are taken from all Indian sects indifferently,[29] from all who wish to give themselves up to the study of divine things.

"The Brahmans pay no taxes like other citizens, and are subject to no king.[30] Of the philosophers among them, some inhabit the mountains, others the banks of the Ganges. The mountain Brahmans subsist on fruit and cow's milk, curdled with herbs.[31] The others live

the only Antonine who can be described as of Emesa. Lassen, however (*ut sup.*, III, 348), is of opinion that it was addressed to Antoninus Pius (A.D. 158-181, an error for 138-151), but as his reference is to Heeren's ed., whose emendation I presume he adopts, I cannot conceive how he arrives at this conclusion.

[29] Megasthenes, as quoted by both Arrian and Strabo, had some indistinct notion that the Indian Sophistai or some of them were not so bound to caste as the other Indians. But Arrian so puts it as if the whole Brahman caste was open. Μονον σφισιν ανειται σοφιστην εκ παντος γενεος γενεσθαι, and this because of the austerity of their lives.—Indica, xi, 7, xii, 9. Fr. Hist. Græc., II, pp. 427, 429. Didot ed. Strabo, on the other hand, that no man can exercise two trades, except he be a philosopher, πλην ει των φιλοσοφων τις ειη, and this because of their virtue.—*ib.*, p. 430. Diodorus omits the passage: doubtless it was ambiguous.

[30] Αλειτουργητοι γαρ οντες οἱ φιλοσοφοι πασης ὑπουργιας, ουθ' ἑτερων κυριευουσιν ουθ' υφ' ἑτερωνδεσποζονται.—Diodorus, II, 400; Fr. Græc., II, p. 405. Menu says, "A king, even though dying, must not receive any tax from a Brahman learned in the Vedas."—cvii, 133. "The temple lands (of Buddhist priests) were invariably free from royal duty."—Hardy, Monachism, p. 68.

[31] "Buttermilk may be swallowed, and every preparation of buttermilk," 10 §. "And every mess prepared with barley or wheat, or with dressed milk," 25 §, c. v, Menu.

on the fruit trees which are found in plenty near the river and which afford an almost constant succession of fresh fruits, and, should these fail, on the self-sown wild rice that grows there.[32] To eat any other food, or even to touch animal food, they hold to be the height of impiety and uncleanness.[33] Each man has his own cabin, and lives as much as he can by himself, and spends the day and the greater part of the night in prayers and hymns to the gods. And they so dislike society, even that of one another, or much discourse, that when either happens, they expiate it by a retirement and silence of many days.[34] They fast often.

"The Shamans,[35] on the other hand, are, as I said, an elected body. Whoever wishes to be enrolled in their order presents himself to the city or village authorities, and there makes cession of all his property. He then shaves his body, puts on the Shaman robe, and goes to the Shamans,[36] and never turns back to speak or look

[32] "Let him eat green herbs, flowers, roots, and fruits, etc.," § 13. "Let him not eat the produce of ploughed land," § 16, c. vi, of the Anchorite ed. But as a Sannyasi, "an earthen water-pot, the roots of large trees, coarse vesture, total solitude,—these are the characteristics of a Brahman set free," § 44, *ib.*

[33] The Brahman student must "abstain from flesh meat," § 177, ii, *ib.* "The Manava Dharma affirms that the Brahman who eats flesh loses instantly his rank."—Tr. Rl. As. Soc., p. 163, iii, v.

[34] As anchorite, "Let him live without external fire,—wholly silent," vi, 25, *ib.* As Sannyasi, "Alone let him constantly dwell for the sake of his own felicity, observing the happiness of a solitary man,—without a companion," *ib.*, 42.

[35] Samanaioi, from the Pali Sammana, found first in Clemens Alexandrinus, seemingly from Polyhistor, and applied to the priests of Bactria.

[36] "The priest can only possess three robes," p. 66. "From

at his wife and children if he have any, and never thinks of them any more, but leaves his children to the king and his wife to his relations, who provide them with the necessaries of life. The Shamans live outside the city, and spend the whole day in discourse upon divine things. They have houses and temples of a royal foundation, and in them stewards, who receive from the king[37] a certain allowance of food, bread, and vegetables for each convent. When the convent bell rings,[38] all strangers then in the house withdraw, and the Shamans enter and betake themselves to prayer. Prayer ended, at the sound of a second bell the servants place before each individual, for two never eat together, a dish of rice; but to any one who wants variety they give besides either vegetables or fruit. As soon as they have done dinner, and they hurry over it, they go out to their usual occupations. They are not allowed to marry or to possess property. They and the Brahmans

the commencement of his novitiate he is shaved," p. 112. "The wearing of the robe is imperative," pp. 114, 122. Hardy, East. Monachism.

37 The regular and usual mode of obtaining food is "to take the alms bowl from house to house," Hardy, *ut sup.*, 94, but as we may gather from the Sacred Books of Ceylon and the Legend of Anepidu (Hardy, Monachism, p. 68, and Buddhism, p. 218), land and food were also provided by kings and rich men for monasteries; indeed under certain circumstances the priest is enjoined to refuse the food "that is given statedly to a temple."—*Id.*, Monachism, p. 97.

38 So in the legend of Sâmgha : "Au bout de quelque temps le son de la plaque de métal qu'on frappe pour appeler les religieux s'était fait entendre, chacun d'eux tenant son vase à la main vient s'asseoir à son rang."—Burnouf, Introd. à l'Hist. du Bouddhisme, p. 320.

are so honoured by the Indians, that even the king will come to them to solicit their counsel in matters of moment, and their intercession with the gods when danger threatens the country."

"Both Shamans and Brahmans have such a notion of death, that they impatiently bear with life, and view it but as a necessary though burdensome service imposed upon them by nature. They hasten therefore to free the soul from the body.[39] And often when a man is

[39] Onesicritus says of them when suffering from disease, *Αισχιστον δ' αυτοις νομιζεσθαι νοσον σωματικην· τον δ' ὑπονοησαντα καθ' αυτου τουτο, εξαγειν ἑαυτον δια πυρος, νησαντα πυραν...ακινητον δε καιεσθαι.*—Strabo, xv, 65. Pomponius Mela more generally, "At ubi senectus aut morbus incessit, procul a cæteris abeunt mortemque...nihil anxie expectant...Prudentiores...non expectant eam sed ingerendo semet ignibus læti et cum gloriâ arcessunt."—III, vii, 40. "On voit...dans l'Inde des hommes se brûler sur un bûcher...Cet usage vient de la croyance...à la métempsycose."—Reinaud, Rel. des Voyageurs Arabes, I, p. 120. Yet Menu rather discountenances, except in sickness, voluntary deaths. "If he has an incurable disease" (for an example see Radja-Tarangini, i, 311-12, note), "let him advance in a straight line towards the invincible north-east point, feeding on air and water till his mortal frame totally decay, vii, 31; but 45 *ib.*, "Let him not wish for life, let him expect his appointed time as a herd expects his wages." Similarly the Buddhist. "The rahats do not desire to live, nor do they wish to die; they wait patiently for the appointed time."—Hardy, E. Mon., 287. But from the answer of Punna (Purna) to Buddha, "There are some priests who from various causes are tired of life, and they seek opportunities whereby their lives may be taken, but this course I shall avoid" (*id.*, Buddhism, p. 260); and from the fact that the perfected priest when "at the point of death would cause his body to be spontaneously burnt" (*id.*, Monachism, 261), we may presume that voluntary deaths among priests even in Buddha's time were not unfrequent and permissible on some occasions, *i. e.*, were as among the Brahmans not very strictly prohibited, and that Megasthenes very fairly states both the doctrine

well in health, and no evil whatever presses upon him, he will give notice of his intention to quit the world, and his friends will not try to dissuade him from it, but rather account him happy, and give him messages for their dead relations; so firm and true is the conviction of this people that souls after death have intercourse with one another. When he has received all his commissions, in order that he may quit the body in all purity,[40] he throws himself into a burning pile, and dies amid the hymns of the assembled crowd. And his nearest friends[41] dismiss him to his death more willingly than we our fellow-citizens when about to proceed on some short journey. They weep over themselves that they must continue to live, and deem him happy who has thus put on immortality. And among neither of these sects, as among the Greeks, has any sophist yet appeared to perplex them by asking, 'If everybody did this, what would become of the world?'"

Thus far Bardesanes on the Gymnosophists. To form

and the practice, *Ουκ ειναι δογμα φησιν ἑαυτους εξαγειν· τους δε ποιουντας τουτο νεανικους κρινεσθαι.*—Geog. Hist. Græc., II, 439.

[40] Megasthenes ascribes no particular virtue to the death by fire: it is merely the death preferred by fiery spirits, *τους δε πυρωσεις εις πυρωθουμενους*, *ib.*

[41] The Relation des Voyageurs Arabes, ninth century, thus describes one of these self-immolations. The man "se met à courir dans les marchés ayant devant lui des cymbales et entouré de sa famille et ses proches."...A crown of burning coals is placed upon his head..."Le homme marche la tête en feu...et pourtant il marche comme si de rien n'était, et on n'aperçoit sur lui aucun signe d'émotion: enfin, il arrive devant le bûcher et s'y précipite."—Reinaud, i, 122.

any just estimate of the value of his information, we must compare it with the accounts given by more ancient writers. The companions of Alexander speak of the Indian sophists and of them as divided into classes, but nowhere mention the Sarmanai[42] by name. Thus Aristobulus,[43] of two Brahmans he saw at Taxila and who in the presence of Alexander displayed each in his own way his powers of endurance, remarks that while the younger wore all his hair, the elder was shaved.[44] And Nearchus[45] distinguishes between the Brahmans who are engaged in political life and are councillors of the king, and those who give themselves up to the study and contemplation of nature, as Calanus. He adds, that with these last women philosophise, and that all lead austere lives. With Megasthenes as we know him from Strabo, Diodorus Siculus, and Arrian,[46] begins our knowledge of the Sarmanai. Of the philosophers generally he says they do no labour, pay no taxes, and are subject to no king; that they are present at all sacrifices whether public or private, and preside over all

[42] Sarmanai, Sans. Çramaná, used by Megasthenes and his copyists.

[43] From Strabo, xv, I, 61.

[44] The shaved head would imply a Buddhist priest, described in the Prabodhatschandradaja as "Kahlgeschirner, Kopfbüschelverzierter, Haarausraufer," p. 39, and whoever compares the whole account of this shaved Brahman, how he came to Alexander and followed him to the end, with Onesicritus's story of Calanus—save that no mention is made of this Brahman's voluntary death—will be inclined to think that he and Calanus are one and the same person.—Strabo, xv, I, 65.

[45] Strabo, *ib.*, 66.

[46] Strabo, xv, I. Diodorus Siculus, II, 35. Arrian, Indica, vii.

funeral rites;[47] and that on New Year's Day they meet in the king's palace and there make known the future of the year, its events and harvests, and that he who thrice fails in his predictions is condemned to a life-long silence. These philosophers he divided into Brahmans and Sarmanai.

Of these the Brahmans were the most honoured, because their opinions were the most fixed and uniform. The Brahman's education began even in his mother's womb. During the period of gestation she was soothed by songs and chaunts in praise of continence, which in proportion as they won her pleased attention beneficially influenced her future offspring. After the child's birth and as he grew in years he was passed on from one preceptor to another, until he was old enough to become an auditor of the philosophers. These lived frugally, abstained from animal food and women, and in a grove outside the city spent their days in earnest discourse, communicating their knowledge to all who chose to listen. But in their presence the novice was not permitted to speak, or hawk, or spit, under the penalty of one day's banishment from their society. At the age of thirty-seven his student life ceased.[48]

47 Menu, III, 124.

48 "The discipline of a student in the three Vedas may be continued for thirty-six years in the house of his precepter, or for half that time," etc. Menu, III, 1. That on his return home he lived more laxly and elegantly may be gathered from §§ 3, 61, 62, *ib.*, and iv, 34. In the chapter on Diet, §§ 25-35, are the rules to be observed in eating flesh meat. Among the Jains, "A student till he is married should tie only a thread round his loins, with a rag to cover his nakedness." But "as soon as he is married, then he may dress properly at his pleasure."—As. Resear. ix. 248.

The Brahman then returned to his home, lived more freely, wore gold rings and silk, and ate the flesh of such animals as were of no service to man, abstaining however from pungent and highly seasoned food. He married too as many wives as he could, for the sake of offspring, but did not admit them to a fellowship in his philosophy.

Of the Sarmanai, he writes that the Hylobioi were the most honoured. They dwelt in the woods, and subsisted on leaves and wild fruits, "wore a vesture of bark,"[49] and abstained from wine and venery. Through messengers they advised with the king on the causes of things, and were employed by him as his intercessors before the gods. Next to them were the physicians. They too lived abstemiously, but not in the open air. They ate rice and flour, which they seem to have got by begging. They made barren women fruitful. They healed by diet rather than by medicine, and of medicaments preferred cataplasms and unguents. Both they and the Hylobioi would remain a whole day in the same posture. Others were diviners, and skilled in the rites to be observed towards the dead, and they wandered as mendicants about the towns and villages. And yet another class, but more urbane and better nurtured than these last, was like them occupied with the things of Hades, in so far at least as they conduced to piety and a holy life. With some of these Sarmanai the women are allowed to philosophise[50] under a vow of chastity.

[49] See on the third and fourth Orders. Menu, vi, 6, etc.

[50] Of the Sanyasi, "Let him repair to the lonely wood, commit-

Another writer, quoted also by Strabo[51] towards the close of the same chapter, speaks of the Pramnæ[52] (no doubt for Sramnæ as Garmanai for Sarmanai), as of a class opposed to the Brahmans, as argumentative[53] and contentious, and as jeering the Brahmans for their love of physiology and astronomy. They are Mountain or Gymnete or Political or Rural (προσχωριοι). The Mountain Pramnæ are clad in skins, and carry wallets full of roots and medicaments, and in their cures use charms and incantations. The Gymnetes as their name implies go naked, and for the most part live in the open air till their thirty-seventh year. They admit women to their society, but both they and the women are strictly chaste. The Political[54] and Rural classes live, the one in the city and are clad in silks; the other in the country and "wear for their mantles the hides of goats."

ting the care of his wife to her sons, or *accompanied by her*, if she choose to attend him."—*ib.*, 3 §.

51 Geogr., xv, I, 70.

52 In a paper on the Religious Sects of the Hindus, I find that the late Professor Wilson derives the term Pramnæ, from Pramana, proof, and inclines to think that they were Bauddhas; the Sarmanai, on the other hand, ascetics generally. As however in his later years he identified, I believe, the Sarmanai with the Buddhist Shamans, his great authority can scarcely be brought to bear against the view I have taken.—As. Res., xvii, pp. 279-280.

53 So in the legend of Sâmgha, when in his wanderings he finds a hermitage with five hundred Rishis, to avoid receiving him they say one to another, "Continuons de nous livrer à nos occupations ordinaires: ces Çramanas fils de Çakya sont de grands parleurs." —Burnouf, *ut sup.*, 323.

54 Menu, vii, 37, and compare 54 and 58, *ib.*

It would appear from these accounts that the companions of Alexander knew of Brahmans only, Megasthenes and our anonymous author of Brahmans and Sarmanai, and that they divided the Sarmanai into four classes. But of these four classes, it seems, that while the first two in both writers pretty fairly correspond with one another, the first of one with the second of the other, the two last have no one point in common, and can scarcely be intended to represent the same members of the same society; indeed, the Political and Rural Pramnæ are much more like the Brahmans of Megasthenes than his Sarmanai—the one to his Brahmans whose novitiate or student life has ceased; and the other to those of them who are philosophers. Moreover the Gymnetes, who go naked and live in the open air, and the Hylobioi clad in bark and subsisting on leaves and wild fruits, bear some resemblance indeed to the Digambara of the Jains[55] and the Brahman Sannyasi as painted by Menu, but very little to the Shaman or Buddhist priest as we know him, who wears and is obliged to wear a robe of a particular stuff and colour, and who lives on rice and grain generally, but who is also permitted when in bad health to eat ghee, oil, sugar, honey, and even flesh meat.[56] Again, the anonymous author speaks of the Pramnæ in no very favourable terms, much as Brahmans might be expected to

[55] In the Prabod'h Chandrádaya the Digambara is thus described: "His disgustful form is besmeared with ordure, his hair in wild disorder, his body naked and horrible to the view."—Act III, Taylor's trs.

[56] Hardy, Monachism, p. 92.

speak of Buddhists; but Megasthenes of the Sarmanai with a respect, an admiration which are so extraordinary for a resident at the court of a Brahminical sovereign, Chandragupta, that one may very fairly question whether his Sarmanai were indeed intended for Buddhist priests.[57]

Take now Bardesanes' account. His Brahmans are hurriedly and superficially sketched, as if his pen had been guided by a Buddhist hand. His division of them into Mountain and River[58] is unmeaning—really a distinction without a difference, for both led the same ascetic lives in the same sort of solitude. But his Samanæoi or Shamans are the Buddhist priests of our day. He shows us their order open to all who wish to take upon themselves its duties. But to enter it the aspirant must give up wife and children and property. He must shave his body and put on the yellow robe, and then retire to some vihâra[59] where having made vows of chastity and poverty he lives supported by the alms of kings and the pious rich, and is thus enabled

[57] Çramanas, evidently Brahmans, accompany Arjouna on his twelve years' retreat in the forest.—Mahabharata, ii, 237. Fauche, tr.

[58] Corresponding with the "Mountain and Plain" Brahmans, probably, of Megasthenes.—Strabo, *ut sup.*

[59] In the early days of Buddhism, according to the "Book of the Twelve Observances" (Burnouf, *ut sup.*, 304), another mode of life prevailed. "L'obligation de se retirer dans la solitude des forêts, celle de s'asseoir auprès des troncs d'arbres, celle de vivre en plein air...sont certainement trois règles primitives."—*Id.*, p. 311. Hardy says, "It was an ordinance of Buddha that the priests, who were then supposed to dwell most commonly in the wilderness, should, during the three months of the rainy season, reside in a fixed habitation."—Monachism, 282, and Burnouf, 285-6.

to pass his days in prayer and discourse on heavenly things. His manner of life is decent, orderly, and temperate even in its austerity, and his retirement is at once cheerful and improving, and contrasts favourably with the sullen loneliness of the Brahman. For though the Brahmans have their agrahâras[60] where the ordinary members of their caste are found collected together, and though the Buddhist ascetic notwithstanding his convents occasionally retires to the solitude of the forest; yet is Bardesanes' account of the two priesthoods in this particular characteristic of the spirit of the two religions. In it we see the Brahman, who lives by himself and for himself, with his strong will conquering the wants and appetites of his body, but indifferent to the wants and miseries of his fellows; and in it the Buddhist not less earnest in self-sacrifice, but not neglectful of the social duties, cultivating a kind and genial nature, and knitting his own good to the good of mankind.

But Bardesanes also represents both Brahmans and Shamans as willingly devoting themselves to death by fire. The self-cremation of widows of the higher castes was, within even a few years and until forbidden by law, no uncommon sight in India; but among men, Brahmans, this sort of death has long fallen into disuse. History tells of a Calanus, who with much parade and

[60] "Agrahara est le nom de tout terrain ou de tout village particulièrement affecté aux Brahmanes. Dans le sud de l'Inde...on ne trouve presque pas d'endroit sans un agrahara habité par des Brahmanes seulement."—Radja Tarangini, I, p. 348, note. Troyer trs.

of his own free will died by fire in the presence of Alexander and his army; and of a Cumarilla,[61] who to purify himself from the slaughter of heretical Buddhists ascended the funeral pile. But in modern times another form of suicide has been preferred. The Hindu pilgrim now toils up the snowy heights of the Himalaya to the sacred source of the Ganges, there to die; or he commits himself to its stream, and thus perishes in its holy waters. He suffers and dies to ensure to himself a happy birth in his next existence. The Buddhist also has freely chosen the death by fire as before Augustus. And if ever Brahmans did so choose to die, and if these their deaths worked at all on the religious feelings of the people, I have no doubt that for every Brahman who so died two Buddhists stepped forward to die beside him, but with other and higher aims. They died not for themselves, but for the honour of their creed. They died as Buddha, who in a former existence laid himself down before a hungry tiger; as the Arya Sâmgha,[62] who flung himself into the troubled sea to save the degraded Nagas; as Purna,[63] who to preach his master's law went forth to an expected death. They died as they had lived, for others' good. Their death was but a last and crowning self-sacrifice. Except in this sense, a voluntary death is contrary to the spirit of their religion and incompatible with its duties.

But the Indian ambassadors also told Bardesanes of

[61] Tr. Royal Asiatic Society, I, 441.

[62] Burnouf, Introduction à l'Histoire du Bouddhisme, p. 317.

[63] *Id.*, *ib.*, pp. 253-4.

a lake in their country, known as the Lake of Probation,[64] and of the use they make of it. When any one is accused of a crime and insists upon his innocence, the Brahmans ask him if he will undergo the trial by water. If he refuse, he is sent away and punished as guilty. If he consent, they bring him down to this lake, and to check frivolous or malicious charges they bring his accusers down with him. Together they go into the water, which is knee-deep for everybody, and together pass over to the other side of the lake. The innocent man walks along without any fear, and is never wet above the knees; but for the guilty, the water rises and rises till it is quite over his head, and he is then dragged out by the Brahmans, who hand him over to be punished in any way short of death. The Indian however rarely pushes matters to this extremity; he too much fears the ordeal by water.

But besides this lake for voluntary, they have also another to try both voluntary and involuntary offences; in fact to probe a man's whole life. Of this lake Bardesanes, and I will quote his very words, has left the following account:—"In a very high mountain, situated pretty nearly in the middle of the earth, there was as he heard a large natural cave, in which was to be seen

[64] Troyer, in his notes to the Radja Tarangini, I, pp. 361-66, describes several sacred and extraordinary fountains in Cashmere which the credulity of the people, favoured by their distance and inaccessibility, may have easily worked up into the lakes of Bardesanes. *See* also Ctesias's account of a fountain, the waters of which became solid, and which when given to drink as water made one tell everything one ever did.—Photius, 147 and 155.

a statue,[65] ten or perhaps twelve cubits high, standing upright with its hands folded crosswise; and the right half of its face, its right arm and foot, in a word its whole right side was that of a man; its left, that of a woman;[66] and the indissoluble union of these two incongruous halves in one body struck all who saw the statue with wonder. On its right breast was engraved the sun, on its left the moon; on its two arms were artistically sculptured a host of angels, mountains, a sea and a river together with the ocean and plants and living things, all that is. And the Indians told him that God, after he had created the world, gave this statue to his son[67] as a visible exemplar of his creation.

65 The Radja-Tarangini has a passage which reminds one of this cave and statue. " La possession de la jouissance de la béatitude éternelle devient le partage de ceux qui dans l'intérieur du sanctuaire de Papasudana (qui détruit tout péché) touchent l'image de bois de l'époux Uma. La déesse Sandya entretient dans cette montagne aride l'eau dans laquelle on reconnait ce qui est conforme et ce qui ne l'est pas à la vertu et au vice."—I, 32, 33, Slokas. Of this passage, however, Professor Goldstücker has favoured me with the following translation :—" There those who touch the wooden image of Siva standing in the interior of the sacred place Papasudana, attain as their reward worldly enjoyment and final bliss, 32. There on the waterless mountain the goddess of twilight (the wife of Siva) places water to show to the virtuous that which will benefit (agree with), and to the wicked that which will injure (disagree with) them," 33.

66 " La réunion de Çiva et de Parvati dans un seul corps est le thème de l'invocation par laquelle commence chaque livre du Radja-Tarangini...Cette forme est l'objet d'une grande vénération dans l'Inde. Je rappellerai parmi les images...de l'île d'Eléphanta une statue colossale, représentant Civa moitié homme et moitié femme avec une seule poitrine."—Radj., II, pp. 326, 328.

67 Τουτον τον ανδριαντα φασι δεδωκεναι τον θεον τῳ υἱῳ ὁπηνικα τον

And I asked them, adds Bardesanes, of what this statue was made. And Sandanes assured me, and the others

κοσμον εκτιζεν.—Stobœus, Physica, Gaisford's ed., p. 54. This expression indicates a Christian author, and indeed Bardesanes has been identified with the great heresiarch of that name, who lived in the second and third centuries, and who gained great celebrity by a work on Fate. In this case the Christian author was still living (A.D. 218, 222). Porphyry (A.D. 233, 304) says of the Bardesanes he quotes, that "he lived in the time of our fathers." But the Christian Bardesanes presented his book, Cedrenus of the eleventh century affirms, to Antoninus Pius (A.D. 138, 161), and Epiphanius (ad. Heres., II, 36, II, v. p. 477) speaks of him as faithful to the Church up to the death of Antoninus Verus (A.D. 169), and of this book as of one of his orthodox works; but this book, Eusebius (A.D. 324) asserts (Hist. Eccl., iv, 24, 30), he presented to Marcus Antoninus, and further adds that he wrote it in consequence of the persecution of the Christians by Marcus (A.D. 167, 177), and about the time Soter, Bishop of Rome, died (A.D. 179). Now between the earliest and latest of these dates, the death of Antoninus Pius and the accession of Elagabalus, there elapsed fifty-seven years, and our author must either have been very young when he wrote his work on Fate, or very old when he published his Indica. Again, the Edessene Chronicle (Assemanni, Bib. Orient., i, p. 47, note, and 389, note), gives the precise date of his birth, July 11, A.D. 154. On this authority he must have been seven years old when Antoninus Pius died, and twenty-five when Soter. And at twenty-five he might have written his book on Fate, and at sixty-four his Colloquy with the Indian Ambassadors. But of late years this "Book of Fate," or rather "Book of the Laws of Countries," has been found in the Syriac original, and in 1855 the Oriental Translation Fund published it in its entirety, together with a translation by the Rev. Mr. Cureton. The work is in the shape of a dialogue. Two youths who have been discoursing on "fate, free-will, fore-knowledge absolute," meet with Bardesanes, and appeal to his superior learning and wisdom. They address him sometimes as lord—a homage paid perhaps to his rank and relationship with the Abgari—and sometimes as father, a deference due only to his age and experience. He too alludes and appeals to former works of his, p. 5. "For it has been said by me

confirmed his words, that no man could tell; that it was not gold or silver, nor yet brass or stone, nor indeed any

in another place." When he wrote this work, then, he must have been a man of at least mid age, and either not born A.D. 154, or his book not written A.D. 179. Again, in the book itself are allusions which may assist us in fixing its date. In p. 30, "Because as yesterday the Romans took Arabia and abrogated all their ancient laws, and more especially that circumcision with which they circumcised." Mr. Cureton, Pref. iii, is of opinion that this passage refers to the conquest of Arabia by Marcus Aurelius (Lucius Verus), but of such a conquest I find no record, not even in the titles, Armeniacus, Parthicus, and Medicus, which the senate so lavishly bestowed on him and which he afterwards dropped. (Life, Smith's Hist.) But on the other hand, Trajan (Eutropius, viii, 3):—"Arabum regem in fidem accepit," and "Arabiam postea in provinciæ formam redegit." But to this conquest (A.D. 116), could Bardesanes, even A.D. 167, allude as "of yesterday?" I think not. Severus, however, A.D. 196, again conquered and reduced Arabia to a province (Eutropius, iii, 18). "Arabos simul adortus est, in ditionem redegit provinciæ modo." Aurelius Victor, xx, 14, 15, "Persarum regem Abgarum subegit, Arabas in deditionem accepit." Severi, Hist. Spartianus, Hist. Aug., I, v, p. 157. But if it is of this conquest Bardesanes speaks, then his book can scarcely have been written till after the death of Severus (A.D. 211), or in the reign of Caracalla (A.D. 211, 217). But as any such date is wide of the several dates ascribed to this work by the early Fathers, and as these dates are themselves wide of one another and very indefinite, we will examine how far such a date is consistent with the circumstances. The Edessene Chronicle gives the date of his birth so precisely, that I should be loath except on evidence to reject it, A.D. 154. His book as we have seen indicates that it was written at least in mid-age, perhaps in old age; if written A.D. 214, it would have been written eighteen years after the conquest of Arabia by Severus—neither too late nor too early for the "but as yesterday," and when he was sixty years of age—when he might well quote other works of his own, and be addressed as lord or father.* But tradition spoke of this

* The several dates in the above notes are at variance with those generally received. When I suggested them to the late

other known material; but that, though not wood, it was likest a very hard and sound wood. And they told how a certain king of theirs had on a time tried to pluck one of the hairs off from about its neck, and how he was so struck down with terror, that he hardly recovered his senses and then only after long intercession of the Brahmans. They said that on its head was the

work as having been presented to Antoninus, and hence the embroglio of dates. Now Bardesanes, a Syrian and of the Abgari, could not but know and be known to the Emesene Elagabalus; and it is neither, improbable that on Elagabalus's nomination to the Empire he should present him, evidently of a religious turn of mind, with a work already of repute and which was Christian rather because it was catholic, than because it contained any special Christian doctrine; nor that when he so presented it, he should address the Emperor as Antoninus—a name he much affected and by which he was in Syria generally known. But if the Christians carefully chronicled the interview of Origen and Mammœa, is it not probable that they would likewise bruit abroad the honour conferred on this work of Bardesanes, and associated too with the name of Antoninus? But the name of Antoninus as applied to Elagabalus, can scarcely be said to have ever obtained in either Greece or Rome—*see*, however, Capitolini Macrini, vii, Hist. Aug. Script.—and in Epiphanius' time was probably only given to Pius and Marcus; what more natural then than that the Fathers, when they heard of this presentation copy, should refer it to one or other of these great Emperors—more especially as the work was not heretical, and must therefore be a work of Bardesanes' younger days? though so far as that goes, it might just as well have been written by a Jew as a Christian.

Mr. Cureton, he summarily rejected them. Merx and Hilgenfeld, in their Monographs on Bardesanes, have, however, approved of and adopted them. Hilgenfeld entirely, v. Bardesanes d. letzte Gnostiker, pp. 12 and 28. Merx, with some hesitation, Bardesanes v. Edessen p. 20, comp. p. 130. Let me add that both are of opinion that the work cannot be by Bardesanes.

image of a god seated as on a throne, and that in the great heats it would run down with such a sweat, as would unless stopped by the fanning of the Brahmans wet the earth around. Well, further on beyond the statue, it was according to the Indians very dark, and those who wished to go so far took with them lighted torches, and went on till they came to a sort of door, whence a stream of water welling out fell into or formed a lake in the deepest recesses of the cave. Through this door those who wish to prove themselves are obliged to pass. For the pure-minded it opens itself out very wide so that they enter easily enough, and within they find a fountain of the brightest and sweetest water,[68] the source of the stream I spoke of. The wicked however struggle long and vainly to get in, for the entrance closes in upon them; at length they are forced to confess their sins, and to ask the others to intercede for them, and they are made to fast a long time.

Sandanes further told, that on a certain day the Brahmans flock to this place; that some spend their lives there, but that others come in the summer and autumn when fruit is plenty, both to see the statue and to meet their friends, and to prove their lives by means of the door. They at the same time examine and discuss the sculptures on the statue; for it is not easy to understand them all, both because of their number, and because no one country contains all plants and

[68] *Φασι δε εξαιρετον αυτοις ειναι μιαν πηγην την της αληθειας πολυ παντων αριστην και θειοτατην, ἧς ουδεποτε τους γευσαμενους εμπιπλασθαι,* Dio Chryso., II, 72.

animals. This then is what the Indians relate concerning the ordeal by water.

This Lake of Probation Lassen connects with the ordeal by water; one of the ordeals[69] which on a deficiency or absence of testimony is allowed and even prescribed by the Hindu law (Menu, viii, 190; and Colebrooke, Hindu Law, I, 503-5). Of the manner in which these ordeals are performed, Warren Hastings has given an interesting account in the first volume of the *Asiatic Researches.* In that by water, which except in that it is by water and conducted by a Brahman, resembles in nothing Bardesanes' Lake of Probation—the accused is made, to stand in water either flowing or stagnant up to his navel, and then holding the foot of a Brahman to dive and remain under as long as a man can walk fifty paces very gently, or till two men have fetched back two arrows which have been previously shot from a bow. If, before the man has walked thus far or the two men have brought back the arrows, the accused rise above the water, he is condemned; if not, acquitted.

In the cave of the second lake, Weber[70] finds the first Greek notice of a Hindu temple, and Lassen[71] sees one

[69] In the Radja-tarangini, the widow of a Brahman applies to the king to punish the murderer of her husband, and names a Brahman whom she suspects, but refuses the ordeal by water. "O radja, cet homme est connu pour être versé dans le fameux art de l'eau, il peut sans crainte arrêter le jeu divin."—iv, 94, p. 121, II, v. Eventually they try the ordeal by flour of rice, and the Brahman is convicted. "Le roi lui infligea toute punition sauf la punition de la mort."—105.

[70] Indische Skizzen, p. 86, note.

[71] Indische Alterthumskunder, III, 351.

of the cave temples so frequent on the western coast of the Indian peninsula. The statue he identifies with that of Siva as Ardhanari, or half-man half-woman, and of Siva also recognised as the Supreme God. The image on the head is that of the Ganges, the angels are Devas, and the characters on his arms are typical of him as the Creator.[72] The door and the great sweat he explains as pious frauds, and the sacrilegious king as a legend invented and promulgated by priests to secure the treasures which they habitually deposited within their statues. On Weber's conjecture I would observe, that the cave is a natural cave and seemingly in its natural state, without pillars or carvings in relief; but nevertheless a cave which the patient fervour of a religious idea may hereafter develope into a cave temple. Lassen's conjectures have an air of probability about them; but still it seems to me that the lake and the cave are each in its kind unique; that with regard to the first, we have no indication whatever of its locality; and, with regard to the second, the very indefinite one,

[72] A statue of Siva and Parvati united, or as Ardhanari, is in the Elephanta cave.—Moor's Pantheon, p. 98. And in plates 7 and 24 of the same work are representations of Ardhanari, two seated and one standing. On each side of the united deities are the bull and tiger, the Nandis of Siva and Parvati respectively, but in pl. 7 interchanged. In all the figures

"From the moon-silvered locks famed Ganga springs;"

but in pl. 7 the goddess is seen personally with the serpent's head over her; all bear the soli-lunar emblem on the forehead, the drum and trident or sword in the hands, and the collar of flowers or skulls about the neck; but on none are to be found the symbolical characters which adorned the statue of Sandanes.

that it is in a very high mountain[73] somewhere near the centre of the earth; not therefore in the country of Sandanes or Sadanes, if he came from Ardjake or the Malabar coast as Lassen supposes. I cannot but think that our ambassadors spoke of this lake and mountain not from knowledge but from hearsay, and that they repeated stories current in their country, which they conscientiously believed perhaps, but for which there was about the same foundation as for that Fontaine de Jouvence so famous in old romance.

But as between India and the Roman empire there never existed any interchange of thought or any common sympathies, the allusions to India in Roman literature are at the most but indications of that curiosity which is excited by commercial intercourse. But that intercourse was in the hands of the merchants of Alexandria and Palmyra. These cities, situated, one on the shores of the Mediterranean, the other in the midst of a desert far inland and halfway between Mesopotamia and Syria, can scarcely be said to have had any direct communication with India. They could not be reached but by a long portage and river navigation: and yet the facilities which the one as the great seaport of the

[73] Perhaps in the north of India, towards Mount Meru, where also is that cave of Pluto, παρα τοις Αριανοις τοις Ινδικοις, described by Ælian, xvi, 16, with its mystic recesses, its secret paths stretching deep underground and leading no one knows whither, but down which, when the people drive them, all sorts of animals willingly hurry never to return; though who will may hear the bleating of sheep, the lowing of oxen, and the neighing of horses, coming up from the depths of the earth.

Roman empire afforded to the transit of western merchandise, and the advantages which the other derived from its proximity to India and the comparatively small cost at which it obtained and delivered the products of India, gave them the monopoly of Roman trade with the East. The Alexandrian route Pliny[74] has traced out. At Juliopolis, the river port and a suburb of Alexandria, our merchants embarked with their goods, and favoured by the prevailing north wind sailed up the Canoptic branch of the Nile, and in twelve days reached Coptos, distant three hundred and three miles, a city of a mixed population, Egyptian and Arabian,[75] and communicating with the Nile by a canal. Here they left their boats, and with their merchandize on camel-back pushed across plains and over mountains to Berenice, another twelve days' journey, travelling mostly by night because of the heat, and regulating their halts by the wells on the road. At Berenice, a seaport on the southern frontier of Egypt, they met the fleet intended for India. The ships of which it was composed were large, well-found and manned, and carried besides a body of armed men as a safeguard against the pirates who infested the Indian seas.[76] From Berenice, about midsummer time or in the begin-

[74] Hist. Nat., vi, 26.

[75] Και ἡ εις Κοπτον διωρωξ, πολιν κοινην Αιγυπτιων τε και Αραβων.—Strabo, xviii, I, 44.

[76] "Sagittariorum cohortibus impositis: etenim piratæ maxime infestant."—Pliny, *ib.* πλει δε εις εμπορια ταυτα μεγαλα πλοια, Periplus, § 56; and see also the description of an Egyptian ship in the Indian trade, from Philostratus' Life of Apollonius, *supra*, pp. 49, 50, and note 9, p. 50.

ning of the dog-days, they set sail, and in thirty days made Ocelis, or Cane, the one on the eastern shore of the Straits of Bab-el-Mandeb, the other on the western coast of Arabia in the frankincense country, and thence or from Syagrus to the north of Cane they struck out through the open sea for Muziris, in Pliny's time the haunt of pirates, or for Necanidon (Nelcyndon) or Barake, a forty days' sail. At Barake they took in pepper, which was brought there in native boats from Cottonara. In the month of December or in the beginning of January they returned taking advantage of the south-east monsoon, and when they entered the Red Sea of the westerly wind. So far Pliny. But when he wrote the trade with India was in its infancy; as it developed itself, in the marts which Alexandrian ships most frequented Greek factories[77] were probably established to which the merchants consigned their goods, and which managed all their business with the authorities and the people. In this way we may account for the Greek names of towns on the Indian seaboard, and for

[77] I have no direct authority for this; but besides such names on the Indian coast as Byzantium, found also in the Periplus, etc., Ptolemy, speaking of the situation of some Indian town, states that he has it from those who had resided in the country some time, *παρα των εντευθεν εισπλευσαντων και χρονον πλειστον επελθοντων τους τοπους και παρα των εκειθεν αφικομενων προς ἥμας.*—Proleg. I, xvii. And though much later in time, Procopius says of Abraham, whom the Homerites elected their king, that he was the slave of a Roman, and lived at Adule as (a ship agent or broker). *Ὁ δε Αβραμος οὑτος χριστιανος ην, δουλος δε Ρωμαιου ανδρος, εν πολει...Αδουλιδι επι τῃ κατα θαλασσαν εργασιᾳ διατριβην εχοντος.*—De Bello Persico, I, 20.

that temple of Augustus near Muziris—if it ever existed—which appears in the Peutingerian tables.

Of the course of trade to and through Palmyra we know little. Palmyra we have every reason to believe had no ships of its own. Arab and perhaps native vessels brought the produce of India up the Persian Gulf to the mouth of the Euphrates; and, if they did not themselves ascend the river, at Teredon they discharged their cargoes[78] intended for Vologesia, which was reached either by land on camels or in vessels of lighter draught by the river; but in what time—the distance was nearly two hundred and fifty miles—I am unable to ascertain. At Vologesia however, a two days' journey from their city, the merchants of Palmyra took up the trade. In its market or fair, held always at some little distance from the town itself, they met the Arab or Indian traders, and exchanged with them by sale and purchase the manufactures of the West for the goods and produce of India. By this traffic Palmyra silently but so rapidly grew in wealth and power, that its prince and king, Odenatus, with his own forces and by his energy and generalship saved the Roman empire,

[78] *Vide* Strabo, xv, III, 5, and Pliny, vi, 22. Very possibly they sailed up to Vologesia itself, for a passage in the *Meadows of Gold* of Masoudi, to which Sir Henry Rawlinson called my attention, speaks of ships from India and China as in the fifth century of our era lying at Hira, a little to the south-west of Babylon, 247, Sprenger's tr., and Reinaud's Observations, pp. xxxv-vi, with note I, Relations Arabes. With Apologus probably, and with Omana certainly, the Hindus in the time of the Periplus carried on a trade in native boats from Barygaza.—Periplus Anonym., § 36.

and for his services to the Roman state was raised by Gallienus, A.D. 266, to the title of Augustus.[79] At his death its queen, his widow Zenobia, ventured to throw off her allegiance to Rome. For a moment she held the sovereignty of the East,[80] but was at length defeated and taken prisoner by Aurelian, who at the same time pillaged and destroyed Palmyra,[81] A.D. 275, and thus put an end to the Roman trade with India through the Persian Gulf.

The Alexandrian trade with India, unlike the Palmyrene, was not broken up by any one great catastrophe. It remained some time stationary; but from the reign of Caracalla it rapidly declined, and when Palmyra was destroyed it was in so languishing a state, that in so far at least as it was a trade directed and controlled by Alexandrian merchants it may almost be said to have died out. Among the circumstances which affected its prosperity, we may reckon:—

I. The privileges accorded to Palmyra by the Emperor Hadrian. The comparatively short sea passage of the Palmyrene route, and the very situation of Palmyra, must have soon drawn to its markets not only such commodities as were intended to supply the wants of the neighbouring districts, but such also as before they were fitted for consumption required the manufacturing aid of the great cities of Phœnicia, as *e.g.* silk, of which the Indian mart was Nelcyndon, and which, if brought

[79] *Vide* Pollio, Hist. Gallieni. Hist. Aug. Script., x, xii, pp. 90, 92.

[80] *Vide* Zosimus, Lib. I, 440.

[81] *Vide* M. Aurelianus Vopisci, xxxi. Hist. Aug. Script., II, 176.

over in its raw state or in the thread,[82] was taken to Berytus or Tyre[83] to be made up into stuffs; or if in stuffs, to Tyre or Sidon to be dyed.[84] The Palmyrene route then once opened must have affected the Alexandrian trade with India, and must so far have counteracted the stimulus given to it, first by Roman protection, and afterwards by the discovery of the monsoons, as to have stayed its further development. But there was ample room for both, and to spare. The Alexandrian people however, filled with the jealousy and hate usually

[82] If it was brought in stuffs was it re-made? Pliny, Philemon Holland's tr. "The Seres kemb from the leaves of their trees the hoary down—'Velleraque, ut foliis depectunt tenuia Seres,' Georgics II, 121—and when it is steeped in water, they card and spin it, yea, and after their manner make thereof a web; whereupon the dames here with us have a double labour both of undoing and also of reweaving again this kind of yarn. See what ado there is about it! What labour and toil it costeth, and how far fet it is, and all that our ladies and wives when they go abroad in the street may cast a lustre from them and shine again, in their silks and velvets."—I, p. 124. From this mention of silk and the Seres we cannot conclude any knowledge of the country, for in an account of London written in the reign of Henry II, twelfth century, we are told of the merchandize found there, "the Seres send purple garments."—Antiquarian Repository, 246, I.

[83] 'Ιματια τα εκ μεταξης εν Βηρυτῳ μεν και Τυρῳ πολεσι ταις επι Φοινικης εργαζεσθαι εκ παλαιου ειωθει. οἱ τε τουτων εμποροι τε και επιδημιουργοι και τεχνιται ενταυθα το ανεκαθεν ῳκουν, ενθενδε τε ες γην ἁπασαν φερεσθαι το εμπολημα τουτο ξυνεβαινεν.—Procopius, Hist. Arcana, c. 25, p. 140, and Ammianus Marcellinus, xiv, 9, 7.

[84] "Quid lineas Ægypto petitas loquar? Quid Tyro et Sidone tenuitate perlucidas micantes purpurâ, plumandi difficultate pernobiles?"—Vopiscus, Carinus, xx, Hist. Aug. Scrip. That the stuffs from Tyre and Sidon were of silk, I gather from the "difficultate plumandi."—χιτων εκ μεταξης εγκαλλωπισμασι χρυσοις πανταχοθεν ὡραινομενος, ἁ δε νενομηκασι πλουμμια καλειν.—Procopius de Ædificiis, III, 1, p. 247, and Ammianus Marcell., xiv, 9, 7.

induced by commercial antagonism, assailed with taunts and sneers and ribald jests those emperors who specially favoured the rival city—Hadrian,[85] who gave it its privileges, and Caracalla and his mother who were almost native there. Hadrian heard and despised their abuse; Caracalla[86] treacherously and savagely avenged it; and his massacre of the people and plunder of the foreign merchants was a blow from which Alexandria did not easily recover.

II. The disturbed state of the Roman Empire from the death of Alexander Severus, A.D. 235, to that of Aurelian, A.D. 275. During this dreary period of Roman story, Palmyra, almost independent, on a distant frontier, and not subjected to the influences of a turbulent garrison and an ambitious general, went on to the very hour of its fall uninterrupted in its career of prosperity. Under its able chief, from a rich but merely commercial city, it became a powerful state. Alexandria, on the other hand, in the very centre of civil discord, was driven on by its excitable people to take a prominent part in every civil war.[87] It itself set up or readily acknowledged as emperor more than one unsuccess-

[85] *Vide* note 6, p. 127, *supra*, from the Hist. Aug. Scrip.

[86] Besides his massacre of the citizens, he compelled all strangers to leave the city, except merchants, and τα εκειvων παντα διηρπασθη. Dio. Cass., c. 22, 77 L. He also took away the Jus Bulentarium conceded to them by Severus.—*Id.*, c. 17, 51 L.

[87] "Sed Alexandria...internis seditionibus diu aspere fatigata, ad ultimum multis post annis Aureliano imperium agente, civilibus jurgiis ad certamina interneciva prolapsis, dirutisque mœnibus, amisit regionis maximam partem, quæ Bruchion appellabatur, *diuturnum præstantium hominum domicilium.*"—Amm. Mar., xxii, 16, § 15.

ful competitor[88] for the imperial purple. Ever on the losing side, it necessarily suffered much, and was indeed once taken and held by the forces of Zenobia, and twice besieged and sacked and its principal and noblest quarter destroyed by Roman armies.[89] Under such circumstances trade was neglected, and that with India as carried on from a distant port so fell away, that it no longer found employment for large fleets of large ships, but was in the hands of a few rich merchants, as Firmus,[90] who probably derived from it more honour than profit.

III. The weakness of the Roman Empire. It was no longer able to repel the incursions of the barbarians, who everywhere pressed upon its ill-guarded frontiers. And the Blemmyes, a fierce people whose heads once

[88] As Æmilianus, xxi, Tr. Tyranni Treb. Pollio. Saturninus and Firmus, vid. Flav. Vopis., Hist. Aug. Scrip., pp. 123, 228, etc., pp. ii, v.

[89] Eusebius (Hist. Eccl., vii) tells of the misery and confusion in Alexandria, A.D. 261, the consequence of sedition and civil war; *ib.*, 22, of the plague which afflicted it; and *ib.*, 32, of its siege and capture, and the destruction of Bruchium. In the Chron. Canon., under Claudius, A.D. 273, "Alexandriæ suburbium post diutinam obsidionem summo excidio deletum est."—p. 392, ed. Maius et Zohrab.

[90] Vopiscus dwells on the wealth of Firmus: "De hujus divitiis multa dicuntur, nam et vitreis quadraturis, bitumine aliisque medicamentis insertis, domum indurisse perhibetur; et tantum habuisse de chartis, ut publice sæpe diceret, exercitum se alere posse papyro et glutino. Idem et cum Blemyis societatem maximam tenuit et cum Saracenis;" and then adds, "*naves quoque ad Indos negotiatorias sæpe misit:* ipse quoque dicitur habuisse duos dentes elephanti pedum denum."—*ib.*, 230, p. II. Vopiscus describes the wealth of Firmus in so far as it was extraordinary, rare, and with this classes his ships to India. After him I cannot anywhere find that ships went from Alexandria to India.

did grow beneath their shoulders,[91] so infested the neighbourhood of Berenice, that Firmus—one of the last of the Alexandrian merchants who sent ships to India—no doubt from motives of interest sedulously cultivated their friendship. They seem to have occupied Coptos and Ptolemais, for Probus[92] (A.D. 279) is said to have recovered these towns from them. But with Coptos—the town where portage on the route to India either began or ended—in the hands of a savage race, Alexandrian trade with India if not diverted into some other channel was impossible; and that for the present it came to a stand the wretched state of Alexandria and Rome leads us to believe; but that in time Indian trade again flowed into Alexandria, though under other conditions and by other means than of old, I shall endeavour to show in another paper.

91 "Blemmyis capita absunt vultus in pectore est."—Pomp. Mela., I, viii, 60. But Rome was able to form a more correct opinion of them after the triumph of Aurelian in which they figured: "prætor captivos gentium barbarum, Blemyes...Indi, Bactriani, Saraceni, Persæ."—Vopiscus, *ib.*, 178, II. The Indi and Bactriani must have been captives from Palmyra.

92 Vopiscus, Probus xvii, *ib.*, 221, II.

ON THE

INDIAN EMBASSIES TO ROME.

Part II.

ON

THE INDIAN EMBASSIES TO ROME,

FROM THE REIGN OF CLAUDIUS TO THE DEATH OF JUSTINIAN.

PART II.

AFTER the fall of Palmyra and the many disasters which about this time overwhelmed Alexandria, the far east ceased to occupy the Roman mind or much place in Roman literature. India and the name of Buddha are however to be met with in Christian controversial writings of the third and fourth centuries directed against the Manichæan heresy. They occur, in Archelaus' account of his disputation with the heresiarch Manes held at Charra in Mesopotamia[1] (A.D. 275-9), in the Catecheses of Cyril of Jerusalem (A.D. 361), and in the heresies of Epiphanius (A.D. 375), which all trace back the Manichæan doctrine to one Scythianus and his disciple Tere-

[1] Vide Archelai et Manetis Disputatio: ed. Zacagnii, p. 1, pp. 93-4. This work written originally in Syriac I refer to, because it is Cyril's and Epiphanius's authority for their notices of Scythianus. Cyril says this heresy sprang up in the reign of Probus (A.D. 276-82), Catechesis, vi, 20. Cedrenus, a mere copyist and a bungling copyist, makes Manes a Brahman and identical with Scythianus, ὁ και Σκυθιανος λεγομενος βραχμανης ην το γενος, but he gives him Βουδας, formerly Terebinthus, for a teacher, to whom he ascribes the four Manichæan books. Hist. p. 455, I, Bonn ed.

binthus, whom they connect with India in this wise. Scythianus, of Scythian descent, but by birth a Saracen of the Saracens of Palestine and thus familiar with the Greek language and literature,[2] was a merchant engaged in the India trade. In the course of his business he had several times visited India, and while there, being a man of an inquiring mind and great natural parts,[3] had made himself acquainted with the Indian philosophy.[4] In his maturer years, having amassed great wealth, he returned homeward, and at Hypsele[5] in the Thebais, fell in with an Egyptian slave girl,[6] whom he bought and married, and who persuaded him to settle in Alexandria.[7] Here he applied himself to the study of and mastered the Egyptian learning,[8] and here formed those peculiar

[2] Σκυθιανου...απο της Σαρακηνης δομωμενου κατα δε τα τερματα της Παλαιστηνης, τουτ' εστι εν τῃ Αραβια, ανατραφεντος· οὗτος ὁ Σκυθιανος εν τοις προειρημενοις τοποις παιδευθεις την Ἑλληνων γλωσσαν και την των γραμματων αυτων παιδειαν. Epiphan. Ad. Hæres, L. II, Tom. II, Hæ., 66, § 1, p. 618, I. v.

[3] "Valde dives ingenio et opibus sicut hi qui sciebant eum per traditionem nobis quoque testificati sunt." Archelaus, *ib.*

[4] Epiphanius, who writes with theological bitterness throughout, alone alludes to his Indian acquirements, but makes him little better than an Indian juggler: και γαρ και γοης ην απο της των Ινδων και Αιγυπτων και εθνομυθου σοφιας, *ib.*, § 3.

[5] πλουτῳ πολλῳ επαρθεις και κτημασιν ἡδυσματων και τοις αλλοις τοις απο της Ινδιας, και ελθων περι την Θηβαιδα εις Ὑψηλην. Epiph., *ib.*, § 2.

[6] According to Archelaus "quandam captivam accepit uxorem, de Thebaide," *u.s.* According to Epiphanius, he took her from a common brothel: ανελομενος τουτ' απο του στεγους (ἑστηκε γαρ ἡ τοιαυτη εν τῃ πολυκοινῳ ασεμνοτητι) επεκαθεσθη τῳ γυναιῳ, *ib.*, p. 619.

[7] "Quæ eum suasit habitare in Ægypto magis quam in desertis," *ib.*, and Cyril, C. vi, c. xxii, την Αλεξανδρειαν οικησας, he thus locates him in Alexandria. *Ib.*, p. 184, I. Reischl, ed.

[8] "In quâ provinciâ cum . . . habitaret, Egyptiorum sapientiam didicisset." Archelaus, *ib.*

opinions which with the assistance of his one disciple and slave, Terebinthus, he embodied in four books,[9] the source of all Manichæan doctrine. Here too he heard of the Jewish Scriptures; and wishing to converse with the Jewish doctors[10] he set forth with Terebinthus for Jerusalem, and in Jerusalem met and in a scornful and self-willed spirit disputed with the Presbyters of the Church, and there after a short time died.[11] At his death, Terebinthus either inherited or seized upon his books and other wealth, and hurrying to Babylon proclaimed himself learned in the wisdom of Egypt.[13] He

[9] Epiphanius, § 2 *ib.*, and Cyril assert that Scythianus wrote these books; Archelaus on the other hand, that Terebinthus was their author. These books Mysteriorum, Capitulorum, Evangelium, (*ου χριστουυπ ραξεις περιεχοντα*, Cyril, *ib.*) et novissimum omnium Thesaurum appellavit." Archelaus, *ib.*

[10] *Επειδη δε ακηκυει πως οἱ Προφηται και ὁ νομος περι της του κοσμου συστασεως*, etc. Epiphanius, *ib.*, § 3: "Placuit Scythiano discurrere in Judæam, ut ibi congrederetur cum omnibus quicunque ibi videbantur doctores." Archelaus, *ib.* Cyril merely mentions that he went to Judæa and polluted the country by his presence: *και λυμηνασθαι την χωραν*, *ib.*

[11] *Ὁ προς τους εκεισε Πρεσβυτερους αντιβαλλειν ηρξατο.* Epiphanius L. II, III, p. 620, places all this in the time of the Apostles, *περι τους χρονους των Αποτολων*, quite impossibly.

[12] Epiphanius will have it that he fell from the house-top and so died—the death also of Terebinthus. Archelaus merely says that arrived in Judea he died; and Cyril, that he died of a disease sent by the Lord, *τον νοσῳ θανατωσας ὁ Κυριος*, *ib.*

[13] Terebinthus dicens omni se sapientia Ægyptiorum repletum et vocari non jam Terebinthums ed alium Buddam nomine, sibique hoc nomen impositum, ex quâdam autem virgine natum se esse, simul et ab Angelo in montibus enutritum."—Archelaus, p. 97. Epiphanius asserts that he took the name of Buddha, *ἱνα μη καταφωρος γενηται*, *ib.* Cyril, omitting the virgin birth, that he took it because he was known and condemned in Judea for his doctrine,

also took the name of Buddha (Βουδδας, Buddas), and gave out that he was born of a virgin, and had been brought up on the mountains by an angel.[14]

Some years after Epiphanius (died A.D. 401), Hieronymus (died A.D. 420) incidentally notices the birth of Buddha. Having enlarged on the honour in which virginity has ever been held, and how to preserve it some women have died, or how to avenge its enforced loss others have killed either themselves or their ravishers, he goes on to say, that among the Gymnosophists there is a tradition, that Buddha the founder of their philosophy was born from the side of a virgin.[15]

Of these writers Hieronymus is the only one who directly refers to the Indian Buddha, and of ancient writers is the first who correctly narrates the manner of

ib., § 23. But Petrus Siculus, A.D. 790, and Photius, 890, give further details: Ὁ μεν Σκυθιανος ετολμησε Πατερα ἑαυτον ονομασαι· ὁ δε Βουδδας υἱον του Θεου και Πατρος, εκ παρθενου δε γεγενησθαι και εν τοις ορεσιν ανατρεφεσθαι. Ὁθεν και δωδεκα μαθητας ὁ αντιχριστος της πλανης κηρυκας απεστειλεν. · Reischl, note to Cyril, *ib.*

[14] Besides this Buddha, Terebinthus, there is a second Buddas, Baddas, or Addas, one of the twelve disciples of Manes, who preached his doctrine in Syria; and a third Bud or Buddas Periodutes, who lived A.D. 570. "Christianorum in Persidi finitimisque Indiarum regionibus curam gerens. Sermonem Indicum coluisse dicitur, ex quo librum Calilagh et Damnagh (Kalilah va Dimna, de bonis moribus et apta conditione animi, Geldemeister de Rebus Ind., p. 104) Syriace reddidit."—Asseman. Bib. Orientalis, III, 219, but as the work had been already translated into Persian by order of Choroes (A.D. 531-579) "Syriacam versionem proxime post Persicam fecit Bud Periodutes."—Asseman., *ib.*, p. 222.

[15] Contra Jovianum Epistolæ, Pt. I, Tr. II, c. 26: "Apud Gymnosophistas inde quasi per manus hujus opinionis traditur auctoritas, quod Buddam principem dogmatis eorum e latere suo virgo generavit."

Buddha's birth from the side of his mother; and yet his notice of him is by no means so full and satisfactory as that of Clemens, written some two centuries before. For Clemens described Buddha as a man and moral lawgiver, and as a man raised to deity by his own supreme majesty and the reverence of his followers, shortly indeed, but how truthfully and characteristically! when compared with Hieronymus, who knows him as the founder of the Gymnosophists, *i.e.*, of the Hindu philosophy, which is as much as if a Hindu should see in Mahomet the author of the western religions.

Again, Hieronymus gives Buddha a virgin mother. But a virgin mother is unknown to the Buddhist books of India and Ceylon, and belongs—derived perhaps from some Chinese or Christian source—to the bastard creed of the Buddhists of Tartary.[16] Under any circum-

[16] According to the Nepaulese "Neither Adi Buddha nor any of the Pancha Buddha Dhyani...were ever conceived in mortal womb, nor had they father or mother, but *certain persons of mortal mould* have attained to such excellence...as to have been gifted with divine wisdom...and these were...Sakya Sinha," Hodgson, Buddhist Rel., p. 68. And the Thibetan books from the Sanskrit, among the qualities required of the mother of Buddha place this one: "elle n'a pas encore enfanté," to which Foucaux appends this note: "Mais il n'est pas dit qu'elle sera vierge." Hist. de Bouddha, tr. de Foucaux. The Sinhalese: "Our Vanquisher was the son of Suddhadana and Maya," Mahawanso, Turner, p. 9, Upham, p. 25. Indeed the Virgin mother seems strange to the Indian mind, *vide* Birth of Parasu-Rama, Maurice, Ant. Ind., II, 93, and of Chrishna, Harivansa Lect. 59, Langlois. According to the Mongols, "Soudadani...épousa Maha-mai, qui, *quoique vierge*, conçut par l'influence divine un fils le 15 du dernier mois d'été," Klaproth, Mem. sur l'Asie, II, p. 61. Whether, however, the idea was borrowed from the Christians by the Tartars, or whether it is original among them may be a question. For I find among the

stances this dogma of Tartar Buddhism[17] could scarcely have reached Hieronymus; and he here writes, it may be presumed, on the authority of Archelaus or Epiphanius and confounds through ignorance the Manichæan with the Indian Buddha.

With regard to the Buddha of Archelaus, Cyril and Epiphanius, when we remember the many points of at least superficial resemblance between Buddhism and Christianity and the proselytising spirit of both religions, we may well wonder that so few of the early Christian fathers have known the name of Buddha; and that of these few Archelaus and his copyists have so little appreciated its religious significance, that they speak of it merely as of a name assumed by Terebinthus, and so assumed Epiphanius asserts, because it is the Assyrian equivalent of the Greek word Terebinthus.[18] They in fact connect the Manichæan heresy with India,[19] not through the name of Buddha, but

Mongols that Alankava, the ancestress of three great Tartar tribes, after a certain night vision, "se trouva fort surprise de cette apparition; mais elle le fut beaucoup plus, lorsqu'elle apperçut qu'elle était grosse sans qu'elle eût connu aucun homme." Alankava. Dict. Orient., D'Herbelot; but *see* Observations, iv, p. 339, *id.* And of the great Lao Tseu, who is somewhat anterior to Buddah, the Chinese believe that his mother conceived him impressed "de la vertu vivifiantedu Ciel et de la Terre." Mailla, Hist. de la Chine, xiii, p. 571.

17 Indeed I suspect that the Tartars were not at this time Buddhists, for of the Buddhist faith Klaproth writes, "elle n'a commencée à se répandre au nord de l'Hindoustan que A.D. 60; et beaucoup plus tard (the 7th century, *id.*, p. 88), dans le Thibet et dans les autres contrées de l'Asie Centrale," u. s., p. 93.

18 Τερηβινθου...μετονομασθεντος Βουδδα κατα την Ασσυριων γλωσσαν, Epiph., *ib.*

19 "Error quoque Indicus Manetem tenuit qui duo pugnantia

through Scythianus and his Indian travels and familiarity with Indian learning.

But if the Indian Buddha was unknown to Archelaus, he certainly was not unknown to Scythianus, who took the name, probably because it was symbolical of his own mission, and of himself as destined to inaugurate a new era in the history of mankind; and because by it he connected his own system of religion, which was eclectic and conciliatory, with the religions of the East. But this notwithstanding, Manichæism, the Gnostic perhaps excepted, is that scheme of Christianity with which the Buddhist faith has the least affinity. For the Manichæan was an essentially speculative, metaphysical creed, or rather a philosophy from and to which a religion and morality were derived and attached, and of which Manes was but the author and expounder. Buddhism on the other hand spite of its real atheism and its Nirvana is a religion eminently practical, formal, and ritual, of which Buddha is the great central sun, and his example, wisdom, and precepts, the world wherein his followers live, move, and have their being.[20]

numina introduxit," Ephrem Syrus from Assemann, though as Assemann very justly observes the two hostile deities are evidence not of an Indian but a Zendian origin.

[20] See, however, Lassen, Ind. Alterthumsk., III, p. 406, who finds traces of the influence of Buddhism in the religion of Manes. 1st. In the two opposite principles of Manichæism. 2nd. In its account of the world's origin. 3rd. In the laws which it supposes determine the several existences of individual souls in their progress towards final emancipation; and 4th. In its final destruction of the world. But without denying that these dogmas may have been borrowed from Buddhism, it must be allowed that they may just as probably be the result of independent thought, applied to

These notices relating to Buddha and extending over some century and a half, I have thrown together for convenience sake and because they show that Roman knowledge of India and Indian matters was on the decline. I return now to the times immediately succeeding the fall of Palmyra.

It would be absurd to suppose that the destruction of Palmyra however much it affected put an end to the Indian trade through the Persian gulf. That would find new channels for itself and live on so long as it proved remunerative to the carriers and merchants engaged in it. It seems in fact as we gather from a passage of Ammianus Marcellinus to have been transferred to Batne. This Batne situated at no great distance from the Euphrates, about sixty miles north of Thapsacus, and a day's journey from Edessa,[21] was when Strabo and even Ptolemy wrote a place of so little importance that it escaped their notice; in the reign of Constantius some seventy-three years after the fall of Palmyra Ammianus describes it as a rich commercial

the great problems of which they are one of a very limited number of solutions.

[21] "Ab Euphrate flumine brevi spatio disparatur." Am. Marc., x, 2, iii, *πολισμα μεν βραχυ και λογου ουδενος αξιον, ἡμερας δε ὁδῳ Εδεσσης διεχον*. Procopius de Bel. Persico, II, 12, 209. Asseman (I, 283) in the opening chapters to his life of S. Jacob Sarugensis has collected a good deal of information about Batne, yet strange to say, he makes no mention of Ammianus Marcellanus' notice of it, far the most important of all that have come down to us, and confounds with it a Batne in Chalcis, which Julian so pleasingly describes in a letter to Libanius, Epistola xxvii. Of *the* Batne, for he visited it also, he could have had no such pleasing an impression. Am. Mar. xxiii, II.

city, and as celebrated for its great fair which took place in the early part of September and was frequented by merchants and all sorts of people from every part of the world, who crowded thither to trade for the products and wares of India and the Seres. How many years after the ruin of Palmyra passed away before Batne reached this height of prosperity we have no means of ascertaining; but however rapid its growth, its decay must have been almost as rapid, for in less than two centuries its wealth and glory were already forgotten and Procopius contemptuously mentions it as a small and insignificant town.[22]

We now turn to Rufinus, born A.D. 330, died A.D. 410, and his short notice of the Indian travels of Metrodorus and Meropius.[23] He speaks of them as philosophers, and of their having gone to India for the purpose of seeing its towns and country, and the world generally.[24] He tells besides of Meropius, that he was a Tyrian and travelled, stirred by the example of Metrodorus; that he took with him Ædesius and Frumen-

[22] Zosimus speaking too of Julian's visit, calls it an insignificant town, πολιχνιον τι. Hist. l. iii, c. 12. From Asseman, u. s., it would seem as if Batne rose or fell according as Persians and Romans were at peace or at war with each other. He shows how it flourished under St. James of Sarug, and there was then peace between Chosroes and the Romans.

[23] Hist. Eccles., L. I, c. ix.

[24] "Inspiciendorum locorum et orbis perscrutandi gratiâ ulteriorem dicitur Indiam penetrasse." *ib.* Schröckh however sends Meropius to Ethiopia only (Kirschengeschichte, vi, 24, as also Socrates, A.D. 439, Hist. Eccles., I, xv, and Sozomen, A.D. 446, II, xxiii), though both evidently writing on the authority of Rufinus. Their India interior is from the context clearly Ethiopian.

tius, lads, "puerulos," his relations and pupils, and that after he had examined and observed every thing in India that was noteworthy,[25] he and his wards took ship to return home. He goes on to say, that on the way their water and provisions failed them, and that they made for an Ethiopian port; and that the inhabitants happening to be at variance with Rome, seized the ship and massacred all the crew and passengers save Frumentius and Ædesius, whom for their youth's sake they spared, and presented to the king. He adds, that in the course of time the king died, and that his widowed queen entrusted his one infant son and successor, together with the government, to the care of Frumentius, who in fact ruled the country till the king came of age, when he gave up his trust and authority together, and asked, and with difficulty got, permission to return to his native land. That he then came to Alexandria, and there visited Athanasius, not long before consecrated its bishop, A.D. 336, and that to him he spoke of the spread of Christianity in Ethiopia, and his labours in its cause; and was by him induced to accept the see of Auxume, the first Ethiopian bishopric.

With the visits of these Roman travellers we may connect an Indian embassy,[26] which reached Constantinople in the last year of Constantine's life, A.D. 336-7,

[25] "Igitur pervisis et in notitiam captis his quibus animus pascebatur."—*ib.*

[26] *Ινδων των προς ανισχοντα ἡλιον πρεσβεις...δωρα κομιζοντες...ἁ δε προσηγον τῳ βασιλει, την εις (αυτων) ωκεανον δηλουντες αυτου κρατησιν· και ὡς οἱ των Ινδων χωρας καθηγεμονες εικονων γραφαις, ανδριαντων τ' αυτον αναθημασι τιμωντες, αυτοκρατορα και βασιλεα γνωριζειν ὡμολογουν.*—Eusebius, de Vita Constant., L. iv, c. 50.

and brought with it strange animals, and all sorts of brilliant and precious stones. These the ambassadors presented to Constantine, in token that his sovereignty extended to their ocean. They told him too of pictures and statues dedicated to him by the Princes of India who thus acknowledged him as their autocrat and king.

I have no doubt whatever that its many and often successful wars with Persia, and its large and continued demand for the products of the East had magnified throughout India the wealth and power of the Roman Empire; and I understand how the appearance of Romans at their courts might probably induce the Hindu kings to express, by an embassy, their respect and friendly feelings for the Roman Emperor; but I cannot easily believe that any independent princes should, of their own motion and with no prospect of gain, thus hurry to bow themselves before Roman supremacy. In the lowly homage attributed to them, I trace the flattery of court interpreters and court newsmen, who would thus raise Constantine to a level with Augustus, as his court-poets had before raised Augustus to a level with Alexander.

To return to the travellers, Ammianus Marcellinus[27] (and he refers to some Book of his History now lost, where the matter was treated at length), in defending Julian against those who charged him with having instigated the Persian war, asserts that that war was

[27] xxv, iv. "Sciant...non Julianum sed Constantium ardores Parthicos succendisse cum Metrodori mendaciis avidius acquiescit, ut dudum retulimus plane."

brought on by Constantius, who too rashly gave credit to the falsehoods of Metrodorus. Now this Metrodorus, Cedrenus, of the eleventh century, has identified with the Metrodorus of Rufinus. He tells us of him, that he was Persian-born and pretended to philosophy; that he travelled to India and the Brahmans, and made for and introduced among them water-mills and baths; and that by his strictly ascetic life, he won their confidence and respect, and was admitted into the very penetralia of their temples, whence he stole pearls and other precious stones. These jewels, together with others entrusted to him by the Hindu king as presents for the Roman Emperor, he offered to Constantine as gifts from himself, and at the same time gave him to understand that the Persians had seized and appropriated a parcel of other jewels which he had sent overland. On this, Constantine wrote curtly to the Persian king, and receiving no answer, put an end to the peace between them.[28]

Valesius is of opinion that Cedrenus has here given us those falsehoods of Metrodorus which produced the Persian war, and the falsehoods to which Marcellinus referred. But I would observe:—

28 τῳ και ετει της βασιλεως του Κωνσταντινου...Μητροδωρος τις Περσογενης προσποιησαμενος φιλοσοφειν απηλθεν εν Ινδιαν και τους βραχμανας, και χρησαμενος εγκρατειᾳ πολλῃ γεγονεν αυτοις σεβαστος. ειργαζετο δε ὑδρομυλους και λουτρα, μεχρι τοτε μη γνωριζομενα παρ' αυτοις. οὑτος εν τοις αδυτοις ὡς ευσεβης εισιων λιθους τιμιους ..ὑφειλετο. ελαβε δε και παρα του βασιλεως των Ινδων ὡστε τῳ βασιλει δωρα κομισαι...και...δεδωκε ταυτα ὡς ιδια τῳ βασιλει. Θαυμαζοντι δε αυτῳ εφη και αλλα δια γης προπεμψαι, αλλ' αφαιρεθηναι ὑπο Περσων. γραφει ουν αποτομως Κωνσταντινος, προς Σαπωρην αποσταληναι αυτα και δεξαμενος ουκ ανταπεστειλε· δια τουτο ελυθη ἡ ειρηνη.—Cedreni Synop., Hist., pp. 516-7, I, Bonn ed.

1st. That Cedrenus' Metrodorus played not upon Constantius, but upon Constantine.

2nd. That while Cedrenus accounts for the Persian war which broke out A.D. 336-7, Marcellinus alludes to that begun A.D. 357; that during which Constantius died. For had he been speaking of the first war, as his object was to exculpate Julian from having instigated it, instead of looking about for Metrodorus and his lies, he would merely have pointed to the date of Julian's birth, A.D. 331,[29] and the accusation would of itself have fallen to the ground. The Metrodorus of Cedrenus cannot be the Metrodorus of Marcellinus.

But how about the Metrodorus of Marcellinus and Rufinus? If we turn to Rufinus' notice of Frumentius, we find that he was consecrated Bishop[30] of Ethiopia about A.D. 326. If we weigh well the adventures of his life from the day he left Tyre, to that in which he landed in Alexandria, we cannot surely crowd them into a less space than twenty-five years. He will then have set out for India about A.D. 302, and Metrodorus, who preceded him, about A.D. 300. But Metrodorus, already known as a philosopher, must have been at the very least twenty-five years old, and above eighty-three when (A.D. 357) with gratuitous and purposeless falsehoods he stirred up war between Persia and the Roman Empire. Malice, no doubt, belongs to every age; but this kind of malice at such an age is not probable—more

[29] V. Smith's Greek and Rom. Biographical Dict., Julianus.

[30] According to Theophanes, ninth century, Meropius in the time of Constantine was the first Apostle of the Ethiopians, Frumentius their first Bishop.—Chronog., p. 35, Byz. Hist., Bonn ed.

probable is it that the Metrodorus of Rufinus is other than the Metrodorus of Marcellinus.

But how if Cedrenus' and Rufinus' Metrodorus were one and the same? Cedrenus, I have little doubt, thought to identify them. And as he brings his hero to Byzantium, and before Constantine, A.D. 327, his Metrodorus and Rufinus' not only bear the same name, but are cotemporaries, and had both visited India; but here all resemblance ends. The Metrodorus of Rufinus was a philosopher and not unknown; Cedrenus', with a Greek name, was a Persian and a charlatan. How, besides, if they were identical, account for the silence of Rufinus as to the adventures of a man who had become famous or infamous, and who must have been known to his informant, Ædesius, at least by report? A gossiping historian, (I hasten to admit that his gossip is strictly ecclesiastic and religious), I do not believe that Rufinus, had he known it, would willingly have let die this story of a Persian and a philosopher; a heathen almost certainly, and if a Christian probably a heretic, from which so pleasing a moral might have been drawn. No, the Metrodorus of Cedrenus stands by himself, his own clumsy creation probably.

But, again, as to Rufinus himself. His chronology is always loose and vague enough at the best, but in this his notice of Frumentius, as gathered from the lips of Ædesius, Frumentius' friend and companion, one might expect some approach to accuracy. Now, reasoning on his own data, I have approximately fixed on the year A.D. 302, confirmed by Tillemont[31], as the year in which

[31] Hist. des Empereurs, notes sur Constantin, n. lxiii.

Meropius, with his wards, set out for India. But Valesius[32] and Neander,[33] while accepting Rufinus' date for the ordination of Frumentius, refer to a letter of the Emperor Constantius to Aizana and Sazana, kings of Auxume, which is quoted at length by Athanasius in his Apologia, and from which it would seem that Frumentius was ordained or consecrated to Auxume,[34] while Athanasius was being judged and condemned for heresy at Antioch, A.D. 355-6. Hence a difficulty which Baronius solves, cutting the Gordian knot with a vengeance, by supposing two Frumentius's, the one a Bishop of Ethiopia, the other of Auxume,[35] but which is in general slurred over by the historian, who satisfies himself with just mentioning this discrepancy of dates and then quietly assuming that Rufinus' is the correct one. But how stands the case? On the one side, we have an official letter from a Roman emperor to the two kings of Auxume, implying the recent ordination of their bishop, and we have that letter quoted, and so far silently acquiesced in, by the ordaining bishop. On the other

[32] V. Valesii Hist. Eccl., Socratis, p. 9.

[33] Kirchengeschichte, II, p. 256.

[34] Constantii Tyrannis Auxum., Epist. in the Apologia Athanasii ad Constantium. Constantius after insisting on the necessity for a unity of faith advises the kings to send Frumentius back to Alexandria, there to submit his life and doctrine to the Ven. Bishop George and the other Egyptian bishops. *ιστε γαρ δηπου και μεμνησθε...ὁτι τον Φρυμεντιον τουτον εις ταυτην την ταξιν του βιου κατεστησεν Αθανασιος μυριοις ενοχος ων κακοις, ὡς ουδεν των...εγκληματων ...δικαιως εσχεν επιλυσασθαι, αυτικα της μεν καθεδρας εκπεπτωκε.*

[35] Theophanis Chronog., p. 346, speaks of the Auxumites *Εξουμιτων* as Jews and converted to Christianity in Justinian's time, in consequence of a vow made by their King Adad, to become Christian should he conquer Damian the Homerite king.

side, we have Rufinus' reminiscences, which are but the reflection of what Ædesius himself remembered and told.[36]

What credit then is due to Ædesius? Schröckh tells of Rufinus,[37] that he was born in Concordia, almost on the Adriatic, about A.D. 330; that he was baptised in 371; that shortly afterwards at Alexandria he made the acquaintance of a noble Roman lady, Melania,[38] whom in A.D. 378 he accompanied to Jerusalem, and then first visited Palestine. At or about this time he must have known Ædesius, priest at Tyre. But Ædesius, if "puerulus" in 302,[39] was in 378 much past eighty, though Rufinus makes no allusion to his age, and his memory, especially as regards dates, could not have been very bright and clear. Between his authority then and that of a royal letter who could hesitate, would also hesitate between Fox's Book of Martyrs and an Act of Parliament.

But, if we accept the letter, we must set aside

[36] Quæ nos ita gesta, non opinione vulgi sed ipso Ædesio Tyri presbytero postmodum facto, qui Frumentii comes prius fuerat, referente cognovimus, x, ix, c.

[37] Kirchengesch. x, pp. 12-14; the Art. Rufinus, in Smith's G. and R. Biographical Dict., v. Rufinus—might be a translation of Schröckh's account.

[38] In his Lausiaca Hist. cxix, Palladius has given a life of Melania, and how the east and west, north and south were not unknowing of her charities. His next chapter is directed to another Melania, a niece of the first, which I recommend to those who would wish to know something of the wealth and possessions of a Roman lady.

[39] Socrates, unde edoctus nescio, calls the children παιδαρια... Ἑλληνικης ουκ αμοιρα διαλεκτης, more than ten years of age probably. Hist. Eccl., *ut sup.*

Cedrenus' narrative as apocryphal, and Rufinus' dates as incorrect; and as Athanasius was condemned by the Arian Council of Arles, A.D. 353, and finally deposed by that of Milan, A.D. 355;[40] but seems to have ordained and consecrated Frumentius while yet only under the imputation of heresy; I conclude that he ordained and consecrated Frumentius between the years 352 and 354 A.D.; and allowing, as we have done, twenty-five years for the events of his life, he will have set out for India under the guardianship of Meropius about A.D. 327-8, but whether immediately after, or as Valesius supposes on the return of, Metrodorus, we have no means of ascertaining.

But if we put aside Rufinus' date, what about his facts? Both from his narrative and the royal letter, we gather that at Auxume there were many Christians, and that the Government also was Christian. But here all agreement ends. The letter is addressed to two kings, the joint sovereigns of Auxume; the narrative knows of but one king, the ward from his childhood of Frumentius, and shows a state of things scarcely compatible with a double sovereignty; unless indeed we assume that this double sovereignty was the result of a revolution which broke out in the short interval between Frumentius' departure from, and his return to, Auxume. But if we see no reason to assume anything of the kind, we must again choose between the royal letter and the senile reminiscences of Ædesius; and for the royal letter I avow a weakness.

[40] Athanasius, Smith's Biographical Dict.

During the reign of Constantius we also hear of Theophilus the Indian. Philostorgius relates of him,[41] that he was born at Dibous, an island of the Indians, that when very young he was sent by his people as a hostage to Constantine, and that, educated in a monastery, he was sent at the head of a mission to the Homerites. Dibous, or rather the Dibenoi, Valesius,[42] and Shröckh after him, have identified with the Diù of the embassy to Julian, and Dibous with Divu, Diù, an island lying off the Indus. But what relation could possibly have existed between the Divi and Constantine, which should have obliged them to send hostages to Rome? I find that Theophilus is often called the Blemmyan, and his mission points to an Arab origin, and I incline to think that Dibous[43] is some Arab island or promontory connected with the Debai or Dedebai of Agatharcides.

[41] ταυτης δε της πρεσβειας (to the Homerites) εν τοις πρωτοις ην και Θεοφιλος ὁ Ινδος, ὁς παλαι μεν Κωνσταντινου...ετι την ἡλικιαν νεωτατος, καθ' ὁμηριαν παρα των Διβηνων καλουμενων εις Ρωμαιους εσταλη. Διβους γ' εστιν αυτοις ἡ νησος χωρας των Ινδων δε και οὑτοι φερουσι το επωνυμον ...τον μεντοι Θευφιλυν...τον μοναυλιον ανελεσθαι βιον. Ecc. Hist. III, 4

[42] Ad locum cita. annotatio.

[43] v, *ib.*, § 5. After having preached much and founded churches among the Homeritæ, and extended his labours even to the mouth of the Persian Gulf, επι την Διβοδ νησον...απεπλευσε κἀκειθεν εις την αλλην αφικετο Ινδικην, and there corrected much that was wrong. Then in the next chapter, 6, εκ δε ταυτης της μεγαλης Αραβιας εις τους Αυξουμιτας καλουμενους απαιρει Αιθιοπας. He tells how they live at the entrance of the Red Sea, and beyond them the Suroi, in whose land grow xylecassia, cassia, and cinnamon, προς μεν δε τουτους ὁ Θευφιλος ουκ αφικετο. But after he had done in Auxume all he had to do he returned to Rome. Does not all this show mere travel in Arabia, up to the Persian Gulf, and the Red Sea? See also Agatharcides de Mare Eryth., § 95.

The next incidental notice of India belonging to these times is to be found in Damascius' Life of Isidorus as preserved by Photius.[44] It is an account of some Brahmans who visited Alexandria and lodged in the house of Severus, Consul A.D. 470. They lived, we are told, very reputably after the manner of their people. They frequented neither the public baths nor any of the city sights, but kept within doors as much as they could. They ate palms and rice and drank water. They were not mountain Brahmans nor yet common Indian folk, but something between both, just agents for the Brahmans in the city and for the city with the Brahmans. What they reported of the Brahmans quite tallied with all one reads about them: as that by their prayers they can bring down rain and avert famine and pestilence and other incurable ills.[45] They told also of the one-footed men, and the great seven-headed serpent, and other strange marvels.

I suspect that the prophetic and supernatural powers of the Brahmans were greater on the shores of the Mediterranean than on the banks of the Ganges. The one-footed men were a favourite Hindu myth and known in Europe from the days of Ctesias. The seven-headed serpent may be referred either to that king of the Nagas who with his seven folds covered the body of

[44] *Vide* Photii Bib., ed. Schotti, p. 1042: *ηκον δε προς τον Σεβηρον και Βραχμαναι κατα την Αλεξανδρειαν, και εδεξατο σφας οικιῳ ιδιῳ*, etc. This visit must have taken place therefore before Severus took up his residence in Rome, and before his consulship.

[45] So Onesicritus: *εφη δ' αυτους και των περι φυσιν πολλα εξετασαι και προσημασιων ομβρων, αυχμων, νοσων*, Strabo, xv, I, 65, and Dio Crysostom, Oratio xlix.

Buddha and shielded him with his crests, or to the seven-headed serpent on which Vishnu reposes.[46] But whatever the tales of these men the question arises, why came they to Alexandria? They were not merchants, or they would have been found in its markets; and they travelled neither for their own instruction nor for that of others, or they would have mixed with the world and not avoided the haunts of men. Whatever might have been their object, they so lived that they could learn nothing, teach nothing.

Of direct notices of India subsequent to the fall of Palmyra I find a short one in a "Description of the Whole World," extant only in Latin translations, but originally written in Greek about A.D. 350 and seemingly by some eclectic in religion. In the farthest east it places the Eden of Moses and the sources of that great river, which dividing itself into four branches is severally known as the Geon, Phison, Tigris, and Euphrates. Here dwell—and we are referred to the authority of some unnamed historian[47]—the Carmani, a good and pious people, who know neither moral nor physical ill. They all live to the age of one hundred and twenty, and no father ever sees his children die.[48] They drink wild

[46] Hist. du Bouddha, Foucaux trans., p. 354, And compare Vishnu Purana, by Wilson, p. 205, where Ananta is described with a thousand heads, with the plate in Moor's Pantheon representing Vishnu on the seven-headed "Ananta contemplating the creation, with Brahma on a lotos springing from his navel to perform it," plate 7.

[47] "Et hæc quidem de prædictis gentibus *historicus ait*," Junioris Philosophi Descriptio totius Orbis, § 21, p. 516, II, Geog. Græci Minores.

[48] Their great age the Carmani share with others: "Cyrnos

honey and pepper, and they eat a bread and use a fire which daily come down from heaven; and the fire is so hot that it would burn them up, did they not run and hide themselves in the river until it returned to its own place. They wear garments of a stuff that scarcely ever soils, and then recovers all its freshness on being passed through fire. Next them to the west are the Brahmans. Like the Carmani, they are subject to no king, and live happily sharing something of their neighbours' felicity. Their food is fruits, pepper, and honey. Then come five other nations, and we have reached now the greater India, whence comes silk (or wheat) with all other necessaries, and the Indians live happily and in a country large and fertile. Next to India Major is a land which is rich in everything; its inhabitants are skilled in war and the arts, and aid the people of India Minor in their wars with the Persians. Bordering on this land is India Minor, subject to India Major; it has numberless herds of elephants which are exported to Persia.

Though our author parades the authorities he has consulted, from Moses and Berosus to Thucydides and Josephus, his work, which is rather a popular description of the world than a scientific geography, is interesting only when it treats of those countries and places, as

Indorum genus Isigonus annis 140 vivere. Item Ethiopas Macrobios et Seras existimat," etc., etc. Plin., Hist. Nat., vii, 2; Strabo, xv, 15. But their other blessings, that they die each in his turn and know no ills, are their own; but hinted at as characteristic also of the happy age of the Mahabharata: "Tandis que la caste des Ksyatryas s'abonnait à la vertu...personne ne mourait enfant."—I, 264, Fouche's Tr.

Syria and its cities, with which he was himself acquainted. Of the far East his account is especially meagre and would be worthless, but that it serves to show how necessary is commercial intercourse to keep alive our knowledge of other and distant countries; and how very soon after that intercourse had ceased India again faded away into the land of myth and fable.

Some few years later (A.D. 360-70) Avienus published a Latin hexametrical version of Dionysius Periegetes' Geographical Poem of the World. And though he nowhere shows any extraordinary regard for his text and never stops at any alteration of it to suit his own taste or the views of his age, I observe that he scrupulously follows it in everything relating to India.

I will but mention Dracontius (died A.D. 450) and Avitus (A.D. 490), who the one in his Carmen de Deo, speaks of India in connexion with spices—

> "India tunc primum generans pigmenta per herbas
> Eduxit sub sole novo."—i, 176.

and with precious stones and ivory—

> "India cum gemmis et eburnea monstra minatur."—307.

while the other, in his Poem de Mosai. Hist. Gestis, glorifies the Indians because they receive the first rays of the sun,[49] and describes them as black, and with their hair bound back off the forehead;[50] and who both—like

[49] . . . . "Ubi solis abortu
Vicinos nascens aurora repercutit Indos," 196, 1.
borrowed probably from Avienus "primam coquit hanc radiis sol," 1308, and Dionysius Periegetes, 1110.

[50] "Cæsaries incompta riget quæ crine supino
Stringitur ut refugo careat frons nuda capillo."

the author of the Description of the Whole World quoted above—place India to the west of Eden, whence the rivers bring down all sorts of precious stones to us common mortals.[51] They add nothing to our knowledge of India, and merely illustrate the common-place axiom, that in an intellectually inferior age fables and myths are preferred to truth, and the most wonderful tales to the best ascertained facts.

To this age, the fifth century, also probably belongs Hierocles. Of his work, Philistores, but a very few fragments have been preserved; and of these, two relate to India and imply that he had himself visited India and in India travelled. The first from Stephanos of Byzantium, under Brachmanes, is to this effect :—" After this I thought it worth my while to go and visit the Brahman caste.[52] The men are philosophers dear to the gods, and especially devoted to the sun. They abstain from all flesh meats and live out in the open air, and honour truth. Their dress is made of the soft and skin-like (*δερματωδη*) fibres of stones, which they weave into a stuff that no fire burns or water cleanses. When

51 "Est locus in terrâ diffundens quatuor amnes," Dracont. 178. The Ganges, one of these, brings down all sorts of precious stones. —So Eudoxus presents to Euergetes from India aromatics and precious stones : *ὧν τους μεν καταφερουσιν οἱ ποταμοι μετα των ψηφων*. Strabo II, III, p. 81.

" Hic fons perspicuo resplendens gurgite surgit,

. . . . . .

Eductum leni fontis de vertice flumen
Quatuor in largos confestim scinditur amnes."—Avitus, I.

52 *Εθνος*, but having before us the opinions of his predecessors about the Brahmans I suspect we should translate " nation," *i.e.* if he be the Hierocles I suppose.

their clothes get soiled or dirty, they are thrown into a blazing fire, and come out quite white and bright." The second from the Chiliads of Tzetzes (VII Hist., 144 to 716): "Then," he says, "I came to a country very dry and burnt up by the sun. And all about this desert I saw men naked and houseless, and of these some shaded their faces with their ears and the rest of their bodies with their feet raised in the air. Of these men Strabo has a notice, as also of the no-heads and ten-heads and four-hands-and-feet men, but none of them did I ever see, quoth Hierocles."

Hierocles' account of the Brahmans is so modest, and his explanation of the one-footed men of Strabo so simple, that his narrative might easily be accepted as the genuine production of one who had visited India; but first: for the asbestos stuff in which his Brahmans are clothed and which we have no reason to believe they ever wore, but which as it was an Indian manufacture[53] and rare and valuable he perhaps substituted for the wonderful earth-wool[54] Philostratus imagined for

[53] "Inventum jam est quod ignibus non absumeretur .... ardentesque in focis conviviorum ex eo *vidimus* mappas, sordibus exustis, splendescentes igni magis quam possent aquis... Nascitur in desertis adustisque sole Indiæ, ubi non cadunt imbres, inter diras serpentes; assuescitque vivere ardendo, rarum inventu, difficile textu propter brevitatem. Rufus color." Pliny, xix, 4. Strabo, however, speaks of it as a product of Eubœa, and in his time also used for napkins: *εν δε τῃ Καρυστῳ και ἡ λιθος φυεται ἡ ξαινομενη και ὑφαινομενη ὥστε τα ὑφη χειρομακτρα γινεσθαι, ῥυπωθεντα δ' εις φλογα βαλλεσθαι και αποκαθαιρεσθαι*, x, I. B., p. 383.

[54] *'Η δε ὑλη της εσθητος, εριον αυτοφυες, ἡ γη φυει, λευκον μεν ὥσπερ το Παμφυλων, μαλακωτερον δε τικτει, ἡ δε πιμελη οἵα ελαιον απ' αυτο*ɹ *λειβεται. Τουθ' ἱεραν εσθητα ποιουνται, και ει τις ἑτερος παρα τους Ινδους τουτους ανασπῳη αυτο, ου μεθιεται ἡ γη του εριου.* Philost., Apoll. Vita, III, xv, p. 54.

them; and secondly: for the monsters he so carelessly attributes to Strabo—and of which so far as I know Strabo is innocent—had Hierocles but told of them as of something of which he had heard, these ten-headed and four-hand-and-footed men would have been identified with the statues of Ràvana and Ardhavan,[55] and adduced as an evidence of a visit to India. As it is, we know him as an untrustworthy writer, and we have only his own word for it that he was ever there.

We have next an account of India[56] written at the close of the fourth or beginning of the fifth century and drawn up apparently at the request either of Palladius, or of Lausius to whom Palladius inscribed his Historia Lausiaca. Its writer states that he went to India with Moses, Bishop of Adule; but found the heat such, the coldest water being set boiling in a few minutes,[57] that

[55] *Vide* plates 54 and 24, Moor's Hindoo Pantheon. And as belonging to the popular legends we hear in the Mahabharata of men: "à trois yeux, plusieurs à un seul œil...les monopedes," etc., II, 54, Fouche's Tr.

[56] Of this tract there are two versions, a Greek addressed to some eminent personage not named, and a Latin attributed to Ambrosius and addressed to Palladius. In the Greek version the author himself visits India, *τα ακρωτηρια μονον*, p. 2; in the Latin it is his brother, Musæus Dolenorum Episcopus, who traverses Serica, now on this side the Ganges, p. 58, where are the trees that give out not leaves but very fine wool, and where he sees the stone columns raised to Alexander; and who at length reaches Ariana, which he finds burnt up by the heat, and so hot that water is seen boiling in the vessels that hold it, and who then gives up his journey and returns to Europe. In this first part I have preferred the Greek, but afterwards I oftener follow the Latin version as the more full and intelligible.—Palladius, ed. Bissæus.

[57] Ctesias of the Indian sea: *το δε ανω αυτης...θερμον ειναι ὥστε μη*

he very quickly returned. He had little to say of his own knowledge; but in the course of his travels he had fallen in with, and heard a good deal about India from, a scholar of the Thebaid, a lawyer, who disgusted with his profession had thrown it up and set out to see the world and more especially the land of the Brahmans. This man recounted, that in the company of a priest he took ship in the Red Sea for the Bay of Adule. Here he landed and went to visit the city and pushed on inland as far as Auxume,[58] where he met with some Indian, *i.e.* Arab, merchants about to proceed for India: he

ιχθυν ζηναι. Photius Bib., p. 144. Strabo, of the heat in India says, lizards crossing the road are burnt up, and water quickly warms, p. 730. This however may have been an extravagant mode of speech merely, for Sidonius, almost a cotemporary of Palladius, when urging his friend Donatius to leave the city, says, "jam non solum calet unda sed coquitur." Epist. II, 2.

[58] I here follow neither the Greek nor Latin version. The Greek: διαπλευσας μετα πρεσβυτερου ταυτην θαλασσαν κατελαβε πρωτον Αδουλιν ειτα την Αυξουμην εν ῇ ην βασιλισκος των Ινδων, vii, Pseudo-Callisthenes, Müller, p. 102, and afterwards Απο της Αυξουμης εὑρων τινας πλοιαριῳ διαβαινοντας Ινδους εμποριας χαριν, επειραθην ενδοτερον απελθειν, viii, p. 103. The Latin: "In rubrio mari navem conscendens navigavit primo sinum Adulicum et Adulitarum oppidum vidit, mox Aromata promontorium et Troglodytarum emporium penetravit; hinc et Auxumitarum loca attigit, unde solvens... Muzirim pervenit, *ib.*, 103. The Greek version is evidently defective, for it never brings our scholar to India at all, while the Latin traces out an itinerary confused and improbable. For after leaving Adule, our traveller makes for Aromata, the most eastern point of Africa, and the emporium of the Troglodytes;—but "Aduliton...maximum hic emporium Troglodytarum etiam Ethiopum;" (Plin., iv, 34)—or suppose it some port in the Adulitic Bay, still he is always retracing his steps till he comes to Auxume, an inland town (διεστηκεναι την Αδουλιν της Αυξουμεως πεντεκαιδεκα ἡμερων ὁδος. Nonnosus, p. 480, Hist. Bizant.), whence he sets sail for India.

joined them, and together they crossed the Ocean. After several days' voyage they reached Muziris, the chief port on this side the Ganges and the residence of a petty Indian rajah. At Muziris our traveller stayed some time, and occupied himself in studying the soil and climate of the place and the customs and manners of its inhabitants. He also made inquiries about Ceylon and the best mode of getting there; but did not care to undertake the voyage when he heard of the dangers of the Sinhalese Channel, of the thousand isles, the Maniolai, which impede its navigation, and the loadstone rocks[59] which bring disaster and wreck on all iron-bound ships. They told him, however, of this island, of its happy climate[60] and its long-lived inhabitants, of its four satrapies and its great king, king of all the Indias,[61] of whom the petty sovereigns of the coast were but the governors. He knew too of its great trade, of its markets thronged with merchants from

[59] Ptolemy knows of the Maniolai and the loadstone rocks, but limits their number to ten, and throws them forward some degrees east of Ceylon, vii, p. 221; and before Ceylon places a group of 1378 small islands, vii, 4, p. 213. And Masoudi, who had traversed this sea, says that ships sailing on it were not fastened with iron nails, its waters so wasted them, p. 374.

[60] So Fa-hian: "Ce pays est tempéré, on n'y connait pas la différence de l'hiver et de l'été. Les herbes et les arbres sont toujours verdoyants. L'ensémencement des champs est suivant la volonté des gens." Tr. de Rémusat, c. xxxviii., p. 332.

[61] *Εν ταυτῃ δε τῃ νησῳ και ὁ μεγας βασιλευς κατοιχει των Ινδων, ᾧ παντες οἱ βασιλικοι της χωρας εκεινης ὑποκεινται ὡς σατραπαι*, de Bramanibus, p. 3. "Huic quatuor moderantur ... satrapes, inter quos unus est maximus cui...cæteri obediunt."—Latin version. These satrapies would be those of Jafna, Malaya, Rohuna, with that of Anarajapura as the chief.

Ethiopia, Persia, and Auxume (Latin version only); of its five great navigable rivers,[62] and perpetual fruit-bearing trees, palms, cocoa, and smaller aromatic nuts. And he had heard how its sheep were covered not with wool but hair, gave much milk, and had broad tails; and how their skins were prettily worked up into stuffs, the only clothing of the people, who would on feast-days eat both mutton and goat's flesh, though their usual food was milk, rice, and fruit.

And the scholar further said: "I tried to penetrate into the interior of their country, and got as far as the Besadæ, a people with large heads and long untrimmed hair, dwarfish and feeble but active and good climbers, who occupy themselves with gathering the pepper from the low and stunted trees on which it grows. They seized on me; and their king, the consumption of whose palace was one measure of corn a year (the year in the Latin version only), whence got I know not, gave me as slave to a baker. With him I stayed six years, and in this time learned their language and a good deal about the neighbouring nations. At length the great king of Ceylon[63] heard of me, and out of respect for the

[62] Ptolemy likewise gives five rivers to Ceylon, ut sup. the Soana, Ayanos, Baracos, Ganges, and Phasis; and after him Marcianus Heracleënsis, Geog. Minor. Didot, p. 534.

[63] This tract is imperfect. The Greek version sends our traveller direct from Auxume into the interior of Africa, where he was not likely to hear anything about the Brahmans; the Latin on the other hand after saying every thing to dissuade him from the voyage to Ceylon, suddenly and without a hint that he had left Muziris sets him down in the midst of its angry and excited population. But it is rarely consistent with itself, for 1st, it describes Ceylon on hearsay as an island of the blest, " in quâ sunt illi quibus

Roman name and fear of the Roman power, ordered me to be set free, and severely punished the petty rajah who had enslaved me."

Of the Brahmans this scholar reported, that they were not a society like our monks but a race, born[64] Brahmans. They lived he said near the Ganges and in a state of nature. They went naked, wandering in the woods, and sleeping on leaves. They had no domestic animals, tilled no land, and were without iron or house or fire or bread or wine; but then they breathed a pleasant, healthful air, wonderfully clear. They worshipped God, and had no slight, though not a thorough, knowledge of the ways of Providence. They prayed always turning,

Beatorum nomen est," and seems to countenance that description, and yet the people our scholar fell among he found a weak, hideous, and inhospitable race. 2nd. It speaks of pepper as the chief produce of the island: "piper ibi nascitur in magnâque colligitur copiâ;" but though pepper certainly grows in Ceylon, it is not and never has been among its staple productions (Ptolemy, viii, p. 212), nor to gather it the occupation of its people. But from their name and description, Sir E. Tennent (Ceylon) has identified the Besadæ with the Sinhalese Veddahs. Let me observe that the name is unknown to the Latin version and belongs to the Greek, which expressly states that our scholar never went to Ceylon: *ου γαρ δεδυνηται ουδ' αυτος εις την νησόν εισελθειν*, lib. III, vii, *ib.*, and appears there in several shapes as Thebaids, Bethsiads, and Bethsads. 2ndly, that the Besadæ are in Ptolemy a people living in the extreme north of India. 3rdly, that the Besadæ, except in those great features common to the ill-fed barbarous races, bear no resemblance to any Sinhalese people. For though like the Veddahs they are puny, ill-shaped, live in caves and recognize a domestic chief, the Veddahs unlike them have no king living in a palace, no political existence, and no arts such as the existence of a baker implies.

64 *Vide* from Bardesanes, *supra*, pp. 152-3.

but not superstitiously, to the East. They ate whatever came to hand, nuts and wild herbs, and drank water. Their wives, located on the other side of the Ganges, they visited during July and August,[65] their coldest months, and remained with them forty days.[66] But as soon as the wife had borne her husband two children, or after five years if she were barren, the Brahman ceased to have intercourse with her.[67]

The Ganges is infested by the Odonto, a fearful monster, but which disappears during the Brahman

65 "In India...December, January, and February are their warmest months; our summer being their winter; July and August are their winter."—Masoudi's *Meadows of Gold*, p. 344. Though Masoudi confirms the statement of our traveller, in fact, the summer in India corresponds with our summer.

66 Among the Buddhists: "Quand venait la saison des pluies ...les Religieux pouvaient cesser la vie vagabonde des mendiants. Il leur était permis de se retirer dans des demeures fixes. Cela s'appelait séjourner pendant la Varcha: c'est-à-dire, pendant les quatre mois que dure la saison pluvieuse." Burnouf, Hist. du Boud., p. 285. The rainy season, however, is not the same on the East and West of the Ghauts. *See* too in the Mahabharata, the observance of times and seasons in the relations between the Brahmans and the widows of the Kshatryas exterminated by them. I, p. 268, Fouche's tr.

67 Suidas, s. v. Βραχμανες, has, with a slight alteration, copied this account of the Brahmans. He says "they are a most pious people (εθνος), without possessions and living in an island of the ocean given them by God; that Alexander came there and erected a pillar (the bronze pillar of Philostratus, As. Jour., xviii, p. 83) with the inscription 'I, the great king Alexander came thus far;' that the Makrobioi live here to 150, the air is so pure...The men thus dwell in the parts adjoining the ocean, but the women beyond the Ganges, to whom they pass over in the months of July, etc." The island of the Indian Makrobioi is probably borrowed from the Atlantic Erythia, where dwelt the Ethiopian

pairing months, and by serpents seventy cubits long. The ants are in these parts a palm, and the scorpions a cubit in length; and hence the difficulty of getting there. The tract then concludes with a series of letters, which purport to have passed between Dandamis, the chief of the Brahmans, and Alexander the Great, and which might have been written anywhere and by anybody, except one who had learned to think or was accustomed to command.[68]

Our author's account of his own experience of India, its great heat, is so absurdly impossible, that we lose all faith in his veracity. I believe neither in his own story, nor in that of his travelled lawyer who seems to me introduced merely to give reality and interest to the narrative. In the narrative itself we first hear of the loadstone rocks attached to the Maniolai, as guarding the coasts of Ceylon. These rocks, which the voy-

Makrobioi according to Eustatius. Com. in Dion. Per., § 558, p. 325, II, Geog. Min.

Ητοι μεν ναιουσι βοοτροφον αμφ' Ερυθειαν
Ατλαντος περι χευμα θεουδεες Αιθιοπηες,
Μακροβιων υἱηες αμυμονες, οἱ ποθ' ἱκοντο
Γηρυονος μετα ποτμον αγηνορος. Diony. Perieget., 558, etc., *ib.*

[68] Of cotemporaries of Palladius, who in their works have noticed India, I pass over Marcianus Heracleënsis (A.D. 401), who as a geographer had necessarily much to say about it, but who as the mere copyist of Ptolemy principally, and occasionally of other writers (Geog. Græc. Min. Pf., p. 133, I, ed. Didot, conf. Lassen, u. s., 288, III), added nothing to the existing knowledge of India: and Justin, Hist. Philip. (Smith's Biog. Dict., s. v., and Ætat. Justini and Testamenta, Valpy's Delphin ed.), to whom we are indebted for much of the little we know of the Greek rule in Bactria and India, but whose history as an epitome of that of Trogus Pompeius belongs really to the Augustan age.

ages of Sinbad have since made so famous, probably owed their origin to some Arab merchant, some Scythianus, who while he amused the imaginations of his wondering customers, at the same time fenced round with terror the trading grounds whence he obtained his most precious wares. Here too we read of a Sinhalese Empire with dominions extending far into the interior of India, and here only; for the Sinhalese annals show us Ceylon ever open to Tamil inroads, sometimes subdued or at best struggling for independence, and at other times prosperous and powerful, but never even then claiming rule over any part of India.[69] And here also we have an account of the Brahman marriage, which, though in one particular, divorce for barrenness, not altogether incorrect, is as a whole quite opposed as well to all we know of Brahman habits as to that ideal of Brahman life on which the Laws of Menu so willingly dwell.[70]

[69] This tract was written about A.D. 400. If the scholar ever existed, he must have travelled and obtained his knowledge of Ceylon some time in the last half of the fourth century, during the reigns of either Buddha Da'sa, from A.D. 339 to 368, or of Upatissa II, A.D. 368-410. From the Mahawanso, pp. 237-9, and the Rajavali, pp. 241-2, we gather, that Ceylon was at this time in a flourishing condition; but we find nothing which can lead us to suppose that its kings held dominion in India. Fa-hian also was in Ceylon about A.D. 410, and his description of the island quite corroborates the statements of its Sacred Books. Foe-koue-ki, xxxviii, 9. Upham's Sacred Books of Ceylon, l. c., and Turnour's Appendix to the Mahawanso, p. 72.

[70] For the marriage duties and the respect due to women, v. Menu III, 45-8 and 55-62. For the marriage duties of women, *ib.* 153, 160, and ix, 74. The ideal of marriage: "Then only is a man perfect when he consists of three persons united, his wife,

About this same time (A.D. 360-420) appeared the Dionysiacs, a poem in forty-eight books, written by Nonnos of Panoplis in Egypt, to celebrate the triumphs of Bacchus and his conquest of India. The first eight books tell of Cadmus, and the loves of Jupiter, and the jealousy of Juno. The ninth, tenth, eleventh, and twelfth recount the birth and education of Bacchus, and his love for, and grief at the death of, the youthful satyr Ampelos;[71] and how Ampelos was then changed into a vine, and how of the grapes Bacchus made wine and drank it, and threw off his old sorrow.[72] In the thirteenth book Iris[73] from Jove calls on Bacchus to drive the arrogant and lawless Indians from Asia, and by great deeds and labours to gain a place in Olympus. It then enumerates the Centaurs, Satyrs, Cyclops, and peoples which gather round the Bacchic standard. In the fourteenth and fifteenth books Bacchus is in

himself, and his son, and thus learned Brahmans have announced this maxim—The husband is even one person with his wife," *ib.* 45. Consequent upon this "A barren wife may be superseded by another in the ninth year, she whose children are all dead in the tenth, she who brings forth only daughters in the eleventh," *ib.* 81.

71 *Ουδε ἑ καλλος ελειπε, και ει θανεν· ὡς Σατυρος δε*
κειτο νεκυς, γελοωντι πανεικελος, οἱαπερ αιει
χειλεσιν αφθογγοισι χεων μελιηδυν αοιδην. xi, 250.

72 *...προτερας δ' ερριψε μεριμνας*
φαρμακον ἡβητηρος εχων ευοδμον οπωρην. 290, xii.

73 He sends Iris to bid him—

οφρα δικης αδιδακτον ὑπερφιαλων γενος Ινδων
Ασιδος εξελασειεν. 5, xiii.

But unlike the Iris of Homer, who always strictly delivers her message, she somewhat varies it, and bids him—

ευσεβιης αδιδακτον αἰστωσαι γενος Ινδων.

Bithynia near the lake Astracis,[74] and he then and there changes its waters into wine, encounters and makes drunk and captive an Indian army under Astrais (αστηρ); and afterwards (seventeenth book) marches into Syria and defeats another and more powerful one commanded by the son-in-law of the Indian king Deriades,[75] Orontes,[76] who in despair kills himself and

[74] ὁ περι Νικομαδειαν κολπος Ασταχηος καλειται. Strabo, xii, 43. Nonnos, ed. de Marcellus, N. N., 100, xiv, 7, xiv.

[75] Δηριαδης, from δηρις, strife, says Nonnos. The name is probably borrowed from the Bassarics of Dionysius, for Eustatius in his Comm. on the Periegesis (606 v, p. 332, II, Geog. Græ. Min.) observes that the Erythræan king was Deriades, an Erythræan τῳ γενει, but who went to India and bravely opposed Bacchus. And then if Dionysius, as Müller is inclined to think, lived in the first century, it may possibly be either a translation or adaptation of the Sanskrit Duryodhana, from "dur," bad, and "yodna," strife, as Professor Wilson in a paper on the Dionysiacs of Nonnos, As. Res., xvii, suggests, and may have become known in Greece through the Greeks who had visited India or the Hindus who visited Alexandria. Or as Duryodhana is the oldest of the Kaurava princes and one of the heroes of the Mahabharata, his name and some notion of the Epic may (spite of Strabo's hint to the contrary, L. xv, 3) have been transmitted to Greece by the Bactrian Greeks, whose relations with India were many and intimate. But in this case it is surely somewhat strange that of all this poem only one name, and that scarcely recognisable, and not the greatest nor the easiest fitted to Grecian lips, has found a place in Grecian literature.

[76] Orontes, Greek form of the Persian Arvanda from "arvat," flowing, Lassen, III, 147, or of the Egyptian Anrata, Rougé, tr. of a poem on the exploits of Rameses by Pentaour. Of this river both Wilson, u. s., p. 610, and Lassen observe that in the belief of Syria confirmed by the oracle of Klaros, it took its name from an Indian chief who died there, and whose coffin and bones indicating a height of eleven cubits were found when the Romans diverted or canalised the river. Pausanias, viii, 2, 3, and see Strabo, xvi, II, 7, p. 639.

gives his name to the neighbouring river, ever since called the Orontes. After this battle Blemmys, king of the Erythræan Indians but subject to Deriades, submits to Bacchus and settles with his people in Ethiopia.[77] The eighteenth book shows us Staphylos, the Assyrian monarch, with Methe and Botrus, his wife and son, doing honour to and feasting Bacchus in their palace, whence after a drunken bout Bacchus goes on his way Indiaward, and at the same time despatches a herald to Deriades, and threatens war unless his gifts and orgies be accepted. The nineteenth book relates the death of Staphylos and the games held in his honour. In the twentieth, Bacchus reaches Arabia, but in the forest of Nyssa, while all unguarded and defenceless, is set upon by Lycurgus, and compelled to take refuge in the Red Sea. The twenty-first book tells of his ambassador's reception at the Indian court, and of the scorn with which Deriades rejects the proffered gift of Bacchus. "He cares for no son of Jove," he says, "his sword and his buckler are his wine and drink, and his gods earth and water."[78] Bacchus learns this answer while frolicking with the mountain nymphs.[79] He prepares for war,

[77] Eustatius, u. s., on the authority either of Nonnos or the Bassarics, gives them the same origin: *Βλεμμυες οὑτω καλουμενοι απο Βλεμμυος τινος, ὁς ὑποστρατηγων τῳ βασιλει Δηριαδῃ κατα Διονυσου συνεπολεμεσε.* (Com. v. 220. p. 255, *ib.*)

[78] . . . . *Δηριαδης γαρ*
ου μαθεν ουρανιων μακαρων χορον, ουδε γεραιρει
Ηελιον και Ζηνα.
. . . .
οινος εμος πελεν εγχος· ὁ δ' αυ ποτος εστι βοειη. 256.
. . . .
μουνοι εμε γεγαασι θεοι και Γαια και Ὑδωρ. 261, xxi.

[79] . . . *ορειασι μιγνυτο Νυμφαις.* 277, xxi.

and calls on the Arab Rhadamanes to equip a fleet and attack the Indians by sea. He himself with his army passes over the Caucasus.[80] In the twenty-second book we have the first battle on Indian ground. Near the Hydaspes in a thick forest the Indian forces under Thoreus lie in ambush but are betrayed to Bacchus, who by a pretended flight draws them out into the open and completely routs them, and then crosses the river to combat with Deriades. Deriades by the advice of Thoreus retreats on his elephants within the city walls. Attis on the part of Rhea presents Bacchus with arms forged by Vulcan, and foretells that not till the seventh year shall he destroy the Indian capital.[81] In the meanwhile Deriades at the treacherous instigation of Minerva marshals his hosts; and the twenty-sixth book gives the names of the cities, islands, and peoples, with their chiefs, which form his army. And on the contents of this book as specially occupied with India we shall dwell at some length. At the summons of Deriades came Agraios (*αγρα*, the chase) and Phlegios (*φλεγω*, to burn) the two sons of Eulæus (river, Ulaï? Marcellus) and with them those who dwell in Kusa[82] and Bagia, near the broad

80 The passage scarce occupies three lines—

και ταχυς ηλασε διφρον Εωιον εις κλιμα γαιης
. . . . αμφι δε πετρην
Καυκασιην λοφοεντα διαστειχων κενωνα . . .
Ηωης παραμειβε πεζαν. 307, xxi.

81 ου γαρ πριν πολεμου τελος εσσεται, εισοκε χαρμης
ἕκτον αναπλησωσιν ετος τετραζυγες Ὡραι.
. . . .
εσσομενῳ δε
ἑβδοματῳ λυκαβαντι διαρραισεις πολιν Ινδων. 363-7, xxv.

82 Those who would identify the different places in the text I

muddy waters of the Indian Zorambos; the people, too, of the well-turreted Rhodoe, the craggy Propanisos, and the isle Gerion,[83] where not the mothers, but the fathers, suckle their children. There, too, were found the inhabitants of the lofty Sesindos and of Gazos[84] girt about with impregnable linen-woven bulwarks. Near them were ranged the brave Dardæ[85] and the Prasian force with the gold-covered tribes of the Sarangi,[86] who live on vegetables and grind them down instead of corn. Then came the curly-haired Zabians with their wise ruler Stassanor; then Morrheus[87] and Didnasos eager to avenge the death of his son Orontes. Now followed the many-languaged Indians from well-built sunny Æthra,

refer to M. de Marcellus' notes to the twenty-sixth book of his edition of Nonnos. They will at the same time see how he has accommodated, and I think not unfairly, the names to the Geographies of Ptolemy, etc.

[83] *Γηρειαν, Ροδοην τε και οἱ λινοτειχεα Γαζον.* Stephan, Byzant., s. v., *Γαζος* from the third book of the Bassarics of Dionysius.

[84] This description of Gazos is borrowed from the *Βασσαρικα* of Dionysius (n. 12, xxvi, B. de Marcellus), and from the same source he probably took his account of Gereion and the Sarangii, for Nonnos is of those poets who repeat but do not invent. Stephanos Byzantinus by the way frequently quotes the Bassarics of Dionysius as a historical authority, e. g., s. v. *Βλεμυες* and *Γαζος*.

[85] *Δαρδαι Ινδικον εθνος ὑπο Δηριαδῃ πολεμησαν Διονυσῳ ὡς Διονυσιος εν γε Βασσαρικων*, Steph., s. v. *Δαρδας*.

[86] *Σαραγγαι δε εἱματα μεν βεβαμμενα ενεπρεπον εχοντες.* Herod., vii, c. 67.

[87] Lassen, u. s., derives Morrheus from *μορρεα*, the material of the vasa murrhina. Prof. W. H. Wilson, *ib.*, suggests Maharajah. Neither derivation seems to me satisfactory,—the first strange and far-fetched, the second scarcely applicable, for Morrheus is no rajah, a soldier of fortune merely, though of high birth, an autocthon: *ηλιβατου Τυφωνος εχων αυτοχθονα φυλην.* 177, xxxiv.

and they who hold the jungles (λασιωνα) of Asene and the reedy Andonides, the burning Nicæa, the calm Malana, and the water-girt plains of Patalene. Next them marched the serried ranks (πυκιναι) of the Dosareans and the hairy-breasted Sabaroi, and Phringos, Aspetos, Tanyclos, Hippouros, and Egretios, then the Ouatecetoi,[88] who sleep lying on their long ears, led on by their chiefs. Tectaphus also was there at the head of his Bolingians,[89] Tectaphus, whom when in prison his daughter suckled and saved from death. From the earth's extremity Giglon, Thoureus, and Hippalmas brought up the Arachotes and the Drangiai, who cover with dust[90] those whom the sword has slain. Habraatos commanded the archers, shamed by the loss of his hair cut off by order of Deriades, and a disgrace among the Indians; he came on slowly and perforce with hate in his heart. He ruled the savage Scyths, the brave Ariainoi, the Zoaroi, the Arenoi, the Caspeiri,[91] the Arbians of the Hysparos, and the Arsanians whose women are wondrously skilled in weaving. Near them were ranged the Cirradioi used to naval warfare, but in

88 So Scylax. Tzetzes Chil., vii, Hist., 144, l. 635.

89 Και τοτε Βωλιγγησι μετ' ανδρασι Τεκταφος ωρτο.—Bassar., Dionys., Stephanos Byz., s. v. Βωλιγγα.

90 "The Dandis and Dasnamis Sectaries of Siva...put their dead into coffins and bury them, or commit them to some sacred stream."—H. H. Wilson, Religious Sects of the Hindus, As. Res., xvii, 176, and in a note: "In the south the ascetic followers of Siva and Vishnu bury their dead (Dubois), so do the Vaishnava (Varangis?), and Sanyasis in the north of India" (see Ward), all the castes in the south that wear the Lingam—*ib.*

91 εν δε τε Κασπειροι ποσι κλειτοι, εν δ' Αριηνοι. Stephanos, s. v. Κασπειρος, from the Bassar. Dionys.

boats of skins; their chiefs were Thyamis and Olkaros, sons of Tharseros the rower. Under Phylites, son of Hipparios, came a swarm of men from Arizanteia, where a certain bushy tree from its green leaves distils sweet honey,[92] while from its branches the Horion[93] pours forth a song like the swan's for melody, and the yellow purple-winged Catreus utters its shrill cry, prophetic of rain. Then followed the Sibai, the people of Hydara, and the Carmanian hosts, with their leaders Kolkaros and Astrais, the sons of Lôgos. The three hundred isles at the mouths of the Indus sent their contingent under Ripsasos, a giant in stature (*εχων ινδαλμια Γιγαντων*, v. 248). Aretos too with his five sons born deaf and dumb obeyed the call of Deriades, with them were ranged the shield-bearing warriors of Pyle, Kôlalla and Goryandos; while under Phylates marched those who dwell in the woody Osthe, mother of elephants, and near them their neighbours from Euthydimeia, speaking another tongue. The Derbicei, the Ethiopians, the Sacæ, the Bactrians, and the Blemyes, also joined the army of Deriades.

The contest then begins. The Gods, as was their

92 *Εστι δε και δενδρα παρ' αυτοις μελι ποιουντα ανευ ζωων.* Strabo, xv, I, 20, Geog. Min. Græc., p. 620, ii.

93 Clitarchus, quoted by Strabo, speaking of the movable aviaries belonging to the Indian kings, says that they are filled with large leaved trees, on the branches of which are perched all sorts of tame birds, and that of these the sweetest songster is the horion, the most beautiful the catreus: *ὧν ευφωνοτατον μεν...τον ὡριωνα, λαμπροτατον δε κατα οψιν και πλειστην εχοντα ποικιλιαν τον κατρεα*, xv, I, p. 690, and Fragmenta Clitarchi, 18 and 18a, Scriptores Rev. Alex., Didot's ed.

wont, take each his side. Jupiter, Apollo, Vulcan, and Minerva, declare for the Bassarids; Juno with Mars, Ceres, and Neptune, for Deriades and his Indians and from no interested motives, for throughout Deriades stoutly disavows all allegiance to them. The fight is carried on with various fortune. Now the Indians flee before Bacchus and his crew aided by the gods; and now, headed by Mars, Morrheus, and Deriades, or Deriades' wife and daughters, and befriended by the stratagems of Juno,[94] they drive him from the field. At length night intervenes (XXXVII.), and Greeks and Indians bury their dead: the Greeks with funeral piles and games, the Indians with tearless eyes, for for them death but frees the soul from earthly chains, and sends it back to its old starting point, to run afresh life's circle of change.[95]

Six years have now passed away, and Rhea has long ago announced that the seventh year and a naval battle shall put an end to the war. The Rhadamanes arrive with their ships. Deriades collects his fleet and goes forth to meet them.[96] The fight is long and doubtful,

[94] Juno drives Bacchus mad. Eustatius in his Commentary on Dionysius, v. 976, alludes to this madness, probably from the Bassarics: Μαινεται Διονυσος Ἡρας προνοιᾳ. Geog. Min., II, p. 386. It is also mentioned by Pseudo Plutarchus, de Fluv. et Mont. Nom., Geog. Min. Græc., II, p. 663.

[95] ομμασιν ακλαυτοισιν εταρχυσαντο θανοντας,
οἷα βιου βροτεου γαιηια δεσμα φυγοντας,
ψυχης πεμπομενης ὅθεν ηλυθε, κυκλαδι σειρῃ
νυσσαν ες αρχαιην. xxxvii, 3 v. v.

[96] Morrheus, xxxvi, speaks of the Rhadamanes as ship-builders:
εισαιω Ραδαμανας, ὅτι δρυτομῳ τινι τεχνῃ
νηας ετεχνησαντο φυγοπτολεμῳ Διονυσῳ. 414 v. v.
but boasts of Indian skill on the sea: Ινδοι

till at length the Cabeirian Eurymedon sends a fire ship into the midst of the Indians, and a general conflagration ensues. Deriades (XL B., 75) escapes, renews the contest on land, and engages in a single combat with Bacchus; but, affrighted by the presence of Minerva,[97] he flies towards the Hydaspes, and, struck by the thyrsus of his adversary, falls and dies in the river. The city and India submit to the conqueror; and Bacchus having raised a monument to those of his troops who have perished distributes the spoils among the survivors, and then returns to Lydia. The remaining eight books tell of the loves and wars and vengeance of Bacchus, and the poem concludes with his apotheosis.[98]

Notwithstanding the probability that through the Bactrian Greeks some knowledge of the Hindu Epics may have reached Greece and our author, I am inclined to think that they were wholly unknown to him.

I. Because his poem speaks of an Indian Empire extending to the shores of the Mediterranean and Red Seas, while the Indian books show us the tide of Indian

---

. . . . Ινδοι γαρ εθημονες εισι κυδοιμου
ειναλιου, και μαλλον αριστευουσι θαλασση
η χθονι δηριοωντες. 465 v.v.

97 Αθηνη
δαιμονι βοτρυεντι παριστατο· δερκομενου δε
δειματι θεσπεσιῳ λυτο γουνατα Δεριαδηος. xl, 74 v.v.

. . . .

98 και θεος αμπελοεις, πατρωιον αιθερα βαινων,
πατρι συν ευωδινι μιης εψαυσε τραπεζης,
και βροτεην μετα δαιτα, μετα προτερην χυσιν οινου,
ουρανιον πιε νεκταρ αρειοτεροισι κυπελλοις
συνθρονος Απολλωνι, συνεστιος υἱεῖ Μαιης. xlviii.

domination rolling ever south and east, and if westward,[99] never passing the Indus.

II. Because, though the names of the Indian cities and peoples in the Dionysiacs, as edited by the Comte de Marcellus, pretty fairly correspond with those given by Ptolemy, Pliny, and Strabo, and are thus accounted for, the names of its Indian chiefs are with but few exceptions, as Morrheus, Orontes, etc., purely Greek.

III. Because his Indian facts, manners, and customs are few, and are:

1st. Such as were long before his time well known to the Roman world; as when he tells of the tearless eyes with which the Indians bury their dead, and of their belief in metempsychosis; and shows them worshipping earth, water, and the sun, and marshalling their elephants for war, and calling their Brahmans to counsel, or employing them as physicians.[1]

2ndly. Such as were not so well known, but for which authority may be found in the Indian books; as when

[99] But compare Gildemeister, Scrip. Arab. de Rebus Indicis, pp. 2, 8, 9. The Mahabharata also knows of world-conquerors who necessarily extend their dominion westward; thus for Yuddhistara, his brother conquered Kalamankas, "La charmante cité d'Akair et la capitale des Yavanas," p. 457; and Nakaula five kingdoms, the Civis, Trigattas, Ambashthas, Milasas, and Karpatas, p. 439; also the Varvaras, Kivatas, Yavanas, Cakas, 440, II, and again 459, v. iv, but these are geographical names merely; there is no indication of any permanent occupation.

[1] And the Brahmans heal the wound with magic chaunt just as in Homer; thus when Morrheus is wounded—

> Ὀφρα μεν ενθεον ἑλκος, ὁ μιν λαχε, δαιμονιη χειρ
> λυσιπονου Βραχμηνος ακεσσατο Φοιβαδι τεχνῃ,
> θεσπεσιῃ μαγον ὑμνον ὑποτρυζοντος αοιδῃ. xxxix, 369.

Deriades disgraces Habraatos by depriving him of his hair—thus Vasichta punishes the Sacas by cutting off the half of their hair, and the Yavanas by shaving their heads;[2] and chooses two soldiers of fortune[3] for his sons-in-law—thus their fathers give Sita and Draupati,[4] the one to the strongest, the other to the most skilful, bowman; and as when Morrheus neglects and deserts his wife, daughter of Deriades, for a Bacchante—thus the Hindu Theatre[5] affords more than one example of kings and Brahmans in love with women other than their wives, as in the Toy-cart, the Necklace, the Statue,[6] etc. But however warranted by Indian custom these several acts, as presented by Nonnos, scarcely associate themselves with Hindu life, certainly not more than the name of Deriades with that of Duryodhana, though they sufficiently remind us of the Greeks of the Lower Empire.[7]

[2] Harivansa, I, p. 68. Langlois, tr., Or. Tr. Fund; and Wilson, Hindu Theatre, 332, II.

[3] Of Morrheus—

νυμφιος ακτημων, αρετῃ δ'εκτησατο νυμφην. xxxiv, 163.

And when Deriades married his daughters, all gifts

. . . . *αγελας δε βοων και πωεα μηλων*
Δηριαδης απεειπε· και εγρεμοθοισι μαχηταις
Θυγατερων εζευξεν αδωροδοκους ὑμεναιους. *ib.*, 169, 170.

[4] With a certain reserve "Un roi puissant ne doit introduire dans un alliance qu'un mortel de la plus haute renommée," says the father of Draupadi. Mahab. II, p. 167.

[5] Wilson's Hindu Theatre, pp. 326 and 364, II.

[6] See the several plays in Wilson's Hindu Theatre, and some observations of Wilson's on the plurality of wives among the Hindus, II, 359.

[7] I do not however know that this inappreciation of Indian life is an evidence of Nonnos's ignorance of the Hindu books, only of

3rdly. Such as are unsupported by Hindu authority. Thus Deriades shows himself skilled in the niceties of Greek mythology, and his wife and daughter Bacchanal-like rush to the battle;[8] and, as if India were deficient in wonders, the fathers in Gereion suckle their children, and Gazos is impregnable with its cotton bulwarks.

The Topographia Christiana (A.D. 535) next claims our attention. Its author, Cosmas, who had been a merchant, and who as a merchant had travelled over the greater part of the then known world, betook himself in his latter years to a monastery, and there, though weak of sight and ailing in body, and not regularly educated,[9] set himself in this work to prove, that our world was no sphere, but a solid plane.[10] He describes it, and illustrates this and indeed all his descriptions by drawings,[11] as a parallelogram lying lengthways east and west, and sloping up very gradually

his want of imagination. With some play of fancy and the faculty of verse Nonnos is essentially without the poet's power. His personages are all conventional, and I suspect that no knowledge of India, not even had he trudged through it on foot, would have made them more Indian, more real, and more lifelike.

[8] In the Hanuman Nataka, nevertheless, the wife of Ravana, to animate his drooping courage, offers

> "If you command, by your side I march
> Fearless to fight, for I too am a Kshatrya."
>
> Hind. Theat., II, p. 371.

[9] *ασθενων ἡμων τυγχανοντων τῳ τε σωματι, ταις τε οψεσι...πιεζομενων—αλλως τε και της εξωθεν εγκυκλιου παιδιας λειπομενων και ρητορικης τεχνης αμοιρουντων.* Lib. II, p. 124. Montfaucon, Nova Collectio Patrum, vol. ii.

[10] *Vide* Prolog., II, pp. 114-5.

[11] *Vide* the Plates at the beginning of Montfaucon's Nova Collectio Patrum, v. ii, Pl. 1.

from its base, but more gradually on its south and west than on its north and east sides, into a huge conical mountain round which sun and moon run their courses, and bring with them day and night.[12] All about this great mass of earth[13] he places an impassable ocean, communicating with it by four gulfs, the Mediterranean, Arabic, Persian, and Caspian Seas,[14] but eternally separating it from a trans-oceanic land, where was and is Eden, the happy birthplace of our race, and whence rise sheer up those mighty walls which arch themselves into the firmament above us. Written with such a theme, enforced by many quotations from scripture misunderstood, and the authority of fathers and philosophers, worthless on this point, the Topographia Christiana is but dull reading, and would long since have been forgotten had it not here and there been lighted up by some sketch of Cosmas's own travels, some notice of what had fallen either under his own observation or that of other trustworthy and competent witnesses, and always told with a simplicity and guarded truthfulness which place him in the first rank of those who know how to speak of what they have seen, and repeat what they have heard, just as seen and heard, without exaggeration and without ornament.

Cosmas had a personal knowledge of three of the four

[12] *Vide* pp. 133-4 and notes, *ib.*

[13] The length he computes to be of four hundred mansions of thirty miles each, its breadth of about two hundred, *vide* p. 138.

[14] Lib. iv, p. 188, and pp. 186-7, and p. 132 : *εισι δε εν ταυτῃ τῃ γῃ εισβαλλοντες εκ του Ωκεανου...κολποι τεσσαρες·...οὑτοι γαρ μονοι οἱ κολποι πλεονται· αδυνατου ὑπαρχοντος του Ωκεανου πλεεσθαι.* P. 132.

inland seas—the Caspian[15] he had not visited. As an occasional resident at Alexandria (p. 124), he knew the Mediterranean well. He had sailed down the Red Sea from Œla and Alexandria to Adule;[16] he had passed the Straits of Bab-el-Mandeb, and had been within sight of, though he did not land at, the Island of Socotora;[17] and thence, if he ever visited India, had stretched across the main to Ceylon and the Malabar Coast, or, coasting and trading along the eastern shores of Arabia, had made for the Persian Gulf and the emporia of the Indus. Once, too, the ship in which he sailed was on the very verge of the great ocean, and then the flocks of birds hovering about, the thick mists, and the swell of meeting currents[18] warned sailors and passengers of

[15] εμποριας γαρ χαριν επλευσα τους τρεις κολπους τουτους, τον τε κατα την Ρωμανιαν και τον Αραβιον και τον Περσικον· και απο των οικουντων δε η και πλεοντων τους τοπους ακριβως μημαθηκως, p. 132.

[16] Adule ενθα και την εμποριαν ποιουμεθα οίον απο Αλεξανδρειας και απο Ελα εμπορευομενοι, p. 140.

[17] Dioscorides ἡν νησον παρεπλευσαμεν ου κατηλθον δε εν αυτῃ, p. 179. Masoudi III, p. 37, speaks of Socotra as colonised by Greeks much as Cosmas does, pp. 178-9; but Masoudi by Greeks sent by Alexander himself, Cosmas by Greeks subjects of the Ptolemies, his successors. But when the Periplus was written the northern extremity only was inhabited, and by Indians, Arabs, and Ethiopians.

[18] Masoudi, in his Meadows of Gold, says of the sea of Zanj, "I have often been at sea, as in the Chinese Sea, the Caspian, the Red Sea. I have encountered many perils, but I have found the sea of Zanj the most dangerous of all," p. 263, and pp. 233-4 French tr. Soc. Asiat., by Barbier, Reinaud, and de Courteille. See also from Albyrouny, by Reinaud, Journal Asiatique, Sept.—Oct., 1844, pp. 237-8. But as indicative of the superior experience and enterprise of his age, compare with Cosmas the description of the same sea by the author of the Periplus; he points out its dangers

their danger, and their remonstrances induced the pilot to change his course.[19] On the continent he had crossed the Desert of Sinai on foot;[20] he was well known at Adule;[21] he had visited Auxume;[22] and indeed had travelled over the greater part of Egypt and Ethiopia and the countries bordering on the Arabian Gulf; and had moreover written an account of them which unfortunately has not come down to us.[23]

at certain seasons because open to the south wind; and also how the danger may be foreseen by the turbid colour of the sea, and how all then make for the shelter of the great promontory Tabor, § 12, I, p. 266, Geog. Min. Græc.

[19] Εν οἷς ποτε πλευσαντες επι την εσωτεραν Ινδιαν (εν τῃ Ταβροπανῃ, εν τῃ εσωτερᾳ Ινδιᾳ ενθα το Ινδικον πελαγος εστι, p. 178), και ὑπερβαντες μικρῳ προς την Βαρβαριαν· ενθα περαιτερω το Ζιγγιον τυγχανει· οὕτω γαρ καλεουσι το στομα του Ωκεανου· εκει εθεωρουν μεν εις τα δεξια εισερχομενων ἡμων, πληθος πετεινων...ἁ καλουσι σουσφα...και δυσαεριαν πολλην ὥστε δειλιαν παντας· ελεγον γαρ παντες τῳ κυβερνητῃ απωσε την ναυν επι τα αριστερα εις τον κολπον, pp. 132-3. And Βαρβαρια κυκλουται ὑπο του Ωκεανου εκ δεξιων, p. 137. And, απο Αξωμεως ἑως ακρων της Λιβανωτοφορου της Αιθιοπιας της καλουμενης Βαρβαριας, ἥτις και παρακειται τῳ Ωκεανῳ, p. 138. The recommendation to the steersman would, therefore, it seems, have driven them further out to sea, unless we suppose that they were just doubling the promontorium Aromata, when it would bring them nearer to the Arabian coast.

[20] Ὡς αυτος εγω πεζουσας τους τοπους μαρτυρω. Of the desert of Sinai, p. 205.

[21] Here Elesboas commissioned him to copy the inscription on the throne of Ptolemy, p. 141.

[22] εξ ὧν τοις οφθαλμοις ἡμων εθεασαμεθα επι τα μερη Αξωμεως εν τῃ Αιθιοπιᾳ, p. 264.

[23] *Vide* Prologos II. I have noticed only those places which Cosmas positively states he had visited, but he insinuates a much wider range of travel. Thus measuring the earth's breadth from the Hyperborean lands to Sasus, he says there are but two hundred mansions: ακριβως γαρ επισταμενοι, και ου πολυ διαμαρτανοντες της αληθειας, τα μεν πλευσαντες και οδευσαντες τα δ' ακριβως μεμαθηκως κατεγραψαμεν, p. 144.

But Cosmas, a merchant and a traveller, mixed much with other merchants and travellers; and while his simple and genial nature won their confidence, his curious and enquiring mind drew from them all they had to tell of or had seen in other lands that was worthy of note. With their information he corrected or confirmed his own impressions and enlarged and completed his knowledge. In this way he first heard from Patricius of the dangers of the Zangian Ocean,[24] and in this way he learned the adventures of Sopater; and in this way, by going among the slaves[25] of the merchants at Adule and questioning them about their people and country, he was able to speak to the correctness of the inscription on Ptolemy's chair.

As a merchant engaged in the Eastern trade, Cosmas was interested in and well acquainted with everything relating to it. He has accordingly noticed the principal ports at which it was carried on, together with the kinds of goods which each port specially supplied. He speaks of China, the country of silk, as lying to the left as you enter the Indian Sea in the furthest East and on the very borders of the habitable world, and yet not so far but that in its cities might occasionally be seen some Western merchant lured thither by the hope of gain.[26]

[24] ταυτα δε παραλαβων εκ του θειου ανδρου...ητοι και αυτης της πειρας, εσημηνα, p. 132.

[25] Captain Burton describes the trade at Zanzibar as in the hands of Arab merchants, who bring with them a train of native porters, some of them as many as two hundred.

[26] αυτη δε ἡ χωρα του μεταξιου εστιν εν τῃ εσωτερᾳ παντων Ινδιᾳ κατα το αριστερον μερος εισιοντων του Ινδικου πελαγεος, and a little before,

Adjoining China[27] to the West was the clove region; then came Caber and next Marallo, famed, the one for its alobandenum, the other for its shells. With Marallo Ceylon seems to have been in communication, as it certainly was with the five pepper marts of Male, Pudopatana, Nalopatano and Salopatana, Mangarouth[28] and Purti, and the other ports further northward on the western coast of the Indian Peninsula, as Sibor and Calliana[29] a place of great trade where ships might load with copper, sesamine wood, and clothing stuffs, Orrhotha[30] and Sindus, which last exported musk and androstachys. These Indian marts forwarded their wares to a great emporium situated on the southern coast of Ceylon, where they exchanged them for the silk, cloves, aloes, tsandana, and other merchandise which came from China and the countries lying eastward, or for Roman gold[31] and the manufactures of the West. In its ports[32] you might see ships freighted for,

ει γαρ τινες δια μεταξην εις τα εσχατα της γης εμποριας οικτρας χαριν ουκ οκνουσι διελθειν, p. 137.

[27] For this account of the countries and ports of the East trading with Ceylon, vide pp. 337-8.

[28] "Mangarat, urbs inter Malabaricas maxima regi gentili obediens." Gildemeister de rebus Indic., p. 184.

[29] Calliana: Lassen, Kaljanî; Hippocura on the mainland, somewhat to the north-west of Bombay.

[30] Orrhotha, Soratha, Surat.

[31] To the universal use of Roman gold Cosmas testifies: *εν τῳ νομισματι αυτων* (*Ρωμαιων*) *εμπορευονται παντα τα εθνη...θαυμαζομενον παρα παντος ανθρωπου...ἑτερᾳ βασιλειᾳ ουκ ὑπαρχει το τοιουτο*, p. 148.

[32] Ibn Batoutah similarly speaks of Calicut, the great emporium of his day. "Un des grands ports du Malabar. Les gens de la Chine, de Java, de Ceylon, des Maldives, du Yaman, et du Fars s'y rendent, et les trafiquants de diverses règions s'y réunissent.

or coming from, Persia, Ethiopia, and every part of India, and in its markets you met with men of all nations, Indians, Persians, Homerites, and merchants of Adule. Answering to this great commercial city of the East was Adule in the West, situated some two miles inland[33] on the southern shore and at no great distance from the mouth of the Arabian Gulf. It was in direct and frequent communication with India. The merchants of Œla and Alexandria thronged to its markets; for there they found, besides the rich productions of the East, slaves, spices, emeralds,[34] and ivory, from Ethiopia and Barbaria.

Besides the sea route from China to the Persian Gulf, Cosmas speaks also of another and a shorter road[35] which led through Juvia,[36] India, and Bactria to the eastern confines of Persia one hundred and fifty stations, and thence through Nisibis, eighty stations, to Seleucia, thirteen stations more, and each station he computes at about thirty miles. That this road was much frequented may be gathered from the quantities of silk always to be found in Persia and which it brought there; but that it was used only by Persian, and not by Roman merchants,[37] I presume from the exaggerated length attri-

Son port est au nombre des plus grands du monde," iv, 89. Dufrémery, tr.

33 *Vide* pp. 140 and 338.

34 *Vide* p. 339.

35 *διατεμνει ουν πολλα διαστηματα ὁ δια της ὁδου ερχομενος απο Τζινιτζας επι Περσιδα, ὁθεν και πληθος μεταξιου αει επι την Περσιδα εὑρισκεται*, p. 138, B.

36 *Ib.* "Vaticanus autem *Ουννια* secundâ manu." Note.

37 Ammianus Marcellinus seems to intimate that in his time

buted to it by Cosmas, and his generally vague account of it.[38]

He speaks of Ceylon as situated in the Indian Sea beyond the pepper country midway between China and the Persian Gulf,[39] and as lying in the midst of a cluster of islands which are all covered with cocoanut trees[40] and have springs of fresh water. On the authority of the natives he gives it a length and breadth of about two hundred miles each, and states that it is divided into two hostile kingdoms. Of these the country of the Hyacinth has many temples, and one with a pinnacle which is surmounted by a hyacinth the size they say of a fir cone, of a blood red colour, and so bright that when the sun shines upon it, it is a wondrous sight.[41] The

this road was travelled by Roman merchants: "Præter quorum radices et vicum quem Lithinon pyrgon appellant iter longissimum mercatoribus petitum ad Seras subinde commeantibus," p. 335.

38 Nisibis and Pekin are on the thirty-seventh and fortieth parallels of north latitude respectively, and the one on the forty-first, the other on the one hundred and seventeenth parallels of longitude; there are consequently seventy-six degrees of longitude between them. But according to Cosmas there are two hundred and thirty stations of thirty miles each, or 6,900 miles. In the same way between Seleucia and Nisibis he places thirteen stations, or 390 miles, whereas there are in fact but four degrees of latitude. Might then these *μοναι απο μιλιου λ'* be *απο μιλιου κ'* of twenty miles, which would pretty fairly give the real distance?

39 "L'île de Kalah," Point de Galle, "qui est située à mi-chemin entre les terres de la Chine et le pays des Arabes." Relations Arabes, p. 93. It was then the centre of traffic both from and for Arabia, 94 *id.*

40 *αργελλια* (p. 336 Cosmas). The narikala of the Hindus, and the nardgyl of the Arabs. Rel. Arabes, LVII Discours Prel.; and for an account of the islands, *id.*, p. 4.

41 Hiouen-Thsang (A.D. 648, some century after Cosmas) thus:

other kingdom occupies the rest of the island, and is celebrated for its harbour and much frequented markets. The king is not of the same race as the people.

In Cosmas's time India seems to have been parcelled out into many petty sovereignties; for besides these two kings of Ceylon he knows of a king of Malabar, and kings of Calliena, Sindus, etc., but all these rajahs seem to have acknowledged the supremacy of, and paid tribute to, Gollas, king of the White Huns,[42] a white people settled in the northern parts of India. Of this Gollas he relates that besides a large force of cavalry he could bring into the field two thousand elephants, and that his armies were so large that once when besieging an inland town defended by a water fosse, his men, horses

"A côté du palais du roi s'élève le Vihara de la dent de Bouddha. . . . Sur le sommet du Vihara on a élevé une flèche surmontée d'une pierre d'une grande valeur, appellée rubis. Cette pierre précieuse répand constamment un éclat resplendissant. Le jour et la nuit en regardant dans le lointain, on croit voir une étoile lumineuse," II, p. 141. Fa-hian, however, who was at Ceylon, A.D. 410: "Dans la ville on a encore construit un édifice pour une dent de Foe. Il est entièrement fait avec les sept choses précieuses," p. 333. Fa-hian thus mentions this Vihara, and, as if only lately built, but says nothing of the hyacinth, probably placed there subsequently to his time, v. Marco Polo, 449, Société Geog., ed.

[42] To Ουννων των Εφθαλιτων εθνος, ούσπερ λευκους ονομαζουσι. Procopius, de Bell. Pers., I, III, p. 15. Εφθαλιται δε Ουννικον μεν εθνος εισι και ονομαζονται...μονοι δε ούτοι λευκοι τε τα σωματα και ουκ αμορφοι τας οψεις εισιν, p. 16, *id.* The valley of the Indus seems to have been occupied by a Tartar tribe, even in the first century of our era. Ptolemy calls the lower Indus Indo-Scyth. Reinaud, Mem. sur l'Inde, p. 81 and p. 104.

and elephants, first drank up the water, and then marched into the place dryshod.[43]

He speaks of elephants as necessary to the state of an Indian monarch, and of the petty rajahs of the sea-board as keeping some five, some six, hundred elephants, and of the king of Ceylon as having moreover a stud of horses which came from Persia and were admitted into his ports duty free.[44] His elephants he bought and paid for according to their size at from fifty to one hundred golden pieces[45] each, and sometimes even more. They were broken in for riding and were sometimes pitted to fight against one another, but with their trunks only, a barrier raised breast high preventing them from coming to closer quarters. The Indian elephants he observes have no tusks and are tameable at any age, while those of Ethiopia to be tamed must be caught young.[46]

As a Christian he naturally observed, and as a monk willingly recorded, the state of Christianity in the East.

[43] Cosmas Indicopleustes. Montfaucon, Nova Coll. Patrum, I, p. 338.

[44] *Τους δε ἱππους απο Περσιδος φερουσιν αυτῳ, και αγοραζει και τιμᾳ ατελειαν τους φεροντας*, p. 339. This importation of horses into India, and from Persia, continues to this day, and is frequently alluded to by Ibn Batoutah; those from Fars were preferred, pp. 372-3, II, but they were then subject to a duty of seven silver dinars each horse, *ib.*, p. 374.

[45] *νομισματα*, p. 339. The word used by Sopater in the preceding page, consequently a gold coin, see Embassy to Ceylon. Procopius observes that neither the Persian king, nor indeed any barbarian sovereign, places his effigy on his coins (II, 417). "The Parthian and some of the Hindu kings did."—Wilson's Ariana Antiqua.

[46] P. 339, u. s., and compare p. 141, with regard to the Ethiopian elephants from the inscription at Adule.

In Ceylon there was a Christian church of Persian residents, with a priest and deacons and other ecclesiastical officers,[47] all from Persia. At Male, Calliena, a bishop's see, and the Island of Dioscorides[48] (Socotora), were Christian communities, also dependent on Persia for their ministers and subject to the Persian metropolitan; and this, though in the case of Socotora the inhabitants, colonists from the time of the Ptolemies, were Greeks and spoke Greek. In Bactria too and among the Huns and other Indians and indeed throughout the known world[49] were numberless churches, bishops, and multitudes of Christians, with many martyrs, monks, and hermits.

He describes and gives drawings of some of the animals and plants of Ethiopia and India. In general he closes his descriptions[50] by stating, either that he has

[47] *και πασαν την εκκλησιαστικην λειτουργιαν*, p. 337, u. s.

[48] So also the Relations Arabes of Socotora: "La plupart de ses habitants sont Chrétiens...Alexandre y envoya une colonie de Grecs...ils embrassèrent la religion Chrétienne. Les restes de ces Grecs se sont maintenues jusqu' aujourd'hui, bien que dans l'île il se soit conservé des hommes d'une autre race," p. 139, and see also note, pp. 217-59, II, v., where Reinaud refers to both Cosmas and the Periplus of the Erythræan Sea; see also Marco Polo, p. 702, Marsden's ed.

[49] Cosmas goes through the several nations in detail; but having to do only with India I omit particulars. I observe, however, that he gives no Christians to China, though Masoudi says of Canton, in the tenth century: "the town is inhabited by Moslims, Christians, Jews, and Magians, besides the Chinese."—*Meadows of Gold*, 324, I. In the space of three, rather two and a half (v. Relations Arabes, p. 13), centuries then Mahomedanism had penetrated to China. At the same rate of progress Christianity should have been known there in the third century.

[50] For these descriptions, *vide* pp. 344-5, and the drawings at the beginning of II, v, Montfaucon's Nova Coll. Patrum.

himself seen what he has been just describing and where and how he saw it, or if he have not seen it, what personal knowledge he has of it. Thus to his notice of the rhinoceros he adds, that he saw one in Ethiopia and was pretty near it; to that of the Cheirelephus, that he had both seen it and eaten its flesh; to that of the hippopotamus, that he had not seen it but had bought and sold its teeth; and to that of the unicorn, that he had only seen a statue of one in brass standing in the four-turreted palace in Ethiopia. But when he comes to speak of the bos agrestis, the moschos, and the pepper[51] and cocoanut trees, animals and plants belonging to India, I observe that he does not even hint at any personal knowledge of them, and I ask myself—Was Cosmas ever in India?

When his ship was nearly carried away into the Great Ocean, Cosmas was then bound for Inner India;[52] and as he calls Taprobane an island of Inner India, by Inner India I presume that, unlike the ecclesiastical writers of his age, he intends not Ethiopia and Arabia Felix, but the Indian Peninsula. Again in another place after having spoken of Ceylon and alluded to the principal marts of India, to the White Huns settled on its northern frontier and the lucrative commerce the

[51] He describes the pepper tree as a sort of vine, very unlike the pepper trees I have seen at Palermo. He probably means the betel. "The betel is a species of pepper, the fruit grows on a vine, and the leaves are employed to wrap up the areca nut."—Heeren, Hist. Res., II, 294. "The betel is found in the two Indian peninsulas, Malabar and Arracan."—*Id.*, 295.

[52] See *supra*, note 19, p. 217.

Ethiopians carry on with them in emeralds,[53] he adds, "and all these things I know partly of my own knowledge and partly from what I have learned by diligent inquiry made at no great distance from the places themselves." But this surely is no evidence of India visited, at least not such evidence as is before us of his having been at Auxume where at mid-day with his own eyes he saw the shadows falling south; at Adule, where at the request of Elesboas he copied the inscription on Ptolemy's chair;[54] or in Sinai, which he trudged through on foot listening to the Jews as they read for him the Hebrew letters sculptured on its boulders.[55] So, notwithstanding that he passed the Straits of Bab-el-Mandeb and lay off the Island of Socotra; notwithstanding his name of Indicopleustes and his vague assertions; and, more than all, notwithstanding his narrative, which is sober as fact and commonplace as reality, I cannot help doubting that he ever was in India.

On a review of these notices of India, it seems: 1st. That for nearly a century after the fall of Palmyra no

[53] *Id.*, II, 339. "Autrefois on portait dans l'Inde l'émeraude qui vient d'Egypte" (Rel. Arabes?), 153, I, 232, II. Olympiodorus, Excerp. de Legat., p. 466, Corp. Byz.

[54] For Auxume, *vide* Cosmas, Montfaucon, II, Col. nova Patrum, II, p. 264. Adule, p. 144, *id.*

[55] δθεν εστιν ιδειν εν εκεινῃ τῃ ερημῳ του Σιναιου ορους εν πασαις ταις καταπαυσεσι παντας τους λιθους των αυτοθι, τους εκ των ορεων αποκλωμμενους, γεγραμμενους γραμμασι γλυπτοις Ἑβραικοις, ὡς αυτος εγω πεζουσας τους τοπους μαρτυρω. ἅτινα και τινες Ιουδαιοι αναγνοντες διηγουντο ἡμιν, λεγοντες γεγραφθαι οὑτως—απερσις του δε, εκ φυλης της δε, ετει τῳδε, μηνι τῳδε—καθα και παρ' ἡμιν πολλακις τινες εν ταις ξενιαις γραφουσιν.—p. 205. Does he allude to the Nabathæan inscriptions: "qui couvrent les parois des rochers de la presqu'île du mont Sinai"?—Reinaud, Mem. sur la Mérène, p. 12, tirage à part; and for these inscriptions, Journal Asiatique, Jan. and Feb., 1859.

important mention of India was made by any Greek or Latin writer whatever. 2ndly. That the accounts of India which then and afterwards appeared, whether in Travels, Geographies, Histories, or Poems, those in the Topographia Christiana excepted, were all in the main made up of extracts from the writings of previous ages and added nothing to our knowledge of India. 3rdly. That of such writings these compilers in general preferred, not those which recorded authenticated facts,[56] but those which worked most on the imagination; and they indeed heightened their effect by new matter of the same character. 4thly. That these writings gradually took rank with, and even displaced the more critical studies of Strabo, Arrian, Ptolemy, etc. Thus the Periegesis of Dionysius,* on which Eustatius wrote a commentary, and the Geography of the anonymous writer who so far as I know first gave locality to Eden, were honoured by Latin translations, and judging from the currency their fictions obtained became the text books of after ages. Thus too the Bassarika of Dionysius for Indian countries and towns is more frequently referred to than either Strabo or Arrian by Stephanos Byzantius; and thus the Apollonius of Philostratus becomes an authority for Suidas,[57] and the Theban Scholasticus for both Suidas and Cedrenus, who borrow from him their accounts of the Brahmans,[58] to which

[56] The description of India in Ammianus Marcellinus must be excepted from this censure, v.

* Bernhardyus places Dionysius at the end of the third or early in the fourth century, the latest date assigned him.—Proleg. Geog. Min., v. II.

[57] *Vide* sub vocibus, Poros et Brahmans. Suidas.

[58] Hist. Comp., 267-8, I, v, Bonn. Here the description of the

Cedrenus adds some particulars drawn, partly from the anonymous Geography probably, partly from the Pseudo-Callisthenes, and partly from some other writer whom I am unable to identify. 5thly. That of Eastern travellers in the fourth and fifth centuries many were priests; as we may surmise from the number of Christian churches[59] in India, which were all subject to the Persian metropolitan,[60] and which all received their ecclesiastical ministers from Persia, or sent them there for education and ordination; and as we gather from the frequent mention of priests in the travels of those ages. Thus the author of the Tract inscribed to Palladius,[61] and the Theban Scholasticus visit India in company, the one of the Bishop of Adule, the other of a priest. And Cosmas travels on one occasion with Thomas of Edessa afterwards metropolitan of Persia, and with Patricius of the Abrahamitic order; and in his latter years he becomes a monk, as does also Monas,[62] who assisted him in copying the inscription on the throne of Ptolemy. 6thly. That notwithstanding the religious spirit which evidently

Brahmans is from Palladius; of the Macrobioi from the Geography; the story of Candace from the pseudo-Callisthenis, III, 23; but whence Alexander's visit to Britain?

59 V. from Cosmas, *supra*, p. 26.

60 Jesujabus of Adiabene, Patriarch A.D. 650 (Assemann, III, p. 313), thus remonstrates with Simeon, Primate of Persia: "At in vestrâ regione ex quo ab eccles. canon defecistis interrupta est ab Indiæ populis sacerdotalis successio: nec India solum qua a maritimis reg. Pers. finibus usque ad Colon spatio 1200 parasangis extenditur, sed et ipsa Pers. regio...in tenebris jacet."—Assemann, Bib. Or., III, 131.

61 Palladius was himself a great traveller, *vide* Hist. Lausiaca, Lauso Epistola, p. 897, III, Bib. Vet. Patrum, ed. de la Bigne, as indeed were the monks and priests of these ages, *ib.*, passim.

62 He entered the monastery of Raithu, Elim. Cosmas, p. 195.

animated the travel writers of these times, their accounts of other and far countries are, contrary to what one might have expected, singularly silent on the subject of the religions of the people they visited. I have already expressed my surprise, that the earlier Christian fathers, who to win the attention of the sleeping nations called up from their tombs the forgotten creeds of Chaldæa and Phœnicia, Assyria and Egypt, should never have appealed to the living faith of Buddha. Its ritual was not unlike the Christian. Like Christianity, it rejected the claims of race and country and in itself found another and stronger bond of brotherhood. Like Christianity, it was a religion Catholic and Apostolic, and to attest its truth not a few had died the martyr's death. It was the creed of an ancient race. It was shrouded too in a mystery which startled the self-sufficiency of the Greek and awakened to curiosity even Roman indifference. It was besides eminently fitted to elucidate Christian doctrines, and therefore to draw to itself the attention of Christian writers;[63] and yet—the name of Buddha stands a phantom in their pages. But then few were the Hindus who visited the Roman world, and all as

[63] Buddhism and Buddhist practices attracted the attention of the earliest travellers of our age. *Vide* Carpinus, in Hakluyt, 64, I, and Rubruqnis, 118, 127-8 *ib.*, Marco Polo, p. 47, S. G. ed., and a summary of what was known of Buddhism in his own time in Maffei, Hist. Indic., p. 169, 12mo. Marco Polo too has given an account of Buddha, pp. 449-50, u. s., with some errors, no doubt, but wonderfully correct and detailed when compared with the short notices in Greek writers. But still none of these early travellers I am bound to say connect, or see any similarity between, the Buddhist and Christian services. Marco Polo only observes of Buddha "si fuisset Christianus fuisset apud Deum maximus factus," *ibid.*

merchants lived buying and selling, though not all were Buddhists. And if here and there one more earnestly religious than his fellows was eager to preach Buddha's law, whom could he address and where find an interpreter for thoughts so far out of the range of the ordinary Greek intellect? Allow however that he had studied and mastered the Greek language. Among his auditory, the merchants with whom he traded, the few men of letters if any who sought his society—that a Christian, one of a small community, should have been found, is an accident scarcely to be expected; and the silence of the fathers is thus in some measure intelligible. But now that we have a Christian church in Ceylon, and Christians who are daily witnesses of the ceremonial of Buddhist worship, who have heard of Buddha's life and miracles and mission, and have visited the monasteries where his followers retire to a life of prayer and self-denial, I cannot understand how it is that no word relating to this wide-spread faith has reached the ears of Cosmas, or has attracted the notice of Syrian bishops, and that these ages are worse informed on Buddhism than was that of Clemens Alexandrinus.

We will now trace the changes which took place in the commercial relations of Rome and India. When Palmyra fell, Alexandria did not as might have been expected inherit its Indian trade and the wealth and power that trade brought with it. For when Palmyra fell, Alexandria was suffering from civil war, recent siege and capture. Its citizens had been given up to plunder and put to the sword, and Bruchium, its noblest quarter, razed to the ground.[64] It was overwhelmed by

[64] See from Ammianus Marcel. and Eusebius, notes, *supra*, p. 166.

its own disasters, and in no condition to engage in distant and costly ventures. But when Palmyra fell, the fleets Arab and Indian which fed its markets did not perish in its fall. The ships and crews lived still, the populations to whose wants they ministered[65] had not disappeared. The old demand remained. For a moment the course of trade is disturbed. A great mart has been destroyed, and others must be found or created to take its place. At first probably the merchant fleets, as was their wont, made for Vologesocerta, and there delivered their cargoes, which perhaps found a way up the right bank of the Euphrates to Apamia, and thence to Antioch and the cities of Syria. But the cost of transit and the want of a back freight must very soon have closed up this route, in so far at least as it was the route to the Syrian sea-board, though doubtless the river remained always the great highway for the supply of Mesopotamia and the neighbouring states. And now it was, that the Arabs and Indians probably began to frequent the ports which, unknown to Strabo and Pliny, studded according to Ammianus Marcellinus the Persian Gulf;[66] hither they brought the products of the East, and hence shipped horses, for which they found a ready sale among the kings and nobles of India and Ceylon. And now too it was that the Arabs[67] turned their attention to the Red

[65] Appian thus describes the Palmyrenes: *Αντωνιος...επικαλων αυτοις, ὁτι Ρωμαιων και Παρθυαιων οντες εφορισι, ες ἑκατερους επιδεξιως ειχον· εμποροι γαρ οντες, κομιζουσι μεν εκ Περσων τα Ινδικι και Αραβικα, διατιθενται δ' εν τῃ Ρωμαιων*, de Bel. Civil., v, ix.

[66] "Cujus sinus per oras omnes oppidorum est densitas et vicorum, naviumque crebri decursus," xxiii, 6, 11.

[67] Some believe the last Permaul (of Cochin) was induced by

Sea route,[68] once in the hands of the Alexandrian merchants, but now neglected. In a deep bay on the western shores of the Arabian Gulf,[69] the first after having entered the straits which afforded shelter and a safe anchorage, they found Adule, the chief port of Ethiopia, though only a neat village in the time of the Periplus. They saw that access to it both from East and West was easy; that it lay beyond the confines, and was not subject to the fiscal regulations, of the Roman Empire; that its mixed population, of which the Arab race formed no inconsiderable part, was friendly and eager to forward their views. On Adule then they fixed as the depôt for their trade, and soon raised it from a village and petty port to be one of the world's great centres of commerce.

But under the immediate successors of Aurelian (died A.D. 275), the Roman Empire was in so disturbed a state, and under Diocletian (A.D. 283-304) Alexandria suffered so fearfully for its recognition of Achilleus, that its merchants were probably compelled, and not disinclined, to leave the whole Indian trade in the hands of the Arabs, who had always been not only carriers by

the Jains (A.D. 378, 52) to proceed to Mekka, at which place many of their faith were established, carrying on a trade with India which subsequently fell into Moorish hands. Day, Land of the Permauls, p. 44, he refers to a paper by Kookel Kelso Nair, Madras Quarterly Journal of Science, no year, volume, or page.

68 It had been known from old time. Agartharchides (2nd cent. B.C.) speaks of the native boats which from the Fortunate Islands (probably Socotora) traded with Pattala, on the Indus. De Mari Eryth., § 133. Muller, Geog. Min., I, p. 191.

69 εμπυριον νομιμον κειμενον εν κολπῳ βαθει...απο σταδιων εικοσι της θαλασσης εστιν ἡ Αδουλις κωμη συμμετρος.—Periplus, § 45 or § 4.

land and sea but traders also, as the story of Scythianus proves; and who, as they travelled from city to city, carried their wares[70] with them and wherever they stopped exposed them for sale and thus supplied the immediate wants of the neighbourhood and the tradesmen of the district. But with the restoration of order, during the long reign of Constantine, the Roman merchant grew wealthy and enterprising; he extended the sphere of his operations, and though, partly from inability to compete with the cheaply built but well manned craft of the Arabs, and partly from long disuse and consequent ignorance of the Indian seas, he does not seem to have again ventured his ships upon them, yet he gradually recovered his old position in the Arabian Gulf, and at least shared in its trade from Adule homeward.[71] To Adule he himself resorted, and at Adule through his agents[72] managed his dealings with

[70] The wealth of Scythianus, when it came into the hands of Manes, consisted *χρυσου και αργυρου και αρωματων και αλλων* (Epiphanius con. Manichæ. 6|7, I) showing that Scythianus's journey to Jerusalem, if undertaken primarily in the interest of truth, was not without some commercial object.

[71] Both by his ships on the Red Sea and his fleets of boats on the Nile. Of Roman ships on the Red Sea we know from Cosmas and Procopius (de Bello Pers., I, 19, p. 101). Of the traffic on the Nile we may get some notion from the ruse employed by Athanasius to escape from his pursuers (Photius, Hoeschiel, p. 1448), and more directly from the wealth Palladius gives an Alexandrian merchant, *ανδρα ευλαβην και φιλοχριστον, δυο μυριαδας χρυσινων πραγματευομενον μετα ἑκατον πλοιων εκ της ανωτερας Θηβαιδος κατιοντα.* LXV, Hist. Lausiaca.

[72] I conclude this from a passage in Procopius already cited in part. Telling of the slaves and adventurers left behind him by Hellesthæus, on his return from the conquest of the Homerites,

the East, leaving to the Arabs and perhaps the Indians all the risks and profits of the ocean voyage.

But that Roman intercourse with India was indirect and kept up by Arab vessels is so contrary to received opinion, that I will now cite and examine the few events and notices[73] bearing on the Indian trade which are to be met with in ancient writers. And,

I. The embassy to Julian[74] (A.D. 361) is scarcely conceivable, unless during his reign or rather that of Constantine some and probably a commercial intercourse existed between India and the Roman Empire.[75] But

he says *οὗτος ὁ λεως συν ἑτεροις τισιν Εσιμιφαιῳ τῳ βασιλει επαναστaντες αυτον μεν εν τινι των εκεινῃ φρουριων καθειρξαν, ἑτερονδε ʽΟμεριταις βασιλεα κατεστησαντο Αβραμον μεν ονομα· ὁ δε Αβραμος οὗτος χριστιανος μεν ην, δουλος δε Ρωμαιου ανδρος, εν πολει Αιθιοπων Αδουλιδι επι τῃ κατα θαλασσαν εργασιᾳ διατριβην εχοντος.*—*Id.*, I, p. 20, 105. And that commercial agents were of old date may be shown from Relations Arabes, I, 68.

[73] From Alexander's conquest of India to the close of Justinian's reign embraces a period of about nine hundred years; from the rediscovery of India in A.D. 1498 to the publication of Maffei's Historiæ Indicæ not a century elapsed; and yet Maffei has given an account of India and China, of the manners, customs, characters, and religions of their peoples with which not all the notices of India collected from nine centuries of Greek and Roman writers are to be compared for fulness and accuracy. Does not this in itself go far to prove that our relations with the East in Maffei's time merely commercial and religious were very different from those of Greece and Rome, which at first purely political were then frequent and intimate, but which in the end became commercial only and must have been confined to an interchange of goods, and that without any intercourse with the people?

[74] *Vide supra*, pp. 125-6.

[75] In a Geographical Tract, Totius Orbis Descriptio, translated from the Greek and written A.D. 350-3, Geog. Minor., II, 520, it is said of Alexandria: "Hæc cum Indis et Barbaris negotia gerit

as for such an embassy, the presence at the Sinhalese Court of any enterprising Roman merchant, a Sopater, and who like Sopater may have reached Ceylon in an Adulitan ship, would fully account,—and indeed its Serendivi, so much more akin to the Serendib of the Arabs than the Salike of Ptolemy, smacks of Arab companionship and must have filtered through Arab lips—I cannot look upon it as indicative of an intercourse either direct or frequent.

II. Epiphanius (about A.D. 375) gives some few details relating to this trade. In his story of Scythianus he speaks of the Roman ports of entry in the Red Sea, Œla, the Alah of Solomon, Castron Clysmatos,[76] and Berenice, and observes that through Berenice Indian wares are distributed over the Thebaid, and by the Nile are carried down to Alexandria and the land of Egypt, and to Pelusium, and thus passing by sea into different cities, *πατριδας*,[77] the merchants from India import their goods into the Roman territory. From this passage, written at the close of the fourth century, it appears:

merito; aromata et diversas species pretiosas omnibus regionibus mittit." But another version, *ib.*, "supra caput enim habens Thebaidis Indorum genus et accipiens omnia præstat omnibus"—thus showing that although dealing in Indian wares its Indians were only Ethiopians.

[76] So called because here the Israelites crossed over the Red Sea. Cosmas, Montfaucon, Col. Nov. Pat., p. 194.

[77] Ὁρμοι γαρ της Ερυθρης θαλασσης διαφοροι, επι τα στομια της Ρωμανιας διακεκριμενοι, ὁ μεν εἱς επι την Αιλαν...ὁ δε ἑτερος επι το Καστρον Κλυσματος· αλλως δε ανωτατω επι την Βερνικην καλουμενην, δι' ἧς Βερνικης καλουμενης επι την Θηβαιδα φερονται και τα απο της Ινδικης ερχομενα ειδη εκεισε τῃ Θηβαιδι διαχυνεται, και επι την Αλεξανδρειαν δια του...Νειλου και επι πασαν των Αιγυπτων γην, και επι το Πελουσιον φερεται, και οὑτως εις τας αλλας πατριδας δια θαλασσης διερχομενοι οἱ απο της Ινδικης επι την Ρωμανιαν εμπορευονται.—Epiphanius, a. Hæres., XLVI, p. 618, I.

1st. That Epiphanius speaks of Indian goods as then imported by sea and through one port, Berenice, into the Roman Empire.

2ndly. That he uses the same terms[78] to designate both the imported goods and the importing merchants, and thus possibly intimates that like the goods the merchants also were "Indian," *i.e.*, Arabs of either Ethiopia or Eastern Arabia, the Indians of the ecclesiastical writers of this age. Indeed one might ask whether it was not owing to their association with Indian wares that these peoples came to be themselves known as Indians.

3rdly. That he makes no mention of Adule. But Adule, however closely connected with the ocean trade between Rome and India, was really an Ethiopic city, and could therefore scarcely find a place in this itinerary which begins with the Roman ports of entry.

III. The presence at Alexandria (some time before A.D. 470) of those Hindus whom Severus lodged in his house.[79] I have already remarked on the inexplicable proceedings of these travellers who, as they were neither merchants nor public officers, could only have travelled for amusement or instruction, and who took every precaution against either.[80] I would now direct attention

[78] *τα απο της Ινδικης ερχομενα ειδη* and *διερχομενοι οἱ απο της Ινδικης.* The lighter and more precious wares are expressed by the word *ειδη*, as spices, pearls, etc. It corresponds with the "notions" of American commerce.

[79] *Vide supra*, p. 189.

[80] Many an English traveller might be cited whose habits abroad very much resemble those of Damascius' Hindus. But then we travel for fashion's sake a good deal, because we must; but a

to the character as well of Severus who received, as of Damascius who has recorded their visit. Both clung to the old superstition: and the one was supposed to favour its re-establishment by his personal influence and the other by his writings, the very dotage of "Platonic Paganism."[81] Both were credulous: and as Severus would without examination and only too eagerly have welcomed as guests any men calling themselves Hindus with whom he became acquainted, so Damascius would have noticed a visit of any reputed Hindus, whether made or not, if said to be made to such a man. The visit is open to suspicion.

IV. The Indian embassy to Justinian. Malalas notices two Indian Embassies, either of which may possibly be Hindu. The first reached Constantinople with its gifts the same year (A.D. 530) that John of Cappadocia was made Prætorian Præfect; the second with an elephant about the time (A.D. 552) that Narses was sent into Italy against the Goths.[82] Now with regard to the first of these embassies, as in Malalas the Ethiopians and Eastern Arabs are called Indians,[83] the question arises whether this embassy does not properly belong to

Hindu who leaves his country travels because he has in him the spirit of travel; he travels as Mungo Park did, Belzoni, Burkhardt, and many others, impelled by the strong desire to see strange men and strange lands.

[81] See Gibbon, Decline and Fall, c. xxxvi, sub an. 468, and the extracts from Damascius, in Photius Bibliotheca, p. 1042.

[82] V. from Malalas, note *supra*, p. 126, and Malalas, p. 484. *Ινδικτιωνος ιγ' πρεσβευτης Ινδων κατεπεμφθη μετα και ελεφαντος εν Κωνσταντινοπολει.*

[83] Malalas, u. s., and p. 457; also Asseman, Bib. Orient., IV, pp. 452-3.

some one or other of these peoples; and to answer it we must enter into some detail. From Malalas and Procopius[84] we gather: that there were seven Indian kingdoms, three Homerite, and four Ethiopian; that the Ethiopians occupied the regions lying eastwards and extending to the ocean, and carried on a great trade from Auxume with Rome through the Homerite country; that some time prior[85] to A.D. 529, Dimnos, Damianus (Theophanes), Dunaan (Asseman), the Homerite king, who with many of his people was of the Jewish persuasion, seized upon some Roman merchants while traversing his dominions in pursuit of their business, confiscated their goods and put them to death, in retaliation as he pretended for the continued persecutions to which Jews were subjected in the Roman states; that the Auxumitan trade with Rome was in consequence interrupted, and that the Auxumitan king, aggrieved by the injury to himself and the wrongful death of his allies, invaded and subdued the Homerites, and in fulfilment of a vow contingent on his success declared himself a Christian. To this Ethiopian sovereign or rather his successor, called Elesboas by Malalas, Hellesthæus[86] by Procopius, on the

[84] Malalas, p. 433. Procopius, de Bello Pers., p. 104. The division of the Indians into kingdoms belongs to Malalas; the slaughter of the Roman merchants and its cause and consequences to both.

[85] In A.D. 522-524, *vide* Asseman, u. s., I, 365, note and text, where is an, if genuine, extraordinary letter of Dunaan's, in which with evident satisfaction he details all the cruelties, and they are fearful, which he has inf'icted on the Christians within his power, no one of whom has wavered in his faith.

[86] The converted king Malalas calls Andas, p. 434, Theophanes

breaking out of the Persian War (A.D. 529), Justinian sent an embassy, and adjured him by their common faith to invade the Persian territory, and breaking off all commercial relations with the Persians to send ships to those Indian ports where silk was to be found and there purchase it, and thence by way of the Homerite country and down the Nile and through Egypt to import it into Alexandria; and as an inducement to attempt this enterprise he held out to him the prospect of a monopoly and the hopes of great profits. But Procopius observes that, though the Ethiopians promised, and exerted themselves, they failed, to gain a share in the silk trade: for they found the ground already occupied by Persian merchants who everywhere forestalled them in the Indian markets.[87] And Malalas concludes his account of this negotiation by stating that Elesboas in return sent an Indian ambassador with letters, *σακρας*, and gifts to the Roman Emperor. Is then our Indian Embassy the same as this one from Elesboas?[88] and does

Adad; Aidog, Asseman, u. s., I, 359, notes 5 and 6. The king of the Embassy, Cosmas like Malalas knows as Elesboas. The ambassador I should have thought was Nonnosus, who left an account of his embassy, and from the ambassador, whoever he was (Procopius calls him Julianus, as also Theophanes, Chronog., p. 377), Malalas derived his information, pp. 457-8 *ib.*, and he gives a graphic description of this barbaric court.

[87] *τοις τε Αιθιοψι την μεταξαν ωνεισθαι προς των Ινδων αδυνατον ην. επει αει δε οἱ Περσων εμποροι προς αυτοις τοις ὁρμοις γενομενοι (οὐ δε πρωτα αἱ των Ινδων νηες καταιρουσιν, ἁτε χωραν προσοικουντες την ὁμορου), ἁπαντα ωνεισθαι τα φορτια ειωθασι.*—Procopius, u. s., p. 106. And in Justin's reign the Turks seem to have taken the place of the Persians, *οἱ Τουρκοι τοτε τα τε Σήρων εμπορια και τους λιμενας κατειχον ταυτα δε πριν μεν Περσαι κατειχον.*—Excerpt. Theophani. Hist. Excerpta de Legationibus, p. 484.

[88] Elesboas having received and entertained Justinian's Embassy,

its first mention refer to its departure from Auxume, its second to its arrival in Constantinople? Or is it to be referred to some one of the Pseudo-Indian kingdoms? Or though unrecorded by any other writer, is it really Hindu? Who shall tell? With regard to the second Embassy: it is noticed by both Theophanes and Cedrenus,[89] but noticed seemingly not because it was any strange sight in Constantinople, but because its elephant, a native of Africa as of India, broke loose and did much mischief. However this may be, a Hindu Embassy in Constantinople was no improbable event, for after Elesboas had at the instance of Justinian ineffectually attempted to open up the trade with India, would he not naturally bring over and forward to the Roman

κατεπεμψε και σακρας δια Ινδου πρεσβυτερου και δωρα τῳ βασιλει Ρωμαιων. Malalas, p. 458, and afterwards, p. 477, incidentally mentions the Embassy we have been examining: εν αυτῳ δε τῳ χρονῳ και πρεσβυτης Ινδων μετα δωρων κατεπεμφθη εν Κωνσταντινουπολει, και αυτῳ τῳ χρονῳ Ιωαννης ὁ Καππαδοξ εγενετο επαρχος πραιτωριων.

89 The chronology of these times is loose and uncertain. According to Theophanes (Chron. 1, 346-7), the Christianisation of Auxume, represented by its kings (they had probably gone back to their old heathen faith), and the events which led to it, occurred A.D. 535, and the Embassy with the elephant, A.D. 542. Cedrenus refers it to A.D. 550. Taking then the dates assigned by Malalas, A.D. 530 for our first, A.D. 552 for the second, Embassy, it is clear that the first Embassy follows too closely on the alliance and engagements of Elesboas, while between these and the second there is too great an interval, to admit of the reasons I have adduced for either one of these Embassies being Hindu. Of Theophanes' dates (he lived early part of ninth century) I scarcely like to speak—the first is so manifestly wrong. But if we take A.D. 542 for the date of the Elephant Embassy, and A.D. 533, Gibbon's, for that of Justinian's to Auxume, then these reasons would be pertinent enough.

court some native Indians, ambassadors or others, as the surest evidence he could give of his good faith and zeal in carrying out his part of the treaty? One of these embassies may be Indian, but it is no proof of any direct intercourse with India. Indeed the whole narrative rather intimates that Roman enterprise extended no further than Auxume, and that all trade beyond was in the hands of some other people.

v. The introduction of the silk-worm into the Roman Empire. According to Procopius[90] it happened in this wise. Aware of the interest Justinian took in the silk trade, some monks from India who had lived long in Serinda (Theophanes[91] says it was a Persian), brought over in a reed (*εν ναρθηκι*) silk-worm's eggs, taught the Romans how to treat them, and by acclimatizing the worm to make themselves in the article of silk independent of the Persians and other people. I incline to think that the monks were Persians; for India was under the Persian metropolitan, and its churches as we learn from Cosmas were served by priests from Persia; and a Persian Christian would be more Christian than Persian, and more likely to benefit his co-religionists than his countrymen. But let the monks be Romans,

[90] Ὑπο τουτον τον χρονον τινες μοναχων εξ Ινδων ἡκοντες γνοντες τε ὡς Ιουστινιανῳ δια σπουδης ειη μηκετι προς Περσων την μεταξαν ωνεισθαι Ρωμαιους, etc.—De Bel. Goth., p. 546.

[91] την των σκωληκων γενεσιν ανηρ Περσης...εν Βυζαντιῳ υπεδειξεν· οὑτος εκ Σηρων...το σπερμα των σκωληκων εν ναρθηκι λαβων μεχρι Βυζαντιου διεσωσατο, etc.—Excerpta Theoph. Hist., p. 484, lived close of the sixth century. The seed was brought overland, as the French, to avoid the tropical heats, are now sending it.—*Times*, May 12, 1863.

and Romans we know did occasionally visit and sojourn in India, and their introduction of the silk-worm is no evidence of any ocean trade with India.

VI. A passage in Procopius which intimates that Roman ships frequented the seas in which were found the loadstone rocks. This passage I will quote at length and examine. After having described the Arabian Gulf from Œla, and told of its islands and the Saracens and Homerites on its Eastern coast, and alluded to the many other peoples living inland up to the very borders of the cannibal Saracens, beyond whom he places the Indians, "but of the Indians leaves others to speak at their discretion,"[92] Procopius returns to Boulika of the Homerites, and notices the calm sea and easy transit thence to Adule. He then proceeds to treat of Ethiopia, but first touches on the peculiarly constructed boats used by the Indians, εν Ινδοις, and on this sea. "They are not," he observes, "painted over with tar or anything else, nor are their planks made fast to one another by iron nails but with knotted ropes, βροχοις, and this not as is generally supposed, because there are in these seas rocks which attract iron *(for the Roman ships from Œla, though iron-fastened, suffer nothing of the sort)*, but because the Indians and Ethiopians neither have any iron nor are able to buy any from the Romans, who are forbidden to sell it them on pain of death. Such is the

[92] οἱ δε 'Ομηριται οὑτοι εν χωρᾳ τῃ επεκεινα ωκηνται προς τῃ της θαλασσης ῃονι, ὑπερ τε αυτους αλλα εθνη πολλα, μεχρι ες τους ανθρωποφαγους Σαρακηνους, ἱδρυσθαι φασι· μεθ' οὑς δε τα γενη των Ινδων εστιν. αλλα τουτων μεν περι λεγετω ἑκαστος ὡς πη αυτῳ βουλομενῳ εστιν.—De Bello Pers., p. 100.

state of things about the so-called Red Sea and the coasts on each side of it."[93] On this passage I will observe—

1st. That as long as it treats of the shores of the Arabian Gulf, where the Romans traded, its language is clear and definite enough, but as vague when it comes to speak of the inland peoples, of whom very evidently Procopius had been able to obtain very imperfect information.

2ndly. That the Indoi with whom the Ethiopians and the Persians seem to have had commercial dealings must have been the inhabitants of a country without iron, and not therefore of India celebrated of old time[94] for its steel, but very possibly of Arabia,[95] into which in the age of the Periplus iron and sometimes from India was regularly imported, and the boats of which[96] quite answered to the description of Procopius.

[93] *τα μεν ουν αμφι τῃ ερυθρᾳ θαλασσῃ και χωρᾳ ἣ αυτης εφ' ἑκατερα εστι ταυτῃ πῃ εχει.*—*Ib.*, p. 102.

[94] Ctesias, p. 80, 4.

[95] Of Arabia or Arabians settled in Ethiopia. Elsewhere Procopius speaks of Ethiopia as India: *Νειλος μεν...εξ Ινδων επ' Αιγυπτου φερομενος*, etc. De Ædificiis, vi, I, p. 331, III.

[96] "Les vaisseaux Arabes n'approchaient pas pour la force des vaisseaux Chinois (Ibn Batutah mans each junk with 1,000 men, 600 sailors and 400 soldiers, iv, 91, French tr.)...construits en général en bois et sans mélange de fer, ils tiraient très peu d'eau ...Les Arabes employaient...dans leurs constructions navales des planches de cocotiers, et ces planches étaient liées entre elles avec des chevilles de bois." And Rel. Arabes, Dis. Prel., p. 56, "Il n'y a que les navires de Siraf dont les pièces sont cousues ensembles," *ib.*, I, p. 91; but Ibn Batutah: "C'est avec des cordes de ce genre que sont cousues les *navires de l'Inde* et du Yaman," and he adduces as a reason why iron is not used, the rocky bottom of the Indian sea against which iron-bound vessels break to pieces, iv, 121.

3rdly. That the last paragraph indicates that Procopius confines his observations to that part of the Red Sea which is inclosed by coasts on either side, the Arabian Gulf, and that consequently the loadstone rocks referred to are not those on the Sinhalese coast, but loadstone rocks in or near the Arabian Gulf.

VII. We have Chinese authority that a great trade between Rome and India existed in the sixth century of our era. Ma-touan-lin, born A.D. 1317, in his Researches into Antiquity, briefly affirms that "India (A.D. 500-16) carries on a considerable commerce by sea with Ta-Tsin, the Roman Empire, and the Ansi or Asæ, the Syrians";[97] and the Kou-kin-tou-chou (Ancient and Modern Times), having alluded to the commerce of India with the West, states that the Roman trade with India is principally by sea, and that by sea the Romans carry off the valuable products of India, as coral, amber, gold, sapphires, mother of pearl, pearls and other inferior stones, odoriferous plants, and compounds by concoction and distillation of odoriferous plants, and then adds that from these compounds they extract the finest qualities for cosmetics, and afterwards sell the residue to the merchants of other countries.[98] We observe—

97 *Vide* Chinese account of India, from Ma-touan-lin, tr. by Pauthier, Asiatic Journal, May to August, 1836, pp. 213-7. For the date of Ma-touan-lin's birth, v. his Life, Rémusat, Nouv. Mélanges Asiat., II, 168, where Rémusat compares Ma-touan-lin's great work to the Mém. de l'Académ. des Inscriptions, and observes that De Guignes in his Hist. des Huns, and the Jesuit missionaries in their several works, owe to it much of their knowledge of China and Chinese literature.

98 Also tr. by Pauthier, Journal Asiatique, Oct. and Nov., 1839,

1st. That silk is not included in the list of Indian merchandise (the ειδη of Epiphanius) sent to the Roman Empire by sea.

2ndly. That this trade by sea necessarily presumes that the goods exported from India were known to be so exported either on Roman account or for the Roman market, but not that they were exported in Roman ships. We have seen that Roman merchants sometimes visited India, that in India Roman money was current, and the Roman Empire known and respected, and we may fairly suppose that that Empire, its trade and its wants and their supply, were often subject of talk in the Indian[99] ports, and would certainly

pp. 278, 389-93. This account seemingly refers to India in the early part of the sixth century (*ib.*, p. 274); but it then goes back to speak of the relations which had before existed between Rome and China; how that (A.D. 166) Antun, Antoninus, sent an embassy through Tonquin with presents, and how the Romans in the interest of their commerce travelled as far as Pegu, Cochin China, and Tonquin; and how a Roman merchant, one Lun (A.D. 222-278), came to Tonquin, and was sent on by its Governor to the Emperor. As Lun and his doings close this short summary of Roman relations with China, I conclude that he was one of the merchants mentioned above, and that they, like him, belong to the period ending A.D. 278, when Roman commerce with the East most flourished,—and as, with one unimportant exception, no further notice is taken of the Roman Empire, I presume that after this time its commerce with these distant regions entirely ceased.

99 When in Bochara (A.D. 1250), Marco Polo meets the ambassadors of Kublai Khan, they press him to visit their master: "eo quod nullum *latinum* usquam viderat, quamvis videre multum affectabat," c. II. And Maffei (Hist. Ind., L. iv) observes of the Byzantine Turks that in the fifteenth century the Indian kings called them "corrupta Græca voce Rumos quasi Romanos." But while this indicates that the memory of Rome survived among the

become known to the Chinese traders there, and would as certainly be spoken of by them on their return home, and would thus find their way into the works of Chinese geographers and historians.

But in order that we may not reason on to a foregone conclusion, hurrying over or explaining away the events and authorities which make against us, we will for a moment suppose that they sufficiently establish the fact of an ocean trade between Rome and India—and then as from the age of the Ptolemies, ending B.C. 46, to that of Firmus, A.D. 273, we know through Strabo, Pliny, the Periplus, Ptolemy, and Vopiscus, that Alexandrian ships sailed for India; we have to show why it is that after that time, though we read of Romans, lawyers, priests, and merchants, who travelled thither and all seemingly through Adule and one of them certainly in an Adulitan craft, we read of none who went in a Roman ship. How too is it, we will be asked, if Roman ships thus crossed the Indian Ocean, that neither they nor their crews are seen among the vessels and peoples which according to Cosmas crowd the port and thoroughfares of the great Sinhalese mart? How, that the Christians of Socotora, an island of Greek colonists,[1] and right in the course of Alexandrian ships *en route* for India, were subject not to the Greek but to the

Hindus, it is no evidence of any commerce between the peoples, no more evidence than is the mention of an Indian princess in the romance of (Peredur?) of a knowledge of India among the Cambrian bards.

[1] Speaking of the inhabitants, the Periplus: *εισι δε επιξενοι και επιμικτοι Αραβων και ετι 'Ελληνων των προς εργασιαν εκπλεοντων.*—P. 281, § 30.

Persian metropolitan?[2] And when Justinian, as Procopius relates, sought to re-establish the silk trade and to wrest it from the hands of the Persians, how is it that he applied, not to his own merchants of Alexandria whose services he might have commanded, and whom had they had ships in those seas he would have wished to encourage, but to the Ethiopian Arabs, whom to the detriment of his own subjects he tempted with the hopes of a monopoly? Again, on this supposition, how account for it, that the loadstone rocks, those myths of Roman geography, which in Ptolemy's time, the flourishing days of Roman commerce, lay some degrees eastward of Ceylon, appear A.D. 400 barring its western approach, and A.D. 560 have advanced up to the very mouth of the Arabian Gulf?[3] Surely an ocean trade with India is, all things considered, all but impossible.

But to return to the loadstone rocks. As in an age little observant of the laws and phenomena of nature, lands unknown save by report and unexplored are ever according to their surroundings invested either with mythic terrors or mythic beauties; and conversely, as all lands in the conception of which the mythic predominates are lands which lie outside the knowledge, and

[2] That the Christian population of Persia was large we may gather from the reasons which Stebocthes, the Persian ambassador, urges upon Justin to dissuade him from breaking the truce with Chosroes. Excepta e Legatis, e Menandri Hist., p. 315, Bonn ed., Byzant. Hist., and that it was loyal to its sovereign its conduct at the siege of Chlomarōn indicates, *ib.*, p. 331.

[3] See *supra*, p. 242, and the Pseudo-Callisthenes, III, vii, p. 103, Didot, and Procopius, *sup.*, p. 38. For Ptolemy's Maniolai Geog. Lib. vii, c. II.

consequently without the sphere of intercourse, of the people who so conceive of them; it follows that these rocks at the very least indicate the extreme limits of Roman enterprise, and the several changes in their position, changes ever bringing them nearer to the Roman Empire, the ever narrowing range of Roman enterprise in their direction. Their changes of position therefore confirm our view of the Roman maritime trade.

But though there is no evidence to show that at this period Roman ships navigated the Indian seas, we know that Indian goods still found their way to Constantinople, and from both Greek and Arab writers that Arab vessels were employed in the Indian trade. So early as the age of the Ptolemies, Agatharchides[4] (B.C. 146) notices a trade between Aden and the Indus, and carried on in native boats, *εμπορικας των προσχωριων σχεδιας*. The Periplus (A.D. 80-90) speaks (§ 26) of Arabia Eudæmon, Aden, as the great entrepôt of Indian commerce in the olden time, before Alexandrian ships ventured across the ocean; and describes Muza, Mokha, as a busy sea-port full of sea-faring men, shipmasters, and sailors, and as trading with Barygaza in its own craft.[5] And lastly, Cosmas (A.D. 535), among the merchant ships to be seen at Ceylon, mentions those of Adule and the Homerites. Arab writers also allude to this branch of Arabian enterprise. Thus Haji Khalfa,[6]

[4] De Mari Erythræo, c. 103, p. 191, II, Geog. Græci Min., ed. Müller.

[5] *το μεν όλον Αραβων ναυκληρικων ανθρωπων και ναυτικων πλεοναζει και τοις απ' εμποριας πραγμασι κινειται· συγχρωνται γαρ τῃ του περαν εργασιᾳ και Βαρυγαζων ιδιοις εξαρτισμοις.*—§ 21, p. 274, I, *ib.*

[6] "Ad qualemcq. historiæ Arabum et Persarum, inquit Hemdani,

in his sketch of the ante-Islamic times, tells of the old Arabs: how they travelled over the world as merchants and brought home with them a large knowledge of the peoples they had visited: and how to the Islanders of Bahrain and to the inhabitants of Omman his age owed its histories of Sinds, Hindus, and Persians. And thus though Masoudi[7] implies that in the early part of the seventh century the Indian and Chinese trade with Babylon was principally in the hands of the Indians and Chinese, yet have we every reason to believe from the Relations des Voyages Arabes, of the ninth century, that it was shared in by the Arabs whose entrepôt was Khanfou.[8]

notitiam sibi parandam nemo, nisi per Arabes pervenire potest... Peragrabant enim terras mercatus causâ, ita ut cognitionem populorum sibi compararent. Pari modo, qui Hiram incolebant, Persarumque............historiam, Homeritarumq. bella et eorum per terras expeditiones cognoscebant. Alii qui in Syriâ versabantur, res Roman. Israel. et Græc. tradiderunt. Ab iis qui in insulis Bahrain et terram Ommân consederant historiam Sindorum, Hindorum et Persarum accepimus. Qui denique in Yemana habitabant cognitionem horum popul. omnium consecuti sunt, utpote regum erronum (Sayya'ret) umbra tecti." Haji Khalfa, tr. Flügel, I, 76, Or. Tr. Fund.

[7] "The Euphrates fell at that time (the time of Omar, died A.D. 644) into the Abyssinian Sea, at a place...now called en-Najaf; for the sea comes up to this place, and thither resorted the ships of China and India, destined for the kings of El-Hirah," p. 246, Sprenger's tr., and I, pp. 215-6, French tr. But Reinaud, who by the way has no great confidence in Sprenger's accuracy, refers these observations to the fifth century. See *supra*, p. 162, Emb. from Claudius to Justinian.

[8] Relations Arabes, p. 12, which gives an interesting account of the dangers and mishaps to which the merchant was liable, and which, p. 68, shows the commerce with China falling away, and

But what in the meanwhile had become of the overland trade with India? When in the second half of the third century, and after nearly three hundred years of Parthian rule, the Sassanidæ. reasserted the Persian supremacy over the peoples of Central Asia, taught by the misfortunes and fall of their predecessors which they might not unfairly trace to a partiality for western civilisation,[9] they eschewed Greek and Roman manners, literature and philosophy. They besides restored and reformed the national faith, the religion of Ormuzd. They cherished old national traditions. They boasted themselves lineal descendants of the old Persian kings,[10] and stood forward as the champions of the national greatness. Their first communication with Rome was a threatening demand for all those countries which, long incorporated with the Roman Empire, had in old time been subject to the Persian dominion.[11] For a moment it seemed as though by force of arms they would have made good their claim, but their barbaric pride proved their overthrow; and after they had spurned his friendship,[12] they were compelled to abate their pretensions in

why. In Ibn Batutah's time, in so far as the Chinese seas were concerned, "On n'y voyage qu'avec des vaisseaux Chinois," iv, 91; but of these the sailors were often Arabs—thus the intendant of the junk in which Ibn sailed was Suleiman Assafady, *id.*, 94; and one of the men was from Hormuz, 96; and I think the marines were from Abyssinia.

9 V. Tacitus, Annal., L. II, c. 2.

10 Reinaud, sur la Mésène, pp. 13-14, tirage à part.

11 Αρταξερξης γαρ της Περσης τους τε Παρθους...νικησας...στρατευματι τε πολλῳ...τῃ Συριᾳ εφεδρευσας, και απειλων ανακτησεσθαι παντα ὡς και προσηκοντα οἱ εκ προγονων, ὁσα ποτε οἱ παλαι Περσαι μεχρι της 'Ελληνικης θαλασσης εσχον, etc.—Dio Cassius: και Ξιφιλινον, 80, c. 3.

12 Sapor, who followed out the policy of his father, and forbade

the presence of the victorious Odenatus, and subsequently to buy a peace of Diocletian by a cession of Mesopotamia and the eastern borders of the Tigris. Thus stayed in their career of conquest and even despoiled of their fairest provinces, they directed their attention to the consolidation of their power and the development of the resources of their kingdom. They anticipated and enforced that cruel policy which in later years was advocated by and has since borne the name of Machiavelli. Under one pretext and another, and sometimes by force of arms, they got within their hands and pitilessly ordered to death the petty kings who owned indeed their supremacy, but whose sway was really despotic and allegiance merely nominal.[13] To the hitherto divided members of their Empire they gave unity of will and purpose. They made it one State, of which they were the presiding and ruling mind. To educate and enlarge the views of their subjects, they did not, like their predecessors, study Greek and speak Greek, but they collected and translated the masterpieces of Hindu literature and Greek philosophy,[14] and

the use of the Greek letters in Armenia, and promised to make Merugan its king if he would bring it to the worship of Ormuzd (Moses Khorene, II, pp. 83-4, tr.), ordered his servants to throw into the river the rich gifts, μεγαλοπρεπη δωρα, of Odenatus, and tore up his supplicatory letters, γραμματα δεησεως δυναμιν εχοντα, and trod them under foot, and asked, "Who and what he was who dared thus to address his lord? Let him come and with bound hands prostrate himself before me unless he is prepared to die, and all his race with him." Petri Patricii Hist., p. 134, Byzant. Hist.

13 V. Reinaud, u. s., pp. 46-7.

14 E. g. of Hindu literature, the Pancha Tantra.—Assemann,

thus nationalized them. They encouraged commerce. So early as the fourth century of our era, they entered into commercial relations with China, which they cultivated in the early part of the sixth by frequent embassies.[15] We hear too of their ambassadors in Ceylon, and with Ceylon and the East they carried on a large ocean traffic, as the many flourishing emporia in the Persian Gulf sufficiently indicate, and as Cosmas distinctly affirms. The old overland route to India also, comparatively neglected in the great days of Palmyra and during the troubled reigns of the last Parthian kings, regained under their fostering care its old importance, and became the great high-road over which silk was brought to Europe. And such was the justice of their rule,[16] and such the protection and facilities they afforded the merchant, that silk worth in Aurelian's time its weight in gold, and a luxury of the rich and noble, was in the reign of Julian sold at a price which brought it within every man's reach.[17] By their treaties

Bib. Orient., III, 222. Plato and Aristotle, of Greek philosophers etc.,—as we may gather from Agathias, II, c. 28, p. 126.

15 "On a eu des rapports avec la Perse au temps de la seconde dynastie des Wei" (à la fin du quatrième siècle). Rémusat, N. Rel. As., I, 248. "Ce royaume, A.D. 518-19, payait un tribut consistant en marchandises du pays," p. 251, *ib.* "Le Roi, A.D. 555, fit offrir de nouveaux présents," p. 252.

16 Agathias, L. II, c. 30, p. 131, though he speaks of the high opinion he held of the Persian rule to refute it.

17 Of Aurelian's time, Vopiscus: "libra enim auri tunc libra serica fuit." Hist. Aug., II, 187. Ammianus Marcellinus observes of the Seres: "conficiunt sericum, ad usus ante hac nobilium, nunc etiam infimorum sine ullâ discretione proficiens." Hist., xxiii, 6.

with Jovian (A.D. 363) and with the second Theodosius, they not only recovered the provinces they had lost, but acquired also, with a not unimportant cantle of the Roman territory, a portion of the much coveted kingdom of Armenia.[18] The overland route was now wholly in their hands, the Persian Gulf also was theirs, and when towards the close of Justinian's reign Khosroes Nushirwan[19] overran Arabia, and gave a king to the Homerites, they may be said to have held the Red Sea and the keys of all the roads from India to the West.

18 The hundred years truce between Theodosius and Bahram concluded A.D. 422. Gibbon, iv, p. 310. The final incorporation of Armenia as Pers-Armenia with the Persian Empire took place at the commencement of the fourth century, *ib.*, 212.

19 V. d'Herbelot, Bib. Orientale, s. v., but Theophanes (Hist., p. 485) seems to place this event in the reign of Justin. Excerp. Hist., p. 485. Corpus Byz. Hist.

INDEX.